SOCIALISM AND SOCIAL SCIENCE
SELECTED WRITINGS OF ERVIN SZABÓ

CONTENTS

ACKNOWLEDGMENTS

The editors wish gratefully to acknowledge the many suggestions and comments received from friends and colleagues, and apologize for not having been able to follow all their recommendations. We wish to thank our typists, Barbara Parker, Sheila Rowswell, Éva Fáró and William E. Taylor, who offered more than mere technical help by deciphering our hieroglyphs and often suggesting better formulations than ours.
Most articles of Szabó were translated from the Hungarian by Mario D. Fenyö; Masses or individuals and The Hungarian Revolution, as well as the correspondence were translated from the German original by J. M. Bak, who also translated all editorial matters. For the permission to reprint J. M. Bak's translation (from the German text) of The agrarian question we are indebted to the editor of 'Peasant Studies' and UCIS, Pittsburgh.

Budapest-Vancouver   Gy.L.   J.M.B.
December 1980

vii

EDITORS' INTRODUCTION

During the two decades of his creative and productive career, Ervin Szabó enjoyed an undisputed reputation as a scholar, wide acclaim as a socialist theoretician, and early and lasting success as a librarian. But he was also beset by continuous frustrations and failures, and was plagued by contradictions he was unable to resolve, as they originated in his personal philosophy, the theories he embraced and the conditions in which he had to live and work.

He was the first systematically trained Marxist in Hungary but also the first 'revisionist' (though not a Bernsteinian). He was a protagonist of extreme revolutionary ideas but found his best friends among liberal democrats in whose circles he felt himself most at home. He was the Hungarian most closely associated with Russian revolutionaries and the best informed about radical movements there, but for a socialist example he chose to turn to the west, to Franco-Italian syndicalism and Anglo-American unionism. His political writings show him as an advocate of all-out class struggle, but as a leader of the Sociological Society and director of the Budapest Municipal Library he defended science and art from immediate political influences.

Three major tensions and contradictions in Szabó's life and work may serve to illustrate the 'field of force' which defined his thoughts and actions: those between theory and praxis, Marxism and ethics, and the author and his audience. All that we can attempt here is to sketch the outlines of these topics, briefly referring to the social, political and intellectual surroundings of Szabó; to do more would amount to an essay on the history of avant-guerre Hungary which would certainly exceed the frame of an introduction.

THEORY AND PRAXIS

Several friends and contemporaries of Szabó wondered whether he was 'deep down inside' a scholar or a revolutionary activist. One of his closest friends - and first biographer - Oscar Jászi wrote that

> his revolutionary convictions were always stronger than his scholarly ambitions. Although he loved and enjoyed scientific truths, he regarded them as a kind of spiritual ammunition in humanity's fight for liberation.... The guiding star

1

of his studies has been to supply the workers with weapons
in the class struggle.(1)

But in another memorial article, a few years later, he stated:
'The librarian and the theoretician were always stronger in him
than the party politician and agitator.' (2) Obviously both assessments contain much truth, and this in itself hints at the puzzle
in Szabó's real character.

These contradictory trends in Szabó's life can be partially
explained by his personal qualities and the conditions of the
times in which he lived. He was of frail health, of weak nervous
disposition, a poor orator, and, although an extremely disciplined
worker, organically unable to fulfil the role of mass leader. Also,
the need for a regular income made him accept a civil service
position early in life which, although hardly against his inclinations, forced him to assure the authorities, however liberal the
Budapest city council may have been, that his 'desires to serve
the cause of socialism are for the time being (sic!) limited to the
scholarly study of the movement'.(3)

Still, it would be a simplification to explain Szabó's reluctant
decision to become the theoretician and not the political leader of
the socialist movement from such motives. He wished to be both,
and does not seem to have ever fully acquiesced in the fact that
he was less and less able to harmonize these divergent intentions.
At the end, however, he accepted that he was neither of them.

To a minor extent Szabó's background and youth defined the
outlines of his future. As the youngest son of an impoverished
small entrepreneur's family, assimilated Jews from a provincial
town, who lost his father as a child, he had to look for a job
promising safe income; the sooner, the better. Commercial careers
must have appeared as unpromising prospects after the father's
failure; many fields, such as government service, were virtually
closed to him, even though he changed his name from Schlesinger
to the 'Hungarian-sounding' Szabó and became a Protestant while
still in his teens.(4) After graduation from secondary school
(Gymnasium) in Ungvár (today: Uzhgorod, Ukrainian SSR), he
matriculated in 1895 at the Faculty of Law and Government in
Budapest, a typical choice for a poor but talented young man in
those times. During his studies Szabó concentrated on political
science and economics, subjects that were rather poorly represented in the conservative faculty of Budapest. This may have
been one of the motives that suggested a few semesters in Vienna
where these disciplines were taught by some of the best-known
economists of the age. During his year there (1898-9) Szabó
attended the course of Karl Menger, the main representative of
the 'Austrian school of economics' and a meticulous methodolo-
gist (5), and of Theodor Inama-Sternegg, author of major works
on economic history and, together with Eugen von Philippovich,
leading statistician of the Austro-Hungarian monarchy.(6) He
learned much of academic economics, but did not become the
'pupil' of either of his Vienna professors.

Budapest was still a provincial city in comparison to fin-de-siècle Vienna, which was an important centre of modern science, art, literature, theatre and politics.(7) Szabó's second, if not first, mother tongue was German, many of his friends and relatives lived in Vienna or at least visited the capital of the monarchy regularly. A séjour in the Kaiserstadt was therefore a self-evident stage in his education, just as it was in that of his fellows. Academic work was only one of the many aspects of it; reading books, meeting people, going to the theatre and galleries were perhaps even more important.

Szabó's acquaintance with socialist thought must have begun first in Budapest in the house of his uncle, Mihály Pollacsek and his wife, the Russian émigré 'Aunt Cécile', the parents of Michael and Karl Polanyi.(8) In their salon (called 'Jungle' by some, à la Kipling) literary and political events, intellectual novelties, such as psychoanalysis, writings of sociologists and philosophers (above all Marx and Nietzsche), were discussed, occasionally with some visitor from abroad. Still, it was in Vienna that Szabó received lasting impulses that moved him farther left than many of his peers. His real home there was the family of the former 'narodnik', Russian socialist émigré Samuel Klatschko. In their house he could meet socialists of different observance, from Social Revolutionaries to Bundists, from Trotsky to Viktor Adler. The circle included many Austrian and Russian revolutionaries among whom Pavel F. Teplov, a leading member of the 'ekonomist' faction became Szabó's best friend and veritable model. According to Jászi:

It was in this Russian atmosphere that he became a revolutionary and a Marxist. From Marxism he received above all the economic theory of development, from the Russian and French revolutionaries the idea of 'révolte': that a new society can only be achieved by a violent uprising of the well-organized and class-conscious working class.(9)

Thus the 22-year-old Szabó, returning from Vienna, would not have been aware of the need to choose between theory and practice, scholarship and politics, since his Russian comrades were all engaged in propagandistic writing, study and organization at the same time. What for them had been a tradition was an inevitable necessity for the Hungarian socialist movement: due to its size and character, the few 'literate' leaders had to be organizers, teachers, writers and editors at once.

The Hungarian Social Democratic Party, although some ten years old by this time, was still not much more than a loose federation of trade unions and workers' self-help organizations. The majority of the older leadership, mostly schooled on the German and Austrian movement, were administrators of workers' health-insurance companies with an essentially bureaucratic outlook; their horizon was defined by attempts at social reform in a country where 12-hour working days were not a rarity and hardly any social legislation

existed. The highly restrictive election system of Hungary,
revised to the disadvantage of the labouring classes in the 1880s,
ensured that no socialist would sit in the Parliament that was still
the domain of great land-owners and the gentry. Socialists were
regarded as seditious elements, and strong police repression did
its best to keep them 'in their place'.(10)

Under such conditions, Szabó, an able young 'student', ready
to work for nothing, was welcomed in the party, especially by a
few younger functionaries, who wished to overcome the inertia of
their elders. Szabó soon became a regular contributor to the
Social Democratic papers, 'Népszava' (People's Voice) and 'Volksstimme'. At the same time, with the help of 'veteran' socialist
intellectuals, he found a job as a librarian; it proved to be a lasting commitment. Thus it seems that he was at first as successful
in harmonizing scholarly and political ambitions as he was in find-
ing his place as a professional in the movement. Financially independent of the Social Democratic Party, he was able to devote his
best to the cause without being bound by employment to the party
bureaucrats.

For two or three years Szabó was the young scholar of Hungarian Social Democracy, editor of what may be termed the cultural
column of the party press, anonymous author of several pamphlets
addressed to workers and students, and also something of a
'foreign secretary', keeping contacts with Adler, Kautsky and,
above all, with revolutionaries from Russia and eastern Europe
(for example, Christian Rakovsky). For years he was the Budapest outpost of several, occasionally mutually opposing, factions
of Russian revolutionaries, assisting in smuggling illegal literature
across the Galician and Romanian border. At the same time he re-
organized libraries, first that of the Budapest Chamber of Commerce, then from 1904 the Municipal Library that now bears his
name. He also published annual bibliographies of economic and
socialist literature, launched an international bibliographical
series and contributed to a score of foreign socialist journals.

His first personal crisis, leading to a 'course correction' in
Szabó's life, became manifest in the winter of 1902-3. 'In order
fully to devote myself to the theoretical study of socialism', as he
wrote to a friend,(11) Szabó resigned from the bibliographical
projects and left his editorial post with 'Népszava'. Soon after-
wards he agreed to serve as one of the editors of the recently
founded (1900) journal of social sciences, 'Huszadik Század'
(Twentieth Century), which was on its way to becoming the auth-
oritative mouthpiece of the democratic-radical intelligentsia.

Szabó's decision to exchange party work for editing a sociological paper seems somewhat paradoxical, if one considers his
deeper motives. He seems to have been more and more dissatisfied
with the narrow-minded reformist spirit of the Social Democratic
Party, where he regretfully noted that the young leaders, his
friends, gradually adapted to the tone and tactics of the 'old
guard', instead of changing them. But his new 'home' was quite
the opposite of the more revolutionary or radical movements that

one would expect; it was an essentially bourgeois, definitely non-
socialist journal and a group of critical, but mostly non-Marxist,
intellectuals had founded and edited it. All this can be better
understood in the context of Hungarian political and intellectual
life at the turn of the century. Szabó's choice had much to do
with his attempts to find an audience which was not only able to
understand and appreciate what he had to say, but also to change,
if only by the force of ideas, the intellectual climate of the
country. The Sociological Society, the sponsor of 'Huszadik
Század' was a centre of such men and women. This circle could
supply him with appropriate scholarly companions, who may not
have agreed with him in all details, but were reliable allies. They
fought a common fight on at least two fronts: against the political
establishment that stood in the way of any consistent modernization of Hungary and, even more, against the parliamentary
opposition which ideologically dominated the country by its nationalist slogans without offering any real alternatives.(12) For
these struggles, Szabó found in his new circles fair, tolerant and
devoted comrades-in-arms. It is actually also true that by his
shift of emphasis to the sociologists Szabó established for himself
a more suitable role in the socialist movement, precisely because
he was now formally outside its organization.

   While both the Social Democrats and Szabó felt increasingly
alienated from each other, no spectacular break occurred; Szabó
remained editor of the annual 'Népszava' almanac, continued to
write in the party press and his great project, the first Hungarian translation of selected works of Marx and Engels, was to be
realized in concert with the party. Szabó's achievements during
the subsequent few years proved the wisdom of his choice. It was
his most successful period during which he gave two major lectures
to the Sociological Society, wrote critical assessments of the international working-class movement and completed the first volume
of his Marx-Engels collection. The former established his reputation as an eminently learned, critical and original socialist among
the social scientists, the latter consolidated his high standing
among socialist workers and functionaries. That he did not slav-
ishly repeat current Marxist commonplaces, but raised some original and critical thoughts, enhanced the former but hardly hurt
the latter.

   Hence, once again, the compromise seemed to work: by writing,
editing and lecturing, Szabó was able to build a much-needed
bridge between a theoretically weak Social Democracy and the
politically isolated intellectuals of his new circle. Even though
Szabó's original idea, to be, just as his Russian friends, an organ-
izer and theoretician-propagandist in one, did not come true, a
new role emerged for him: that of a 'spiritual leader' of the
socialist movement, who does not engage in the day-to-day work
and the minor squabbles, but serves as guardian of the purity of
party politics and theory. However, such a position, which would
have somewhat resembled Kautsky's role in Germany or Plekhanov's
in Russia, demanded more orthodoxy, more tactful compromising

and less urge to intervene actively 'for the true cause' than
Szabó could muster.

On the other hand, he was not suited to be a high priest of one
theory. He was a searching scholar, whose motto, 'de omnibus
dubitandum', obliged him to consider all new Marxist and non-
Marxist theories regardless of their orthodoxy. On the other hand,
his critical findings about the faults of the party vexed him
enough to continue co-operating with oppositional factions and
movements - both within Social Democracy and without. Thus his
1903 decision proved to be inconsistent: Szabó remained, inevitably, and maybe sometimes even *malgré lui*, the grey eminence of
the gradually growing left-wing opposition in the Hungarian Social
Democratic Party. He accepted the editorship of their journal,
wrote theoretical, but very topical articles on the role and structure of the party (see pp. 106-20) and guided by remote control
the struggles for inner-party democracy at the annual congresses,
which he never attended. As long as the Social Democrats did not
subordinate their entire programme and organizational work to the
parliamentary struggle - which in early twentieth-century Hungary meant the fight for general suffrage that might enable the
Socialists to elect members to the Lower House - Szabó may have
found sense in working within, or at least with, the party, even
if from an oppositional stance. The decisive defeat of the opposition at the 1905 congress destroyed any hopes for a turn in the
spirit of Szabó and his friends.(13)

During the constitutional crisis of 1905, however, the Social
Democratic Party proved to be on its way to becoming a political
organization. While it still remained outside of Parliament (where
the first Socialist deputies did not sit until 1922), it was a political
force that had to be contended with, both by the government and
the different shades of the opposition. While in a party still basically engaged in the organization and education of the workers,
Szabó could imagine a place for himself as theoretician and prop-
agandist, the political party was certainly beyond the pale for
him. Actually he foresaw this development, when he wrote in
1904: 'To develop the consciousness of the working class: that is
the most successful tactic of socialist parties.... Whichever party
deviates from this road... deserves to be burned!' (see p. 119).
In 1907 he raised the rhetorical question 'whether parliamentary
socialism and the present theory and practice of Social Democracy
are indeed the ideology of the working class and the correct road
to socialism',(14) only to answer it in the negative. None the less,
he admitted that Social Democratic parties, at least in backward
eastern and east-central Europe, can fulfil a legitimate task in the
struggle for democracy and civil liberties, but if they pretended,
as they did, to fight for socialism then they were sailing under a
false flag. He refused to participate in such an enterprise. At the
same time he admitted that adherence to the Social Democratic
Party - or, for that matter, any party - is only an obstacle to
serious theoretical or scholarly work.(15)

Still, Szabó could not give up his initial loyalty to the working-class movement before another last try at 'practical' work. Since 1902 he had been in touch with German, Italian and French synd-icalists; he agreed with their criticism of 'German' Social Dem-ocracy and saw in their class-oriented, anti-etatist, anti-centralist position the alternative he was looking for.(16) It is, however, somewhat of an overstatement to class Szabó's synd-icalism as an issue of praxis. While he had been quite active in earlier anarchist educational projects, to which we shall refer later, his syndicalist conviction was wisely tempered by his real-ism and his knowledge of the level of consciousness among Hungarian workers. It is obvious from the introductory essays to the second volume of his Marx-Engels collection (1909) and some articles from 1908 onwards that he had fully embraced the revo-lutionary syndicalist programme, but he gave up attempts at any such organization in Hungary after a very brief trial run.

Around 1910 no existing political group could offer Szabó a field of action. No practical work could be combined in avant-guerre Hungary with the radical theories he now professed. Thus, this theoretically most 'practice-oriented' among the young Hungarian intellectuals, this advocate of 'action directe', was condemned to retirement into theory.

The failure of the syndicalist experiment marked another dec-isive 'change of course' in Szabó's life. He formulated his motives in these words:

> Every practical movement is a den of disillusionment and
> repeatedly sobering experiences because it is rare that a
> successful movement can accomplish its aims in a manner
> propagated during the fighting stage. Therefore there is
> need for, at least a few, such people who remain devoted
> to the great aims of the far future and are courageous
> enough to unfold these to the wide masses... by doing so
> they can serve as the gadflies of today's mass movement,
> as the flag-bearers of the morrow and the day after tomor-
> row, building a bridge from the daily frustrations of the
> present to the promises of the future.(17)

He wanted to be one of these few 'prophets'. He chose to fulfil this task by becoming something of a silent signpost pointing ahead, instead of an active teacher-agitator, because, as he ad-mitted in 1913, he was reluctant to accept the role of the surgeon, when the cure for the ills is not known.(18) Having said so, not only political activity, but even a theory oriented on praxis be-came problematic for him.

As to 'activity' he spent the remaining years almost exclusively on his public library which he made into the most advanced work-shop of social science in Hungary. This resignation into librar-ianship did not mean that he would have made a refuge out of his position. As Jászi put it, 'he walked around his library just like a general does during a war in a well-functioning ammunition plant'.(19) Szabó did his best to ensure that his 'factory'

supplied the right 'ammunition' and passed it on to the right
'soldiers'. In this field learning and social activity could be
easily combined. There are many writings in which he outlined
the desirable character of public libraries: neither 'popular' collections of cheap trash 'good enough for the common people', nor
secluded laboratories for academics (see, for example, pp. 198-
201).(20) In 1911 he became the director of the Municipal Library
and a very conscientious director to wit.

But in general terms, theory and practice, scholarship and
politics were now seen by him as different and distinct fields. In
the 1912 presidential address of the Sociological Society (see pp.
189-97) Szabó advocated a social science that did not aim at immediate practical use and did not search for actual remedies of social
ills, but followed its own logic, and only in the far future might
it converge with the active work for the transformation of society.

In an overview, then, one may note the correlation of Szabó's
theoretical metamorphoses and his role in active politics. The
early years of party work were accompanied by more or less
orthodox Marxism; the time of Szabó's theoretical leadership in
the movement was accompanied by an increasingly critical approach
to determinist and materialist Marxism; and his last, resigned
period, was characterized by a more ethical rather than political
approach to societal change, implying, to a certain extent, a turn
away from Marxism. Or, in other words, his philosophical development moved him away from socialist activity and, by being
removed from the field of political action, he was, in turn, in-
duced to embrace new theoretical positions.

MARXISM AND ETHICS

When Szabó appeared in Budapest socialist circles and in the
Sociological Society, many must have noted that with his deep-
seated, piercing eyes and drooping moustache he strikingly resembled Nietzsche. Few would have known that since his student
years he was as much influenced by Zarathustra's questions as
by the answers offered in the writings of scientific socialism. In
retrospect it seems that Nietzsche's 'Kulturkritik', anti-etatism
and the ethical model of his superman's overpowering personality
were the most consistent ideals that accompanied Szabó through
his life, and his Marxism was from the outset 'tinted' by a search
for ethical norms instead - or at least besides - the teachings on
historical necessity.

As early as in the lecture on historical materialism (1903, see
pp. 25-34) and the seminal article on party discipline (1904, see
pp. 106-20), Szabó expressed his reservations on Marxist economic determinism, emphasizing his belief that 'all development in
history has been the result of the actions by critical individuals'.
Subsequently, in the editorial comments to the Marx-Engels selections and in his correspondence with Kautsky on his long
planned and never completed book on classes and class struggle,

he questioned those Marxist positions of his time, which he could not accept, and even certain tenets of Marx himself.(21) He found that the 'subjective element', the role of the individual and the impact of ideas on history have not been sufficiently elaborated in Marxism (e.g. p. 59). At this stage he believed that the principles of these problems and the main teachings of ethics were contained in the Marxian oeuvre, only they had not been developed sufficiently since. Later he seems to have doubted even that, an issue which is still very much debated among Marxists of different observance.

Szabó's dissatisfaction with Marxist perceptions of history and theories of revolution may have partly originated in his sympathy with the ethically motivated revolutionaries and anarchists of the Russian socialist movement. Impressed by their personal courage and their tactical concepts based on individual actions, he was looking for a general theory that would accommodate the 'great men and women' more adequately than Marxism did. It seems that Szabó's questions went beyond those which had been answered by Plekhanov, exactly in response to the ideas of many Russian revolutionaries on the role of the personality in history.(22) In fact, he called for a genuine Marxist ethics, in a way very much akin to the discussions of the time in Germany and Austria between socialists and neo-Kantians,(23) although his point of reference was, besides Nietzsche, the Russian revolutionary and philosopher, Petr Lavrov.(24)

For the task of including 'the subjective dimension' into Marxist theory, Szabó expected much from the study of social psychology. Kautsky's warning to him not to slide off into the direction of overestimating the mental and spiritual factors (see below, pp. 60ff) was perhaps not quite unfounded. What kept him from embarking on psychological speculation was, above all, his belief in the paramount importance of class struggle. His image of a dynamic action of the working class, organized and led by highly motivated individuals who fought in the lines with the workers, but also as a vanguard, pulling the laggards to the fore (see below, pp. 103-5), was such an ideal, in which the individual's ethical qualities could play a historical role without negating the mass movement and its underlying determinants.

Szabó's quandary about the significance of the individual in history was in the last resort a search for a Marxist philosophical concept of man. Many a question that surfaced in more recent discussions on Marx's 'anthropology' was already touched upon in Szabó's writings. He doubted that the answers might be found in the early Marx: although he knew many of the pre-1848 writings, he consciously excluded them from his collection, not only because he found them too difficult or too polemical, but because they sounded to him 'too Hegelian'. What he meant by that can be gauged from a remark in the lecture on historical materialism; while admitting that he is not particularly versed in philosophy, Szabó explicitly stated that to his mind dialectics were not essential to the thought of Marx and Engels and could easily be bracketed out.

Szabó's remarkable statement on dialectics should not be under-stood as an expression of his philosophical 'ignorance'. Its motives may have been manifold. It is not impossible that he was influenced by the anti-dialectical conviction of those Marxists who, such as Max Adler, tried to build a bridge to Kant and emphas-ized the need for socialist ethics. Also, Szabó may have suspected dialectics from an ethical stance and feared that the method could be used or misused for 'explaining away' such conflicts as bet-ween worthy aims and unethical means, an issue to which he returned later in life. Used to debating with social scientists of rather eclectical methodological background, he preferred the pragmatic discourse, and as a moralist he was inclined to categor-ical judgments. Still, it is ironically true that Szabó's aversion to dialectics led him not infrequently into positions as rigidly black-and-white as those he used to criticize in 'German Marxism'.

Szabó's ethical preference must have also played a role in his critique of what became of Marxian dialectics in the Marxism of the Second International. From his early lectures onwards, he was anxious to qualify the then-current 'strict determinism' of most Marxist authors. Fighting on two fronts, against non-Marxists and Bernsteinian revisionists, he defended the importance of economic determinants in social development, but also emphasized the significance of human activity and consciousness. In this res-pect he disputed the validity of Marx's 'theory of collapse' ('Zusammenbruchstheorie') and the political consequences that have been drawn from it. The state of capitalism around the turn of the century seemed to have refuted Marx's expectation that the economic determinants in the history of the liberation of the work-ing class - concentration of capital and economic centralization - would develop faster than the subjective factors, the organization and consciousness of the workers. Szabó believed that the oppo-site, in fact, occurred, which meant not only that the belief in 'strict determinism' had to be qualified but also that the concepts of class struggle had to be revised accordingly.

The emphasis on the 'subjective factors' implied to Szabó that the political class struggle and, in particular, the parliamentary politics of the Social Democratic parties was not the correct way towards socialism: the fight for government power would have made sense only as the legal completion of a development that had run its course in the economy. If that was not so, as it apparently was not, then the direct actions of the working class - that is the 'subjective' element - were on the agenda.

Following this train of thought, Szabó saw in the organizational principle of German-Austrian (and, of course, also Hungarian) Social Democracy, in its 'strict discipline' a reflection of their 'strict determinism'. Based on his belief in the value of voluntary and individually motivated fighters in the class struggle, he rejected the Social Democratic image of a 'disciplined army' à la Prussia. Thus followed from Szabó's reservations about 'objective determinism' his break with Social Democracy which he saw as quietist, bureaucratic and unduly concentrated on politics. The alternative for which he opted implied a greater emphasis on spontaneous 'human activity' predicated not only by the development of the working class, as he saw it, but also by his Nietzschean ethics and Russian revolutionary sympathies.

The theoretical as well as organizational re-orientation did not stop at the confines of history and 'Revolutionstheorie'. Szabó also revised his views, typical for socialist movement of the time, on the place of art and literature in society and on the role of the intellectuals. Although in his younger years as a 'Népszava' editor he supported painters and poets whose work, even though not necessarily first class, appeared to be immediately mobilizing and propagating socialist ideas, in a debate in 1914 he advocated a socialist cultural policy based on the autonomy of art and on co-operation between responsible artists and the movement. His acid critique of 'proletarian poetry' and 'vulgar Marxism' (see below, pp. 202-7) denied, once again, the need for 'disciplined' party directives, this time in literature, science and art, calling upon the ethical engagement of the intellectuals as a guidance for their creative work. In the face of the crisis of the First World War, in one of his last writings he again stressed the paramount role and responsibility of a moral elite (see pp. 208-11).

Once he had written off – in the name of ethics – economic determinism, party discipline and propagandistic art, Szabó was consistent enough to raise doubts about the basic tenets of the materialist concepts of philosophy and sociology as well. In his war-time lecture on Imperialism and Lasting Peace he states 'as a fact' that 'the primacy of economic over political structure is by no means as obvious as many used to believe'.(25) Finally, in the 1918 anniversary address on Marx (see below, pp. 93-100), Szabó, true to his new – and at the same time oldest – position, built a bridge of sorts between his two ideals: regretting the 'political misuses' of Marx, he presented him to the audience as an example of that 'heroic life' which Friedrich Nietzsche esteemed so highly.

In this light it is not surprising that among the 'older' leaders of the Sociological Society Szabó alone expressed open sympathies with the younger 'ethical idealists', such as George Lukács. In a debate in 1918 Fogarasi and Lukács raised the question of 'Sein' and 'Sollen', and opted for the ethically motivated voluntary action in contrast to accepting the deterministic 'objective development'. They found that German Social Democracy's determinist quietism caused the movement to stagnate; they could be sure of Szabó's approval of this diagnosis. Szabó seriously considered their challenge and granted that 'progress and development has to be tried in the court of ethics', but wanted to perceive 'Sollen' not in an arbitrary manner, but as the 'socially possible'. Even though Lukács's circle opposed the basic belief of his generation in materialist-evolutionary philosophy, Szabó had apparently revised his Marxism to the point that he was in concert with them regarding the primacy of ethics. He went as far in rejecting unethical 'necessities' that he said: 'Rather the bad should stay than be changed by evil means.' In a final account-taking with

..

his former comrades, Szabó wrote in early 1918:

> From the point of view of the highest aim of society, the categorical imperative of human perfection, certain democrats, parties and politicians are more dangerous to democracy than its enemies. Those, whose daily politics disregarded the ethical demand of harmony between aims and means... who were ready to bargain about essential points of their programme - and who believe that it was permissible to do good by unethical means, who support and even commit abominable things, if only to get something good out of it.... Verily, I say, profoundly rotten and malicious are those who achieve their aims... by such means. And the democracy that they will have attained by brawls, cheats and intrigues shall not be better than what its critics maintain: political democracy - maybe; but social, human, intellectual or spiritual democracy? Never.(26)

Anybody familiar with Lukács's famous article written in the Fall of 1918 on Bolshevism as an Ethical Problem will recognize the indebtedness of the later Communist philosopher's first major political credo to the last ethical confession of the former revolutionary Socialist. Lukács, however, soon went beyond Szabó, when he chose the words of Hebbel's Judith as his guidance: 'When God placed the sin between me and the deed, who am I to recoil?' Still, in his first Communist years Lukács followed many of Szabó's lines of thought when he emphasized the class-party dichotomy, advocated proletarian democracy and postulated the - almost messianistic - self-redeeming action of the working class in 'History and Class Consciousness'.(27) Even though from the late 1920s he critically - and self-critically! - rejected much of what he had inherited from Szabó, it was no doubt the ethical dimension of Szabó's teachings which made the old Lukács state that 'he was somehow the father of us all'.

AUTHOR AND AUDIENCE

While the contradictions and tensions within Marxism and between Marx and Nietzsche originated in the theories themselves, and the quandaries between theory and practice were to a great extent problems common to many a radical intellectual, Szabó's search for an audience, for friends and allies - and his frustrations and failures in this respect - were essentially defined by the social and political conditions of Hungary around the turn of the century.(28)

In the course of his different types of activity at the crossroads of politics and scholarship, and of the metamorphoses of his theoretical orientation, Szabó addressed different segments of Hungarian society. However, only two strata could be seriously considered as Szabó's audience: the organized workers and the critically inclined intellectuals. The commercial bourgeoisie and the majority of professionals, parochial and conservative in outlook, were unlikely listeners and Szabó, who despised both, never tried to talk to them. Though he felt a certain affinity to rural folk, the eleven million peasants and landless labourers, still the majority of Hungarian society (62 per cent around 1900), were beyond the reach of an urban author.

The Establishment and the political opposition, both actual and former land-owners and their 'hired pens', were, of course, the obvious adversaries: chauvinist nationalists, anti-Socialists and anti-Semites, so to say, by definition. By the time Szabó entered public life they had abandoned even the limited liberal views some of them may have held in the era of the Austro-Hungarian Compromise (1867).(29)

Once he embraced Socialist ideals, it was logical that Szabó's prime audience, the one he wished to address first and wanted to educate in a revolutionary spirit, were the workers. The working class and its organizations in Hungary were still rather primitive. Although the rapid economic growth of the last decades of the nineteenth century had quickly swelled their numbers (to about 700,000 by 1900) it was a heterogeneous population. Skilled workers from German and Czech lands and recently proletarized Hungarian peasants, still tied to their rural background, had hardly made their first steps towards becoming a 'class in itself'.(30) As we have seen, their party reflected these conditions.

Throughout his life Szabó was anxious to keep lively contacts with the workers; he always had some personal friends among them and many more readers. He did not idealize the working class and did not try to 'rub shoulders' with them. The main channel of contact was through his writings, many anonymously published in the Socialist press, which reached thousands. He wrote clear, simple, popular but informative articles of high quality on the Socialist view of history, literature, politics, religion, science and art; a type of literature that did not exist in Hungary before. His pamphlets and leaflets issued in the course of strikes or against police brutality excelled in their mobilizing style. Lectures in workers' educational courses augmented Szabó's teaching and propagandistic work.

The Marx-Engels collection was in a way a continuation of the same mission on a higher level. With this Szabó set himself the task to produce a representative collection which would serve the education of intelligent workers and introduce interested intellectuals to the classics of socialism. Szabó's circumspect planning, careful editing and especially his original and up-to-date introductions made the two volumes more than a mere translation into one of the minor languages of Europe. By his selection and editorial comments Szabó related the writings of two German exiles to the political realities of east-central Europe and the debates of the mid-nineteenth century to the issues of the early twentieth. 'I am convinced', he wrote in the Preface, 'that there is not a single piece in this collection that an intelligent working man

would not understand and read with both mental profit and enjoyment' (see below, p. 70).

All this was received with approval, even gratitude within the
party and among workers keen on education. The same cannot be
said about those articles and pamphlets in which Szabó attacked
the party's 'German jackboot-style', its organizational principles
and political orientation. His advocacy of basic reforms, the
demand for open inner-party debates were rejected not only by
the bureaucrats but also by Social Democratic workers who happened to read them, proud and protective as they were of their
organizational and economic achievements. It was hence an easy
task for the leadership and the local shop-stewards – with whom
Szabó had little contact and never managed to win for himself – to
represent his group's critical stance as 'intellectuals' squabbles'
and discredit it as 'student jokes'.(31) In these matters Szabó
could count only on a small group of young Socialist professionals
in the party, only a few years his juniors, but often called
'Socialist students', for whom he was the source of Russian-type
revolutionary ideas and true internationalism. Late-night meetings
of the 'Revolutionary Committee' were to prepare a vanguard for
the attack on the rigid leadership of the party; even a few young
members of the executive attended. But they were neither effic-
ient nor influential enough to achieve their aims.

The Hungarian Social Democratic Party was anyhow rather un-
friendly to 'intellectuals' within its ranks, and even more to
those without – a feature not uncommon in Second International
parties. Szabó's followers were actually caught between two fires,
as their master himself was quite critical about the role of intellectuals in the leadership of the working-class movement. Lack of
unity and loyalty among them finally broke up the group and, as
mentioned above, the opposition was defeated. Hardly any of them
were able to follow Szabó in his total break with the party and to
his syndicalist position. Here the place for intellectuals was even
more problematic. The anti-intellectualism of most syndicalists
was well known, hence even Szabó's closest comrades were under-
standably alienated by the prospect of participating in a movement
that would grant them little esteem.

Szabó was still not alone in this last phase of his political career.
For some time there had been a minute anarchist movement in
Hungary grouped around the Tolstoyan Jenö Henrik Schmidt,
which managed to influence certain radical movements of agrarian
labourers. Szabó, who kept in touch with this group, though continuously debating with them, was closest to one of its strange
aristocratic members, Count Ervin Batthyány and through him to
foreign anarchists, such as Pierre Ramus and even Kropotkin.
Batthyány financially supported many Hungarian anarchist publications, founded, with Szabó's help, a modern school for peasant children on his estates and, even after his move to England,
assisted Szabó during his travels in search of a cure for his ail-
ments. It was from this anarchist grouping that a few workers
and intellectuals, dissatisfied with the sterile daydreams of 'ideal

anarchism' seceded and founded with Szabó a Syndicalist Propaganda Group. The propaganda, including Szabó's manifesto To
the Workers of Hungary, demanding the foundation of trade
unions independent of the Social Democratic Party found apparently very little resonance. But the core of the group, a few
devoted and actively self-educated workers, remained near Szabó
and became one of the nuclei of revolutionary groups during the
last years of the war.

After the failure of the syndicalist attempt at reaching the
workers by circumventing Social Democracy, Szabó saw himself
forced to face his frustration. In 1913 he asked himself:

> How should I know whether it is true what I write? Where
> can I test the truth of my words? Not in Hungary. But
> farther away they do not carry. Let us therefore wait until
> the time of testing arrives in this country. And until then,
> let us speak about something else, let us try something else,
> maybe less important, certainly less burning issues, but no
> less true and good.(32)

Actually he did his best to test his words abroad, where they
may have been more appropriate: he wrote in a score of German,
French and Italian socialist journals, from the orthodox 'Neue
Zeit' to the syndicalist 'Mouvement Socialiste'. But, of course,
this could not satisfy him. He had to find an audience at home.

This audience was to be the public that had listened to him for
at least a decade by the time he wrote these words, but one to
which he had a rather ambivalent relationship: the intelligentsia
that regarded itself to be 'on the Left'. They were the subscribers of 'Huszadik Század', the literary journal 'Nyugat' (The
West) and the radical-bourgeois daily 'Világ' (Light), the members and friends of the Sociological Society or of the university
students' left-wing Galilei Circle, the people attending the
Society's courses and the most loyal readers at Szabó's Municipal
Library. This social segment may be seen as the 'replacement' of
a class-conscious bourgeoisie that had been sorely missing in
Hungary. Out of some 100,000 professionals (in census terms)
they may have counted at the most two or three thousand. Most
of them were 'free-thinker' sons of those Jewish petty bourgeois
and capitalists who did their best to become acceptable to the
'establishment'.(33)

The 'true and good' causes Szabó had in common with them included the fight against the bulwarks of backwardness from which
the ruling agrarian classes tried to keep the economic, political,
social and intellectual life of the 'great wasteland' of Hungary
under near-feudal domination; the struggle for the democratization
and cultural modernization of the country; the liberation of scholarship, literature and art from the fetters of official academic
nationalism and conservative clericalism - in a word, efforts to
transform public life and thought in the country. Together with
Oscar Jászi and others Szabó became one of the creators and

acclaimed leaders of that 'counter-culture' of avant-guerre
Hungary that managed to unite nearly all valuable intellectual
forces by establishing its own set of values and making it the
only acceptable reference for the cultural elite, rejecting and
despising the norms of the established authorities. Writers were
made on the pages of 'Nyugat', social scientists on those of
'Huszadik Század', not at the academy or the university. 'The
sure sign of Hungary's manifest progress is that stubborn resistance which the old powers mobilize against everything new...
which in turn proves that we have indeed genuine art and scholarship in this country' wrote Ignotus, director of 'Nyugat' in
1908.(34)
     Szabó's particular contribution to this veritable collective effort
of a whole generation was manifold. First, in spite, or maybe
because, of his 'revisionism' and distance to Social Democracy he
was and remained for the intellectuals, well beyond his death, the
most competent representative of Marxism and authentic prop-
agandist of the Marxian method in the social sciences. Second, he
was the first to apply this method to Hungarian history and society, especially to the central issue of national consciousness, the
1848 revolution; Szabó's anti-nationalist position, highly critical
of Kossuth and the nobility (see pp. 157-77) inaugurated an
entirely new tradition of assessment. Third, with the example of
the Municipal Library and his project for a network of public libraries he presented such an educational conception which attempted
to breach the wall between 'high' and 'mass' culture. Fourth,
and not least, Szabó alone rose to the position of an incorruptible
thinker and moralist, who, even at the expense of remaining a
solitary man, was ready to eschew the cliques and parties, prepared at any time to revise his own positions and to express
unpopular truths to his own friends. Although a Marxist, he stood
for an impartial scholarship; although a revolutionary, for autonomous art and literature; although a materialist, for the paramount
significance of ideas and the responsibility of the intellectuals.
These qualities made him into a central figure for all progressive
men and women, and commanded general esteem even among his
adversaries.
     During the war, particularly towards its end, when the world-
wide spiritual crisis left hardly any authority untouched, Szabó's
prestige multiplied. Suddenly, his ethical position and the ideas
he himself may have feared to be utopian - 'action directe',
workers' democracy, anti-militarism and anti-etatism - appeared
more realistic than anything else. In the last months of his life a
wide spectrum of surging new forces found their way to Szabó. He
was the guiding spirit for the young revolutionary socialists mobilized by the Russian revolutions, such as Ilona Duczynska (later
Mrs Karl Polányi), Otto Korvin and Imre Sallai, martyrs of the
Communist movement under the counter-revolutionary Horthy
regime and a good number of others who came to play leading
roles in the revolutions of 1918-19 and beyond. He became the
point of orientation, not only to his old comrades from the left of

the Social Democracy, but also for 'activist' artists such as
Kassák, for the 'ethical idealists' around Lukács and Béla Balázs
and even for many non-radical pacifists. And in far away Moscow
he was elected to the Socialist Academy of Soviet Russia.

He died barely a month before the first Hungarian Revolution
posed most of the problems of revolutionary action which Szabó
tried to clarify in theory. Szabó's premature death on 29 September 1918 spared him of the most trying dilemmas of practical
politics. His funeral became the overture of revolutions; the
workers of Budapest, whom he always wanted to mobilize, stopped
work for a few minutes in his memory, and at the graveside the
Social Democrat Zsigmond Kunfi could say in truth that 'all those
in Hungary who have anything to do with socialism are the pupils
of the rich, courageous, relentlessly honest and creative spirit of
Ervin Szabó'.

The subsequent dramatic months, during which democratic and
socialist ideas and institutions were for the first time put into
practice in Hungary, have shown that the 'pupils' perceived the
master's teachings in very different and often quite opposite
ways. However wide and devoted the circle of those who regarded
themselves as Szabó's followers may have been, no 'school' survived him, not even a small sect. There was in November 1918,
just preceding the foundation of the Communist Party, an ephemeral 'Ervin Szabó circle' that attempted to sustain his revolutionary ideas and his opposition to Social Democracy. But neither
they nor others managed to analyse the complex situation and
define the priorities in the light of his ideas. In those days of
revolutionary action none of the active participants was able to
apply the manifold, more ethical than practical-political, more
strategical than tactical teachings of Szabó. His adepts and followers from the increasingly polarizing political scene could find
justification for as varied and contradictory decisions as sub-
scribing to Leninism in the name of his syndicalism or maintaining
that Szabó alone could have averted the proclamation of the
Soviet Republic in Hungary.

It is, of course, a futile and sterile enterprise to speculate
about what Szabó would have done in 1918 and 1919.(35) Béla Kún
went as far as to see in him 'one of the possible leaders of the
Third International'; the Hungarian Soviet government made him
into one of its 'saints' and placed his bust next to those of Marx
and Engels on the May Day parade in 1919, named the Municipal
Library after him and decreed the edition of his works. But when
the majority of his pupils, almost self-evidently, joined the new
Communist Party, the lack of a 'school' became sadly obvious.
They carried with them their devotion to the revolutionary personality of their master, but not his critical thinking, his sociological scepticism and his ethical standards, which might have
equipped them with means to counterbalance Kún's uncontrolled
voluntarism and the uncritical optimism of the revolution attempting to solve all social ills at once.

The character of Szabó's work and message emerged only in

the course of the debates and discussions of the decades following the defeat of the revolutions, in the sixty years in which
either Communists or Social Democrats or bourgeois radicals
attempted to revive, revise and appropriate his teachings. First,
the democratic and socialist exiles and Szabó's former pupils who
stayed in Hungary competed for his heritage. To be sure, it was
Oscar Jászi, the former Minister of the 1918 Károlyi government,
who published, in exile, Szabó's only major monograph, the book
on 1848. From this rather sterile competition of claims the Communists opted out first: beginning in the later 1920s in the course
of the Bolshevization of the Comintern and the Hungarian Communist Party, they classed Szabó among the 'Social Democratic
traditions' which were to be overcome. Even their later re-
orientation to Popular Front tactics was accompanied by continuous polemics with Szabó's ideas. In these times only a few small
Trotskyite factions kept his anti-centralist, anti-bureaucratic
teachings alive. Later, while searching for their radical traditions
in the midst of the anti-Fascist struggle, the Social Democrats
began to rediscover Szabó's memory, forgetting about conflicts
of the past.

When, after 1945, the People's Republic of Hungary established
its new pantheon, Szabó was half-hidden in a nook left for Social
Democrats and their likes. Offical assessment has split the person
and his teachings, just as it did with Rosa Luxemburg: while the
man received some praise for his revolutionary stance and his
merits in disseminating Marxism, his writings and ideas were
buried in silence. Mátyás Rákosi, 'Stalin's best Hungarian pupil',
is reported to have said that the anarchist Szabó was worse than
the right-wing Social Democrats.

Only since the 'thaw' of the mid-1950s, or rather since 1956,
has the democratic and ethical dimension of Szabó's concept of
socialism been rediscovered and appreciated. The last twenty
years or so have seen the gradual edition of most of his works
and correspondence, and the publication of studies and monographs on his life and work.(36)

In summary, then, Szabó's life and message may appear to have
been but a series of failures and frustrations. His critique of
Social Democracy was not unfounded, as the parties of the Second
International did become mass parties of democracy, rather than
socialism. But his diagnosis has been surely too harsh: the enemies of freedom were not the Socialists, but rather those radical
elements of the left and right which occasionally even profited
from syndicalist and other criticism of the old parties. The working class of western Europe and America did not, as Szabó hoped,
overthrow capitalism in mass strike and direct action; rather the
capitalist system was replaced in mainly agrarian societies of
eastern Europe and Asia in revolutions and civil wars led by parties that were even more 'disciplined armies' than German Social
Democracy. Even in his own country Szabó failed to dismantle
many of the nationalist prejudices and the glorification of noble

heroes; Kossuth, whom he, together with Marx, showed to have been a rather inconsistent democrat, has still a higher place in official and popular memory than himself or his radical-critical friends. Jászi, who after 1919 became increasingly critical of Marxism and socialism, noted the lack of definite answers of Szabó to the many questions he himself had raised: 'He never got beyond criticism and did not arrive at a closed, reflected and constructive alternative.'(37)

However, we are nowadays less interested in perfect answers and closed systems than Jászi was, nearly sixty years ago. What we note above all is that Szabó was a superb asker of questions, disregarding accepted norms and dogma. He raised the problems of historical necessity and subjective will, mass movement and the individual, party discipline and personal liberty, party and class, socialism and freedom, scholarship and politics, Marxism and science and art, tactics and ethics. Many of these were new then – and are scarcely obsolete now.

NOTES

1 O. Jászi, Erwin Szabó und sein Werk. Ein Wort der Erinnerung, 'Archiv für Geschichte des Sozialismus und der Arbeiterbewegung', vol. 10 (1921), p. 29 (henceforth: Szabó).

2 O. Jászi, Ha Szabó Ervin nem hal meg... (Had Ervin Szabó not died) 'Századunk', vol. 3 (1928), p. 530.

3 E. Szabó to J. Körösy, February 1904, in Gy. Litván and L. Szücs (eds.) 'Szabó Ervin levelezése' (Correspondence of E. Szabó) (Budapest, 1977) vol. I, p. 438.

4 On the problem of Jewish assimilation in late-nineteenth-century Hungary see, for example, V. Karady and I. Kemeny, Les juifs dans la structure des classes en Hongrie, 'Actes de recherches en sciences sociales', vol. 22 (1978), pp. 25-59.

5 On K. Menger see, for example, J. Schumpeter, 'Ten Great Economists' (London, 1960).

6 On Inama-Sternegg and Philippovich see V. Müller, 'Karl Theodor von Inama-Sternegg. Ein Leben für Staat und Wissenschaft', Vienna 1967; A. Amonn 'Jahrbücher für Nationalökonomie und Statistik' 3rd Ser., vol. LIV, pp. 158-63.

7 C. E. Schorske, 'Fin-de-siècle Vienna: Culture and Politics' (New York, 1980). The following was written with less insight but full of details: A. Janik and S. Toulmin, 'Wittgenstein's Vienna' (New York, 1973).

8 A brief sketch of the family and their friends is given in L. Congdon, Karl Polanyi in Hungary 1900-1919, 'Journal of Contemporary History', vol. 11 (1976), pp. 167-83.

9 O. Jászi, 'Szabó', p. 37.

10 See, for example, E. S. Vincze, The Struggle for the First Independent Proletarian Party, in H. Vass (ed.), 'Studies on the History of the Hungarian Working Class Movement 1867-

1966' (Budapest, 1975), pp. 19-54; T. Erényi, The Activities of the Social Democratic Party of Hungary in the First
Decades of the Century, in Vass, op. cit., pp. 55-88.

11 E. Szabó to Gy. Mandello, 11 November 1902, in Litván and
Szücs, op. cit., vol. 1, p. 245.

12 On the political and intellectual scene the best overview in a
foreign language is Z. Horváth, 'Die Jahrhundertwende in
Ungarn: Geschichte der zweiten Reformgeneration 1896-1914'
translated by G. Engels (Budapest-Neuwied, 1966); O. Jászi,
'The Dissolution of the Habsburg Monarchy' (Chicago, 1929),
esp. pp. 133-260; cf. L. Congdon, The Moralist as Social
Thinker: Oscar Jászi in Hungary 1900-1919, 'Historians in
Politics' (London, 1974), pp. 273-313; J. Gabel, Hungarian
Marxism, 'Telos', vol. 5 (1975), pp. 185-91; L. Congdon,
Endre Ady's Summons to National Regeneration in Hungary
1900-1919, 'Slavic Review', vol. 33 (1974), pp. 302-22; P.
Hanák, Pathfinders of a Revolution, 'The New Hungarian
Quarterly', vol. 3, no. 6 (1962), pp. 204-17.

13 See T. Süle, 'Sozialdemokratie in Ungarn: Die Rolle der
Intelligenz in der Arbeitebewegung 1899-1910' (Cologne-Graz,
1967), esp. pp. 48-111; F. Mucsi, Die Kämpfe für die organ-
isatorische Reform der SDU, 'Études historiques 1975'
(Budapest, 1975), vol. 2, pp. 107-44.

14 A szocializmus átalakulása (Transformation of socialism)
'Budapesti Napló Albumnaptára' (Budapest, 1907), p. 52.

15 Német és francia szocializmus (German and French Socialism)
'Huszadik Század', pt 1 (1909), p. 294. Szabó wrote these
words in reference to the high quality of Max Weber and
Werner Sombart's 'Archiv für Sozialwissenschaft und Sozial-
politik'.

16 See J. Jemnitz, La correspondence d'Ervin Szabó avec les
socialistes et les syndicalistes de France, 'Le Mouvement
socialiste', vol. 52 (1965), pp. 111-19.

17 Kellenek-e forradalmárok? (Is there need for revolutionaries?)
'Társadalmi Forradalom', 24 December 1910.

18 Cim nélkül (Untitled) 'Nyugat' part 2 (1913), p. 65.

19 Jászi, 'Szabó', p. 39.

20 On Szabó's work on librarianship, see below, pp. 198-201; cf.
also L. Remete, Ervin Szabó und seine Beziehungen zu den
deutschen Bibliotheken, 'Zentralblatt für Bibliothekswesen',
vol. 92 (1978), pp. 257-64.

21 Some of the ethical issues which particularly vexed Szabó
have been discussed by A. Heller, A szükségszerüség árny-
ékában (In the shadow of necessity), 'Történelmi Szemle',
vol. 14 (1971), pp. 356-405.

22 G. V. Plekhanov, 'The role of individual in history' (London,
1940)

23 Cf. H. J. Sandküer and Rafeal de la Vega (eds.), 'Marxis-
mus und Ethik' (Frankfurt, 1974).

24 P. L. Lavrov (1823-1900), Russian social scientist and revolutionary, editor of 'Vpered' (1873-6), and of 'Narodnaia

volia' (1883-86). His famous Historical Letters written in
exile were edited with an introduction to the German translation (Berlin, 1901) by Charles Rappoport; see 'Enc. of
Soc. Sc.', vol. 9 (1964), p. 201.

25 'Freihandel und Imperialismus. Vortrag in der Soziologischen
Gesellschaft in Graz 1918' (Graz-Leipzig, 1918), p. 9.

26 Szociáldemokrácia és politikai erkölcs (Social Democracy and
political ethics), 'Népszava', 24 March 1918.

27 In general: G. Lichtheim, 'Lukács' (London, 1970); cf. also
Editor's Introduction, G. Lukács, 'Political Writings 1919-
1929: The Question of Parliamentarism and Other Essays',
trans. by M. McColgan, ed. by R. Livingstone (London, 1972)
and R. Dutschke, 'Versuch, Lenin auf die Füsse zu stellen',
(Berlin, 1974), pp. 144-54, 180-98; a new biography by
F. Fehér is in preparation.

28 See above, n. 12.

29 Besides the references listed in n. 12, cf. 'Die Habsburgermonarchie 1848-1918', vol. 2 (Vienna, 1975) passim; P. Hanák,
Hungary in the Austro-Hungarian Monarchy, 'Austrian History Yearbook', vol. 3, no. 1 (1967), pp. 260-302.

30 See I. T. Berend and Gy. Ránki, Die Wirtschaftliche Entwick-
lung, in 'Habsburgermonarchie', (op. cit.) vol. 1 (1973),
pp. 462-527; I: T: Berend and Gy. Ránki, Das Niveau der
Industrie Ungarns zu Beginn des 20. Jh...., 'Social and
Economic Research on the History of East-Central Europe'
(Budapest, 1970; Studia historica, 62), pp. 29-49.

31 See above, n. 13.

32 'Nyugat', part 2 (1913).

33 P. Hanák, Skizzen über die ungarische Gesellschaft am
Anfang des 20. Jh., 'Acta Historica Acad. Sc. Hung.', vol.
10 (1963) pp. 1-43; cf. also W: O: McCagg, 'Jewish nobles
and geniuses in modern Hungary' (Boulder, 1972).

34 See also M. D. Fenyö, 'Nyugat' versus the Establishment,
'East Central Europe/Europe du Centre-Est', vol. 7 (1980),
pp. 1-16.

35 On the revolutions see now, P. Pastor, 'Hungary between
Wilson and Lenin' (New York, 1976); T. Hajdu, 'The Hungarian Soviet Republic' (Budapest, 1979; Studia historica, 109).

36 Several selections of Szabó's writings were published in
Budapest, from 1960 onwards; the two volumes of his correspondence (see above, n. 3) are now complete; a short biography by Gy. Litván was published in 1976; some of the
special studies are listed above in n. 16 and 20, and below,
pp. 55 and 198.

37 Jászi, 'Szabó', p. 49.

Part I
ON MARX AND MARXISM

ON THE MATERIALIST CONCEPT OF HISTORY

This first major public presentation by Szabó was prepared
for the discussion held in January 1903 in the Budapest
Sociological Society about Recent Trends in Sociology. The
main speaker was the 'sociologist' Gustáv Leopold, who represented the 'teleological school' of Rudolf Stammler. The
debate focused on the merits and shortcomings of the 'organic
theory', which had been the prevailing approach to society
in Hungary. The majority of the speakers criticized this
school and the discussion amounted to its final defeat. Szabó's
intervention marked the first occasion of the presentation of
Marxism at a scholarly gathering with complete scientific
argumentation. At the same time, he included his doubts
about the strict determinism, characteristic of the German
Marxist school of the age, and thus offered a stringent, but
not rigid, system of social laws to the Hungarian social scientists, instead of the obsolete biological model of explanations.
  The discussion was published in 'Huszadik Század', pt I
(1903): Szabó's address is on pp. 353-60.

Honourable Members of the Sociological Society! You have
appraised and criticized the presentation of Mr Gustáv Leopold
from various points of view; in particular, the adherents of the
organic theory of society, which the speaker has deemed to be on
the decline, defended their stand strenuously. I, too, would like
to speak in defence of a sociological trend which Mr Leopold has
attacked and sentenced to death: the materialist concept of history.
  Before I attempt, however, to defend the substance of this
theory, I have to rectify two errors of fact, principally because
they have a definite bearing on the Marxist theory of society.
One of these rectifications pertains to something Mr Wolfner has
already pointed out, though I am afraid he misunderstood the
speaker. For the speaker did not claim, as Mr Wolfner said, that
the conflict between the reformist and the revolutionary socialists
extends to historical materialism, but he explicitly stated that the
attacks of the reformists are directed against the economic and
political tenets of Marxism. This distinction is rather important,
because it indicates that socialist economics, politics and tactics
can be separated from historical materialism, that is, there is no
necessary connection between them. We have seen that in Italy,
for instance, Turati, the originator and leader of the reformist
tendency, has not rejected the materialist concept of history;

what is more, in his famous pamphlet on theory ('Il partito socialista e l'attuale momento politico') he conceives of the struggle between the two tendencies as a positive factor. On the other hand, it is well known that Ferri, who represents the most rigid orthodoxy in matters of class struggle, tactics, etc., departs considerably from the Marxist doctrine in his basic sociological views. In Russia we note another strange phenomenon: one socialist faction, the so-called 'ekonomists', has interpreted the basic tenet of historical materialism - to wit that economic forces are decisive in social conflicts - in such a literal way that it has included in its Marxist programme nothing but the economic organization of the working class, and has thus arrived at an evaluation of the means of class struggle not unlike that of Bernstein, the very leader of reformism! In contrast, another socialist party, that of the 'socialist revolutionaries', while definitely rejecting Marxism as a theory, nevertheless, in practice, fights with all the weapons of orthodox Marxism, not excepting its revolutionary slogans. The contradictions in the theories of these two groups, the economists and the social revolutionaries - the latter best described as Lavrovists - are exactly inverted when it comes to their practice.

The other necessary correction of facts regards the oft-held assertion that Marx's theory originated in England and came to light in that country. This assertion, even though wrong, seems, at first glance, hardly worth mentioning. Yet this mistake has led to some of the most alluring arguments against Marxism. It has been claimed that Marx, as he moved from the petty economic life of Germany to the imposing environment of the grandiose British world economy, has naturally been led to conclude in his social theory that economic factors play a primal role as the motor force of social development; hence, that Marxist theory has value only as the product of an almost ephemeral impression. However, even from the point of view of subjective reality (for objectively this makes no difference to the validity of Marxist theory), it has to be noted that the materialist concept of history, and the basic Marxian tenets in economics in general, did not originate in England at all but, as can be deduced inter alia from the Preface to 'A Contribution to the Critique of Political Economy', were conceived much earlier - at the time when Marx became the editor of the 'Rheinische Zeitung' and first began to concern himself with economic matters. His notions received confirmation and assumed a more definite form during his visits to Brussels and Paris; that is still before his move to England. Thus if Marxism, as some claim, is excessively concerned with the economy, this cannot be debited to England.

But the real purpose of my intervention is to defend historical materialism against the attacks by our colleague, Mr Leopold. The speaker has grouped the arguments against historical materialism into some ten categories. It is not clear from his presentation whether these are also his own objections, or merely a collection of the most powerful arguments. But since in his conclusion the speaker has arrived at a notion of sociology that is diametrically opposed to Marxism, I am inclined to consider these as his own objections to Marxism. In order to observe the limits of the debate, I will forgo the tempting occasion to expound here historical materialism and attack the opposing theories, and will rather restrict myself to a rebuttal of Mr Leopold's arguments.

It is, however, true that it would be necessary to provide a systematic explanation of Marxist social theory since we do not have a fully elaborated, systematic discussion of historical materialism in all its ramifications. There are works on historical materialism, but none of them summarizes the views of Marx and Engels, the founders of the doctrine. This lack explains - and excuses - the fact that the critics of the materialist concept of history rarely attack, as they should, the doctrine in its latest and most complete form. They rather focus on quotations torn out of context. The speaker is guilty of the same mistake: it is obvious that the historical materialism he had in mind was but its first conception, merely the kernel of the subsequent theory, in which the autocracy of economic forces was still being emphasized in a rigid, one-sided way. True, the doctrine has been applied in this manner by some of Marx's disciples. But there is no longer any excuse for such a procedure. Today we are familiar not only with Marx's Preface to 'A Contribution to the Critique of Political Economy', but also numerous later declarations by Engels on the subject. I am referring in particular to those letters published quite some time ago, which have been recently reprinted by Bernstein.

But even if these materials were not available to us, we should consider, in my opinion, not whether the doctrine did receive a systematic elaboration, but whether it is capable of elaboration, whether it has the potential of being developed further? We shall see that noteworthy attempts have taken place in this sense, that the doctrine has evolved considerably beyond the frame in which it had been attacked in the past, and that these more recent additions have by no means detracted from the original doctrine. Just the opposite: they have widened its base and thus strengthened it. I grant that to some orthodox adepts of Marxism these additions appear sacrilegious, and they reject them firmly. Such rejection, however, does not diminish in any way the intrinsic value of those additions; Engels himself warned against some of these young 'Marxists'.

Now let me address myself to the speaker's attacks point by point. I have little to say about his first point. I am not well acquainted with Hegelian philosophy; hence I cannot give a fair estimate of its significance. I would say this much, however: in my opinion Hegelian dialectics are not so essential to historical materialism that they cannot be dispensed with. The materialist concept of history remains true whether we construct it according to the rules of dialectics, or otherwise.

It seems likewise unnecessary to reflect at length on the second argument of the speaker, that Marxists have not yet demonstrated the validity of their doctrine by historical research. First of all, this is untrue since, in addition to the works mentioned by the speaker himself, to which I would add Marx's 'Eighteenth Brumaire', there is a whole series of historical works and studies based on the method of historical materialism. Among these we may list the socialist histories of the French Revolution, of the Viennese Revolution, and of the Commune. But even if all these had not been written, this would not suffice to forge an argument against a theory that today is almost exclusively represented by socialists; that is, by persons who do not dispose of the material means, the time, or the scholarly apparatus needed for historical research which are provided only by universities to their professors. I am convinced that this gap will be bridged as soon as the number of such people as Werner Sombart and Karl Lamprecht will increase.

As his third argument the speaker pointed to great inventions which have come about, he argued, independently of economic conditions. Possibly so. In my opinion, however, it would be too mechanistic an interpretation of historical materialism if this was a valid counter-argument to it. The materialist concept of history does not deny the possibility of individual invention or discovery but holds that, from the point of view of social progress, such discreet occurrences have little significance. This is best demonstrated by the commonplace of the inventor's tragic fate: many inventions have acquired practical significance only when they coincided with the economic necessities of the age.

The fourth objection – a favourite argument against historical materialism – is that religion has evolved from animism, that is for a psychological reason. Yet if we study the relationship between religion and the economy we must make strict distinctions between the various phases of their evolution. The origins of all religion have to do with puerile notions of nature and of man, and, indeed, it would be difficult to show the influence of economic factors at this stage. True enough, these origins are no more than the product of a fear derived from utter ignorance regarding nature and man, from superstitions in which the influence of the economy is at best negative: the primitive economic activities are in harmony with primitive perceptions, including primitive religious notions. But at the higher stage of religious development, when religion broadens into a world-view and becomes the metaphysical code of a total system of ethics and government, it becomes clear that the commandments or prohibitions of religion are closely related to the prevailing economic and social conditions, and actually represent their powerful sanctions. Undoubtedly, however, certain religious teachings tend to develop roots and continue to hold man captive long after the original economic and social base has been whittled away. How religions can be transformed, retaining their name, is, in turn, evident from a comparison of present-day and primitive Christianity.

The speaker's fifth argument, the reference to Belfort Bax and the specific development of the British labour movement, has

always had a strange sound to me. Not merely because, as you
know, for many years Bax has been hurling anathema at Bernstein and continually demanding his expulsion from the Socialist
Party, but because it was also Bax who selected as the motto of
his journal 'The Social Democrat' that 'in every historical epoch,
the prevailing mode of economic production and exchange, and
the social organisation necessarily following from it, form the
basis upon which is built up, and from which alone can be explained, the political and intellectual history of the epoch'. As
far as I know, it was in accordance with this principle that Bax
found the causes of the specific development of the British labour
movement in the particular international economic position of
Great Britain; namely, in the fact that when British industry and
commerce dominated the world markets, it was its interest in the
continuity of exchange and the undisturbed profiting from the
continuous boom which prompted the British bourgeoisie, by
means of concessions, to take away the edge of those conflicts
which threatened the relationship between the bourgeoisie and the
proletariat and which, when prosperity receded - as it did quite
recently - broke out again and again. Class conflict and class
struggle - though in forms different from those on the continent -
did exist in Great Britain as well, and this is crucial. That British national character and traditions may also have been obstacles
to the spread of socialism in that country is not denied even by
the most dogmatic Marxists, but those are hardly crucial issues.

I must to a large extent agree with the speaker when he argues
that Marxism leads to fatalism and quietism; but I prefer to discuss this matter when I speak of the relationship between Marxism
and Lavrov.

In contrast, I definitely disagree with the speaker as regards
his seventh objection, according to which Marx was guilty of
scientific carelessness in tying his entire social philosophy to his
materialist world-view even though materialist philosophy had
been shaken to its very foundations.

This is undoubtedly one of the most interesting issues in connection with historical materialism. Materialism and idealism have
been of such lively interest for so long to philosophers and lay-
men alike, and especially to the 'political man' - after all, historical materialism is eminently practical, being a theory that actual-
izes itself in day-to-day political struggle - that we must speak of
it in some detail.

Here I must begin by warning, however, not so much the members of this Society but rather those outsiders who do not as yet
have a clear idea of the meaning of these concepts: when speaking
of materialism and idealism one must always distinguish clearly
between the two as philosophical concepts and as ethical concepts.
It should be obvious that philosophical materialism can coexist well
with idealism in its ethical sense, while philosophical idealism is
far from constituting a guarantee against an ethically rather materialistic life. The superficial contrasting of these two terms originated with the German philistine who attempted to camouflage his

lack of ethical idealism by praising philosophical idealism to the
skies.

Furthermore, I should emphasize that it would be a most futile
undertaking indeed – as my friend Oscar Jászi pointed out in his
recent work – to continually contrast materialism and idealism.
Everybody agrees by now – Belfort Bax as well as Haeckel, for
instance – that this would be an artificial dichotomy and, considering monism, totally unnecessary. There can be no matter without force (spirit, idea), and no force without matter. Thus, if
we take into account Marx and Engels rather than the writings of
the modern Marxists, the issue is simply: what kind of materialism was theirs? I dare to assert as an undebatable fact that Marx
and Engels have modified philosophical materialism in certain
rather essential respects and that, furthermore, their materialism
has nothing to do with the rather crass materialism of a Büchner,
a Vogt, or a Moleschott. Engels directed sharp criticism against
their view, calling it mechanistic, as it disregards the chemical
and organic processes, and takes no cognizance of the continual
transformation of matter. Granted that Marx and Engels have
retained the terminology of materialism, and maybe more of it than
we are inclined to accept nowadays; but that theirs was something
altogether different from vulgar materialism can easily be demonstrated.

Along these same lines, the materialist concept of history not
only should be distinguished from materialism in general; it
actually allows, from the very start, for the operation of ideological factors in social life. It might be almost enough to refer to
the fact that both idealist utopians and orthodox Marxists believe
that the determining influence of economic factors, that is their
influence on all aspects of intellectual life, will cease once socialist
society is established. As far as the past and present are concerned, however, we may also quote from Marx, who wrote that
when necessity, that is the compulsion of economic needs, does
not operate, because these needs of the society have been met,
then 'human effort, which is an end in itself, the true realm of
liberty, will begin'. It is then that the intellectual, aesthetic life
of man, a life he already had in him originally in germ form, can
truly begin.

And this is where we reach the objection most often raised
against the materialist concept of history; namely, that it would
exclude the influence of ideological factors on social life.

It should be clear from what precedes that Marx's philosophy of
history has certain temporal limits. Just as in his theory of values
he has found the key, not to human economy in general but to
capitalist economy in particular, his historical theory does not
apply to man in isolation – as does the value theory of the Menger-
Jevons school – but only to society; second, he considers the
economic factor of primary importance only as long as the economic needs of a sizeable group of persons remain unsatisfied.
Because this has always proved to be the case ever since the end
of primitive communism, and will be as long as there are classes

and class struggle, in the final analysis it is the economic factor which determines the social, political and intellectual contents and tendencies of an age. To be sure, by economic factors we do not mean 'the iron determinism of economic relations', as the speaker has described it, but rather the prevailing mode of production, exchange and reproduction of goods. All this, however, certainly does not exclude the influence of ideological forces. In a society based on private property, classes emerge as a result of the division of labour, and develop conflicting interests. Among these classes struggle ensues including, of course, struggle on an ideological plane: this brings about the state, the laws, the prevailing morality. These ideas or ideologies survive and evolve according to their inner logic even while the social conditions which formed their base, the struggles themselves, or the economic relations may alter considerably. Ideologies become autonomous and, in turn, affect the economic base, even modifying it to a certain extent. This was the position of Marx and Engels, which, at the same time, can also answer the argument of the speaker, borrowed from Stammler; namely, that the reform attempts of contemporary socialist parties do not jibe with the theory. They do very well, indeed. The state is an ideological factor, just as is law, morality, etc.; to influence this factor and use it to modify the current conditions to a certain point, namely up to the main points of economic conflict and of conflicts of class interest, is entirely possible. To strive for this much does not contradict historical materialism. It would be a contradiction if Marxists expected everything from the state, if they were to suddenly neglect economic and social evolution, if they were to disregard the class character of the state and, much like certain utopians, were to expect the realization of the socialist society from a fiat of the government. When there are some who expect a transformation in this manner, neither Marx, nor Engels, nor their followers are at fault.

The speaker's ninth objection is that Marx had forgotten about the idea-provoking influence of man's natural environment. My reply will be brief. Both Marx and Engels have time and again referred to either the direct influence of natural factors, or to nature as a category of the economic factors; that is they have conceded at least the indirect influence of nature. This applies particularly to prehistory, while later man does manage to free himself increasingly from the domination of nature. In this regard Marxism is in total agreement with Buckle and with Hellwald but, of course, goes beyond them.

The speaker has left until last the basic argument of Stammler against historical materialism, one that attacks the doctrine at its very foundation. Stammler claims that the representatives of historical materialism are constantly forced to set up objectives whenever they apply the doctrine; in other words, to lead individuals in a certain direction. But teleology is incompatible with the law of causality; hence causality itself, this cornerstone of historical materialism, is faulty. The assumption underlying this

attack, therefore, is that causality would exclude the conscious
expression of the will of the individual, and leads to fatalism or
quietism. We know that this charge has often been raised against
Marxism.

I would rather not deal with the first part of this issue, whether
causality exists or not. I prefer to leave this terrain to others
better versed in philosophy; I will simply assume that causality
does exist, and that without such an assumption all social science
becomes impossible. Here I am only interested in deciding whether
historical materialism indeed excluded conscious will and the set-
ting up of objectives; in other words, whether it eliminates the
subjective element from the evolution of society, whether it considers this evolution as a purely objective phenomenon.

And here, in contrast to Mr Wolfner, I am quite willing to concede that historical materialism has been so interpreted not only
by its enemies but even by many of its adepts, and that both
Marx and Engels had, for a long time, emphasized the objective
factors almost exclusively. While they did not belittle at all the
role of the man of action in practice – after all, they themselves
were outstanding propagandists – they nevertheless almost completely neglected this role in their theory. They made no attempt
to construct either a psychology of the individual, nor even a
mass psychology of the materialist theory of history. But it is
easy to see why this had been the case. In contrast to the then
predominant Hegelian social idealism, they had to lead social
science back onto its materialist foundations, and to reconstruct
it on that basis. They had to emphasize the basic doctrine against
their enemies; in the midst of this struggle, the reflexive forces,
including man, were naturally relegated to the background. But
Engels himself reproached some of his disciples for having misunderstood the doctrine, for having applied it in a one-sided
manner; and he refused to identify with these 'Marxists'.

The issue, therefore, is whether man can be organically incor-
porated into historical materialism? I am grateful to the speaker
for having mentioned the name of Lavrov. I have long yearned to
make this Russian philosopher, so little known abroad, better
known at least in our country; because, in my opinion, in his
works we can find that which hitherto has been missing from the
theory of historical materialism, namely an elaboration of the subjective psychological aspect.

The speaker is completely wrong in classifying Lavrov among
the teleologists. He may have been led to this conclusion by the
Introduction which Charles Rappoport wrote to the German translation of Lavrov's 'Historical Letters', an otherwise excellent piece
which, however, is somewhat biased when it comes to Marxism; in
my opinion, it does not provide an entirely accurate description
of Lavrov's philosophy, but seems to have been written with a
mind to loosen the relationship between Lavrov and Marx. Lavrov
claimed to be Marxist – albeit with certain reservations – and
surely he must have had good reasons for his claim. His reservations concern the inadequate consideration of the subjective

element. Incidentally, Lavrov does recognize that social development is based on economic conditions, but the ideas formed in this
process have a creative, active role in further development. And
the subjects of this process are the bearers of ideas, that is
human beings who select their ends and act intentionally.

Engels argues the very same thing: again and again we meet
with the phrase 'men make their own history'. He sets up the distinction between natural and social determination: 'In nature...
things do not occur for consciously willed purposes.... However,
in the history of society the actors are all human beings with
consciousness, who act out of consideration or emotion towards a
definite goal; nothing happens without purpose or without a will
to an end.' And further: 'Men make their history, whatever may
come out of it, in so far as each pursues his own consciously
chosen end, and the result of these several divergently active
wills and their manifold impact on the world around them is history. It depends, therefore, on what the many individuals will.'

Already in 1845 in his 'Theses on Feuerbach' Marx wrote what
can be taken as the kernel of his later theory: 'The main defect
of all hitherto existing materialism... is that the object, the reality, sensuousness are perceived of only as the form of the object
or of contemplation but not as human sensuous activity or practice ['Praxis'], not subjectively. Hence it happened that the
active side, in contrast to materialism, has been developed by
idealism'. Thus he and Engels clearly saw the function of the
active man; the trouble was that, since they had to polemize with
adversaries all the time, they only emphasized those factors which
were the causes of men's actions and ideas. This, as I have said,
was admitted by Engels himself.

The difference between Lavrov, on the one hand, and Marx and
Engels, on the other, is that Lavrov wrote philosophy of history,
and considered history not from the point of view of causes and
causality, but from that of goals and means, subjectively, as the
product of man's intentionality. Marx and Engels, on the contrary,
considered history objectively, and sought to analyse causes.

Yet Marx did not exclude idealism, while Lavrov did not disregard the material foundations of ideals. His ideals are not
arbitrary ones, but the products of scientifically controlled vol-
ition. In order to have an intelligent will, we must know not only
what is possible to will but also what is worth willing.

In my opinion, Lavrov provides a theory that is complementary
to Marxism in which the subjective element did not receive appropriate weight; not in principle but in its elaboration. And here I
can conclude my intervention. I have limited myself to the speaker's attacks against historical materialism, and did not intend to
present the theory as a whole. I only meant to justify my conviction that the materialist theory of history, the way it had been
outlined by Marx and particularly by Engels in their last writings,
and the way it was rounded out by Lavrov, provides an altogether
satisfactory, although as yet unelaborated, explanation of social
existence. This theory can never be replaced by teleology, all the

less so as, in my opinion, teleology not only cannot be a social science, but is not even a science at all.

SOCIALISM

Szabó's exposé on Socialism was his opening lecture in a
series of discussions organized by the Sociological Society
in 1904 on The Direction of Social Development. Since, as
the introduction stated, 'even the educated in Hungary
accept such cliches as Liberalism = Manchester, the exploitation of the poor by the economically powerful, Socialism =
land distribution (!) and Conservatism or Christian Socialism = black cassocks and bleak reactionaries', the Society
wished to present the major contemporary trends in western
social thought. The main speakers represented Liberalism,
Anarchism, Socialism and Conservatism (with a focus on
Christian Socialism). In twelve sessions more than thirty
scholars and politicians spoke on the topics. The debates
focused very much on socialism, not only because of the significance of the issue but also because Szabó's lecture was
unquestionably the best of all. Hence, he did not overstate,
when, in his closing words after replying to the diverse
objections and opposing views, he stated: 'One social ideal
stands out that clearly falls into the direction of social progress: the socialist ideal.' The debate was published in
'Huszadik Század', vol. II (1904) and also separately as
'A társadalmi fejlődés iránya' (Budapest, 1904); Szabó's
lecture is on pp. 37-66 of the latter. The last part of the
lecture was also published in German as Psychologisches
zur Frage der Freiheit in der sozialistischen Gesellschaft,
'Neue Zeit', pt 2 (1903/4), pp. 414-6.

'Modern socialism is the product, on the one hand, of the class
conflicts between the haves and the have-nots, wage labourers
and bourgeois and of the anarchy prevailing in production, on the
other.' These were the words with which one of the most outstanding representatives of modern socialism, Friedrich Engels, introduced his polemics against that new brand of socialism which
Eugen Dühring tried to launch in Germany in the 1870s.
    When it became my task - a task above my capacities, I am
afraid - to represent socialism in front of this honoured Society,
I could not find a more appropriate point of departure than that
of Engels. I believe that if I should succeed in demonstrating just
one thing, namely that socialism does not derive from the arbit-
rariness, caprice, or ignorance of some, but is the necessary
consequence of certain social facts that can be established by

experience and verified by science, then I will have accomplished my most important task. And no matter how pale or hesitant the application of the proven basic principles in the various areas of the socialist movement may be, they will not weaken the validity of socialism. It is from this expectation that I derive the courage to represent here a cause, which is undoubtedly the most burning and most central issue of every school of the social sciences, as well as of policy in our days.

In formulating my task thus, I am anxious to adhere to the scientific spirit of this Society. For the essential goal of social science is to determine that social phenomena are also subject to laws; that the intricate structure, the relationship between persons and objects - which we call society - is not the product of chance or some metaphysical caprice, but the necessary consequence of the realization of the trends inherent in certain factors of society. Hence it is impossible to understand any kind of social fact without reducing it to its causes and determining its connections to other social factors, which exert mutually modifying reciprocal influences on it. The task of the social sciences is to reveal the causal connections between social phenomena.

If we adhere to this notion of social determinism then the occurrence of socialistic theories and experiments in the history of all civilized nations, from the most ancient times to the present, will warn us against those who believe that they can easily dismiss the whole theory and movement by high-handed references to it as a 'demagogy'. They should not forget that every new theory was at the time of its appearance decried as mad by its enemies, and that all saviours of people have been called crazy by the supporters of the status quo. Christ was not the last to be mocked and crucified by the 'scribes'. We in Hungary should recall the saying of Baron József Eötvös, that communism has not been accused of a single sin which would not have been hurled at the early Christians. It is striking that even the works of Count István Széchenyi have been thrown on a bonfire, and he, too, was declared lunatic by the scribes of his age. One could, of course, continue the list of martyrs of social progress ad infinitum.

Those, however, who can only evaluate principles and social movements from the point of view of their own subjective interests will never perceive social phenomena in the manner I have described above. Their concepts or interpretations can be changed only by the success of a principle or the victory of a movement. But just as we do not measure the worth of an individual by his external achievements, but rather by the inner motives which guide his thought and his actions, the true nature of a social movement - or, what amounts to the same, its validity - can only be correctly assessed by examining its underlying social motivations.

I

First of all, we must answer the question: what is the cause of
social movement? History indicates that it is a continuous process
of development, the content and tendency of which are determined
by the emergence of groups, their integration, and the changes
in their position within society as a whole. Thus social movement
is the endeavour of one group of people to change its position
within society and thus its relationship to other groups in society.
What prompts people to strive for such change? In my opinion,
the most appropriate answer to this question was offered by that
school of social science which is known as historical materialism,
the founders of which have also been the most influential theoretical and practical leaders of modern socialism. According to
historical materialism the social struggles in every historical
period are determined by the economic relations of that period,
that is by the discrepancy between the forces of production and
the distribution of wealth, and the endeavour to achieve harmony
between these factors of the economy. Since economy is a matter
of relations between people, the representatives of the conflicting
factors of the economy are also people, or rather groups of people:
classes. The conflict between the forces of production with the
relations of production is manifested in the conflict of classes.
The history of societies is the history of class struggles. The
properties and property-less, masters and slaves, serfs and lords,
wage-earners and capitalists struggle against each other, as the
representatives of different modes of production and the conflicting sources of income. Social struggles derive from economic
relations, and these class struggles, in turn, determine eventually
the social and political ideals of the period, the content and trend
of morality, science and the arts.
Of course, in the limited frame of this lecture I cannot prove
the validity of historical materialism through historical examples.
With regard to our question I only need to show that the modern
social movement is the necessary consequence of the present state
of economic production, and that the forms of production and of
distribution of income in the prevailing economic order necessarily
orient contemporary class struggles toward one class embracing
the principle of collectivity.
That new force of production, which gave rise to a new mode of
production and hence to the two great opposing camps of contemporary class struggle, was the *machine*. The second half of the
eighteenth century in England has been appropriately referred to
as the age of the industrial revolution. Indeed, while blood did
not flow in this revolution, there has hardly been a more radical
and profound transformation in the history of mankind.
Time does not permit me to discuss in detail the economic and
social order of the Middle Ages, in order to show its contrast to
modern economy and society. We must content ourselves by des-
cribing the Middle Ages in general as that period of industrial
production when the producer owned the means of production,

hence what he produced was indeed completely the fruit of his own labour. Production was carried out with simple tools, the main role being played by manual labour. There was barely any distribution of labour. Hence the final product was the embodiment not only of the producer's own labour, but also of his diligence, ability, ingenuity and taste. On the other hand, the limits to the volume of production were imposed by the amount of human labour force available.

How does the machine differ from the tool of the artisan? In that 'it is a mechanical tool which need only be brought into motion, and which performs the same operations with its tools which earlier were performed by the workers and their tools' (Marx, 'Capital', vol. I, sec IV, ch. 13). But while in handicrafts the number of tools was limited by the number of workers, the steam engine provides the machine with such driving power that a series of identical machines may operate in the same place, at the same time, together and alongside each other.

This process, however, simply multiplies the capacity of work. 'Where, however, the object of labour goes through a connected series of various gradual processes, performed by diverse but complementary chains of machines' (Marx, op. cit.), in such an uninterrupted, interconnected process where the human hand does hardly more than retrieve the finished product from the set of machines - there the function of the machine in multiplying labour and destroying men becomes quite obvious.

While the tremendous increase in the forces of production, on the one hand, liberates human labour, on the other hand, it immensely extends the area for the application of labour force. The transformation of one branch of industry entails the transformation of another, complementary branch. The penetration of the machine into every branch of the satisfaction of economic needs makes it necessary to increase manifold the production of raw materials. The machines themselves give rise to a new and incredibly differentiated and developed branch of industry: the major industry of manufacturing machines. Mass production, which does not serve the satisfaction of individual needs but rather the competition in the market-place, also requires the transformation of the means of communication and transport. Roads and canals are built; the railway, the steam ship and the telegraph replace the stage-coach, the sailing ship and the messenger.

I cannot give here a detailed description of the conditions that followed the development of machines. However tempting it may be to sketch the orgy of the passion for profit that repressed all human feelings, the frightening misery, the exploitation of women and children surpassing all imagination, the concomitant crimes, and immorality of the metropolis and thus to exert an impact of the feelings of my audience, I have to pass over this opportunity. It may perhaps suffice to refer to the descriptions in the novels of Charles Dickens. I rather wish to indicate the economic and social factors which have necessarily elicited the yearning for socialism. And these factors were not born from misery. They are the results of higher and more complex processes of evolution.

Misery itself, the most direct impact of the machine on the working class, has elicited in them but the negative feelings of blind rage and bitterness. The early history of the industrial era in Britain is filled with food riots and the smashing of machines – not at all in harmony with socialism, which strives towards the highest degree of productivity. When the working class became aware of the futility of riots it resigned itself to its fate and could barely be mobilized for a long time. The utopists, the first prophets of socialism, called upon it in vain, as they also addressed in vain the bourgeoisie. Carlyle's words were very appropriate: the great, silent class lies deeply buried like Enkelados who, to complain of his pains, must cause an earthquake.

In order for socialism to become the feeling and will of the masses the intuitive insight of great men was not enough. The new economic order had to settle to a certain extent, while the soul of people adjusted to the new conditions.

The change in the workers' position affected them first of all through their function as the means of production within the economy. The artisan created his product himself from start to finish: he could include all the elements of his knowledge, his ability, his strength in it; he created a whole, and he liked his work with the feeling of the producer. His product was unique, and the feeling and consciousness of individuality reigned in his soul. The worker working at the machine could feel nothing of all this. The finished product went through a hundred machines and a hundred hands; and the hands had but a minor role: the bulk of the work was done by the machine. The worker who threw the first piece of steel into the smelter in the screw mill never saw the finished screw, and those who retrieved the finished screw from the machine knew nothing about the first phases of the process. On the other hand, he could feel that his work depended on the work of many others; that he was an easily replaceable member of a giant co-operating organism, a member who could achieve nothing without the others. He also saw that in this co-operation the most important role was played not by the human mind, ability, zeal, or strength, but by the inanimate machine which, wherever it may be set up, will continue to work. All men need do is establish the necessary link. What is socialism but the extension of this principle of co-operation from the single factory to the factories of a city, of a country?

The master worked alongside the artisan, in the craft shop. They started and finished at the same time, rested together, ate from the same kitchen, the only difference in the outcome of their work being that the master already had his house and family, whereas the journeyman only hoped to have one. In the factory not only did the reciprocal role of the owner of the means of production and of the worker become entirely different, and not only did direct co-operation and collaboration cease; the outcome of the work differed conspicuously for the entrepreneur and the worker. The worker realized that the person who contributed not an iota of physical work to the production was the master of the goods, the beneficiary of all kinds of pleasures; whereas he, bent under the monotonous, nerve-wracking, tiresome work from early morning to sunset with hundreds and hundreds of companions, could not even earn his daily bread. Lacking capital, he had no expectation to ever leave the ranks of the proletariat. The same applied to thousands of companions, who lived around him in the miserable slums which seemed to be separated from the well-to-do neighbourhoods by iron walls. Such a contradiction in the results of work necessarily feeds the yearning for a distribution of goods that would be proportionate to the work. This is socialism in the area of the distribution of income.

The dissatisfied masses kept on growing. An invisible force drove thousands of bankrupt small entrepreneurs and impoverished peasants into the towns. Whenever a crisis broke out the same invisible force pushed thousands of more-or-less secure factory-hands into the throes of unemployment. Earlier people used to know more or less what to expect upon awakening in the morning. But industry added to the heavy burdens of those who were suffering the persistent feeling of terrifying insecurity. What freedom means to the person whose needs have been guaranteed - namely the possibility to change his circumstances and the opportunity to make profit - meant servitude to the worker. For the wage-earner a guaranteed livelihood became the most exquisite formulation of freedom: and this is what he expects from socialism.

Why would he believe that it is impossible to upset the economic and social order? Each day humanity was surprised by the news of a new miracle. Every day was the birthday of some invention that radically changed the lives of thousands and hundreds of thousands: the steam engine, the railway, the telegraph, the steam ship! Earth-shaking revolutions, the collapse of kingdoms, the birth of new nations. Daily surprises in the natural sciences. It seems that the human capacity for production and creation has no limits. Religious faith has been shaken. The divine and human orders are obviously not eternal. Nothing is impossible!

Thus economic transformation prepared the mind of the working class, and the teachings of the first scientific proponents of socialism fell onto this fertile soil. Much as the present conscious and systematic formulation of socialism could never have come about without the insight of certain individuals of genius, it is equally certain that had the mind of the masses not developed the capacity to receive, a capacity derived from their economic and social situation, the word of these geniuses would have remained without an echo - a cry in the wilderness.

Let us skip over those fifty-two years which separate the first appearance of conscious socialism, the Babeuf conspiracy, through the period of Owen, Saint-Simon, Fourier and Weitling, to the publication of the 'Communist Manifesto', in which we can hail the first truly influential proclamation of scientific socialism.

Why do we call the socialism of Marx and Engels scientific? Why not the socialism of Saint-Simon and of Fourier? After all, the former refer innumerable times to the connections which tie Marxism to utopian socialism. Because Marx and Engels were the first to attempt to integrate the modern socialist movement into the general laws of society in a scientifically exact manner. It can be said that while Saint-Simon and Auguste Comte were the founders of sociology, Marx was the first to give sociological investigation a basis which not only remains valid, but only now begins to occupy the place it deserves in the social sciences. We mean the teachings of historical materialism.

We call it scientific because it was Marx who recognized and determined that socialism, like every social phenomenon, is subject to social laws that are above individual will and that have an effect similar to natural laws; therefore, once we have determined by the rules of social causality that it must exist it is no more possible to speak of its annihilation than it would be to deny the law of gravity, regardless of the beautiful speeches.

This lecture is not meant to be an apology for Marxism. In my opinion, both science and life have disproved a number of the theoretical tenets as well as practical applications of Marxism. But within this Society, dedicated as it is to examining all social phenomena, including socialism, from the point of view of social determinism, it would be impossible to bypass that conception of socialism which stems from the same principle. All the less so as, in my opinion, Marxism has made not only mistakes (and many have chosen to perceive only the mistakes) but has tied socialism to sociology, thanks to a number of teachings which have become part of our scientific arsenal. But I will mention only those that also happen to be basic to modern socialism.

Modern socialism differs from old socialism on two basic issues. One is that modern socialism is permeated by the conviction that industrial development is driven by inherent forces in a direction which inevitably creates the economic conditions necessary for socialist production; the other is the conviction that the liberation of the working class can only be achieved by the working class itself. The first is the doctrine of the concentration of industry; the second, that of class struggle.

'The perishing middle class!' 'Save the small enterprise!' Our press keeps reiterating these slogans more than any other. It has gripped the mind of the people to such a extent that I cannot even describe it as ignorance; it has become such an unconscious reflex to demand simultaneously, in the same paragraph, the development of factory industry, and the support of small enterprises. My previous arguments, as well as the very essence of capitalist development, make it clear that the two are incompatible.

We need only to throw a glance at the large plants and the small craft shops. The shops operate with a limited, working capital, primarily in a hand-to-mouth sort of way, purchasing a small amount of raw material and paying wages. In the large plants, on the other hand, we have constant capital invested in expensive machinery and installations. In the shops the distribution of work involves a few persons; in the large plants co-operation is divided among hundreds of machines and workers, making use of the smallest advantage offered by specialization. The shops produce on commission, for immediate consumption; the factories for storage, hence they can wait for the opportunities of the most profitable sales. The shops play the role of the small consumer in the purchase of raw materials; the large plants purchase wholesale and cheaper.

The superiority of the factories is so obvious that perhaps we do not even need lengthy statistics to demonstrate that competition by the small shops becomes impossible not only in the newer branches, where the production depends on machines, but has penetrated the old branches as well, forcing out the craft shops from the market. This process keeps accelerating. In general, large capital and large plants are more productive, more competitive than the small ones: hence it follows that they destroy not only the craft industry, but at an ever increasing speed the larger factory destroys the smaller one. Industrial development signifies the triumph of the largest capital and the largest plant.

The process is enhanced by the other maladies of capitalist production. Production that disregards consumption and the excessive competition sometimes results in a saturation of the market. This is called 'overproduction', or crisis in production. The enterprises that dispose of a large capital weather through the storm of such a crisis more easily. Every crisis entails the disappearance of masses of smaller enterprises; and the industrial production after the crisis is characterized by a higher degree of concentration.

The technical superiority of the big-factory industry and the confusion or anarchy in the capitalist mode of production inevitably lead to an ever-increasing concentration of capital and of firms. The theoretical climax of this process - which, however, the continual birth of new branches of industry keeps postponing into a distant future - is that a few giant corporations dominate each branch of industry, or the production of each country.

From the point of view of socialism the most important aspect of this development is that the form of production on which socialism is also based, that is social production, also increasingly forms the basis of capitalist industry.

But while the production of the medieval artisan was indeed individual production, and the product was the fruit of his own work carried out with his own means of production, the capitalist, who concentrates the means of production into factories and converts them into truly social means of production, deals with the products of this social production as if they were the fruits of his own individual work, and not those of appropriated labour. From this contradiction, the contradiction between social production and individual expropriation, derives the contradiction between the proletariat and the bourgeoisie. The task of socialism is to resolve the contradiction between the social form of production and the individual form of distribution.

Industrial development is essentially a passive process which goes
on even without anyone's conscious intervention. The process
which will resolve the contradiction between production and distribution is active: the purposeful will and action of people. It
will be the outcome of the proletarian class struggle.

Class struggle! This term elicits greatest anxiety among sentimental souls. This term brought on resentment against the
workers' movement, 'patriotic' anger and contempt, as well as
'humanitarian' complaints and commiseration. Class struggle is
seen as worse than war, more despicable than treason. Class
struggle is perceived not as a civil war that erupts spontaneously
and ends rapidly, but rather as consciously instigated, permanent
internecine fighting. Some of its enemies are willing to forgive
Marxism everything, except the doctrine of class struggle. They
are not aware that the historians of the bourgeoisie - Mignet,
Guizot, Thierry, Niebuhr - knew full well that the entire French
Revolution was nothing other than the climax of the aspirations of
one class, the bourgeoisie, intended to transform the social order
to suit its own interests. This was class struggle. The same was
perceived by Lorenz von Stein and, in our own country, Béla
Grünwald, and Győző Concha, neither of whom received the idea
from Marx or Engels. But they did not 'invent' the process, as
some would like to believe; and the nightmare vision of violence
and fratricide is least applicable precisely to the Marxist formulation of class struggle.

What is important from the point of view of social science is that
Marx and Engels have organically included the phenomenon of class
struggle into the mechanics of social development, which to the
historians was but a unique phenomenon. Even more important
from the point of view of socialism: they thus provided the modern
socialist movement with a sound basis. I see the greatest and most
lasting contribution of Marxism, its most productive achievement
on behalf of socialism precisely in this connection between socialism and social science.

The place people occupy in the process of production and distribution determines the relationship of groups or classes to one
another; from this tenet they have demonstrated, with the help of
historical examples, that the social orders did not change through
peaceful agreements between all members of society, but came
about as a result of struggle between the ruling class and the
ruled. History knows no example of a class voluntarily surrend-
ering the privileged position it has occupied in the economic and
social order. The ruling class has given in only as a result of the
peaceful or violent pressure from the subjected classes. The working class, which intends to replace the present social order based
on the private ownership of capital by a free and co-operative
social order based on public ownership, cannot expect the promotion of such a change by the ruling class, but only from itself,
from its own efforts, by its own action. The liberation of the
working class can only be the task of the working class itself.

The validity of this doctrine is confirmed not by the practical

successes attained by the workers' parties based on the theory of
the class struggle. Those labour parties which do not adhere
very strictly to the principle of class struggle may have been
'more successful' in recent times. Perhaps the wages workers
earn are higher and their hours are shorter, or perhaps these
parties exert a more direct influence on legislation and government than those which interpret the principle of class struggle
more strictly. But I believe that this is an optical illusion; that
these parties are further away from socialism than the stubborn
'negativists'; that is so because the practice of class struggle has
not had that educational impact in which I see the greatest contribution of class struggle.

It is well known that no social order can be maintained for long
merely by force. It is necessary that people adjust to the external
needs of society, that they themselves strive for what society
strives for, and that they should wish to achieve this end in
accord with the economic forces of society. Only then do people
feel themselves free; and without a feeling of freedom a society
cannot survive. The most serious social dislocations are caused
by the conflict of one class's view of freedom with that of another.
The presently prevailing system of economic and social co-
operation, known as liberal, that is free, is indeed based on the
principle of free enterprise. But this kind of freedom implies
misery and insecurity for the working class; that is servitude.

The order of economic co-operation in a socialist society means,
outwardly, the subjection of individuals to the will of the community, in which the individual will seldom prevails. According to
the concepts of the present ruling class, this would be the most
unbearable form of servitude.

There is no doubt that economic development will necessitate the
transition to a socialist social order; it is equally certain that the
more ties there are between the modes of thinking of the working
class and of the ruling class, the more the former's concepts of
good and evil, of licit and illicit, of useful and harmful, that is its
moral, legal and scientific ideology, depend on the ideology of the
ruling classes, the more difficult will be the transition, the more
infantile diseases the new social order will have to go through.

It follows that the working class has to adjust psychologically to
the future order well in advance. In order not to feel the socialist
economic order as a constraint but to conceive of the new type of
operation as an act of free will, it will become necessary to adapt
at once if possible, those concepts and feelings, that is that consciousness, which can only become fully developed in a socialist
society. If the workers do not have an inclination towards this,
the transition will indeed prove very difficult, and may even
require more serious struggles between segments of the working
class than against the ruling class.

These feelings, this consciousness consists of the feeling and
consciousness of social solidarity: of the conviction that our
entire life, from the cradle to the grave is entirely dependent upon
lives and actions of other human beings in all their manifestation.

Hence a happy and perfect life can only be the result of voluntary collaboration determined by the always purposeful order of society. All co-operation demands some sacrifice, resignation and subjection to the general needs of society. As a consequence of this principle of social solidarity the greatest virtue of a socialist would be the development of all his talents to the utmost, but also the highest perfection of self-discipline.

The principle of class struggle requires that every member of the working class recognizes the solidarity with a larger group, the class, immediately. It demands now that he conducts not a personal and wild fight of life and death against his class members, but that he subjects his individual interest to the class interest, sacrifices his possible individual advantages, and struggles for the common benefit of his companions. In a society based on the catch-as-catch-can principle of free enterprise, the class struggle implants into every class-conscious worker the greatest virtue of self-discipline, by deliberate day by day effort. The class struggle in all its forms is the most powerful school for socialist consciousness.

If, on the other hand, we pretend that the working class, and all the rest of us, may attend this same school by conscious work in the service of the *entire* contemporary society, we are at best indulging in wishful thinking. In a society divided into antagonistic classes the common and general interests of all society are negligibly small. An 'idealist' operating in any area of social life so often collides with the diverse but very real social interests, that the force of the facts would undoubtedly wear him out so cruelly that not only the desire to serve all of society, but the willingness to perform any kind of social work would die in him. I assume, what is psychologically impossible, that we would be able not only to conceive a general ideal of society that stands above all class interests and unites them, but also to carry this into the masses. One may encounter the most frustrated social hangovers and the decadent cult of perfect passivity exactly among such 'idealist' apostles of 'harmony'.

The educational impact of class struggle is also extremely significant from another point of view. If the struggle brings out the best possible qualities of a socialist in members of the working class, it also inculcates that most worthwhile element of individualism which I would like to term 'self-making'. The class-conscious proletariat does not appeal to the kindness of the ruling classes, nor to the leniency of the state but, on the contrary, greets with distrust everything that they give voluntarily, and accepts the greater or lesser mitigation of social evils, that is the so-called reforms, only if he is convinced that it is a concession wrung out by its organization, its discipline and its determination. This attitude of the conscious proletariat permits him to partake of the noblest sources of human perfection: the confidence in one's own strength, the awareness of the worth of one's own work and creativity. And we can obtain well-rounded human beings only if their work is in harmony with the noblest talents and desires of

their bodies and souls. This is the impact of class struggle upon
the working class. If liberalism indeed subscribes to individualism
for its own sake, and supports it because it means all-round
human beings, genuine individuals, then it should advocate the
principle of class struggle most devotedly.

II

So far I have endeavoured to demonstrate that the striving for
socialism, as every social movement, is a social necessity con-
ditioned by economic progress, and that it takes place necessarily
in the form of class struggle. I could thus regard my task to be
completed. If, however, I may count on your attention for a while,
allow me to give a sketch of the specific means by which modern
socialism strives to achieve its goals.

I have pointed out both the objective and subjective factors
which guide social progress necessarily in the direction of socialism. One was the concentration of industry, the other the class
struggle. What determines the attitude of the socialist parties to
these phenomena?

If the increasing socialization of production in capitalism is an
economic and psychological prerequisite for socialism, the socialist
parties would naturally have to desire the rapid growth of large-
scale industry. Indeed, socialists of today have everywhere emancipated themselves from that kind of sentimentalism which dis-
regarded the need for economic progress, and fought for the
protection of small autonomous economical entities. The socialist
parties now openly advocate that the workshops, the small busi-
nesses should be absorbed by the big, because this process
brings us closer to socialism. Hence they view favourably all
economic trends which direct progress in the direction of industrial concentration. They are concerned about the formation of
monopolies and cartels only because these may place new burdens
on the working masses of consumers, and because they may prove
more powerful opponents to the organization and struggle of the
working class than their predecessors, the separate corporations.
Nevertheless, the attitude of the socialist parties to the promotion
of large-scale industry is rather passive, because artificial promotion, achieved by subsidies and protective tariffs, often serves
the interests not of large-scale industry, but the privileges of
certain groups of big industrialists, at the expense of the public.
This point of view largely determines the commercial, tariff and
tax policies of the socialist parties.

Those activities of the socialist parties which fulfil the requirements of class struggle are much more significant. Class struggle
is but the frame which receives content by the conscious acts of
the persons constituting the class. Class struggle is the cornerstone of the modern socialist movement, both as the process
transforming the objective elements of society towards socialism,
and as a means of mental adjustment or education. The public, as

well as many social democrats, stress two elements of the practical
programme of modern socialist movements. On the one hand, they
talk of the struggle of the working class for the conquest of political power, in other words, for the political dictatorship of the
proletariat. On the other hand, by influencing legislation they
expect to initiate and develop the protection of the workers, that
is to effect social reforms.

I believe that this concept of the content of proletarian class
struggle was adequate only for the early stage of the workers'
movement. Then, because of the small numbers of the proletariat,
their lack of organization, and especially because of the fledgling
nature of certain economic formations, no general objectives could
be set, not only because the workers lacked sufficient strength,
but also because the economic conditions for an awareness of
those objectives did not yet exist. More recently, however, it
seems that one of the most significant sayings of Marx warrants a
broader application than that of earlier socialists. Marx said that
the new and higher relations of productions cannot replace the
older ones until the material conditions for them have been conceived in the womb of the old society. Previously, the Marxist
interpretation was simply that socialism could not come about until
industrial concentration had reached the highest possible degree
within a capitalist society. Socialism was presumed to be dependent
strictly on the degree of industrial concentration.

I have already mentioned that industrial development is mostly
a passive process, hence it is but a negatve factor in mental
adjustment. I have pointed out that class struggle is the positive
factor. But it now seems that class struggle can find effective
weapons not only in industrial concentration and in intellectual
and political areas, but it can find even more powerful ones in the
economic area.

The economic organizations (trade unions) of the workers, until
recently shrugged off by certain Marxists, have become powerful
weapons for obtaining the very advantages which the same Marxists until recently wanted to achieve purely by political struggle.
Shorter hours, higher wages, improvements regarding working
conditions, and even the political freedom of the worker have
become ever more frequently the fruits of the economically organized direct action of the workers. Much more so than the products
of political struggle or of legislation: legislative acts correspond
increasingly to the principle of class struggle, as they have truly
become concessions wrung by the strength of the organized
workers. Thus, in addition to the educational impact of the economic struggle, which serves to indicate the path of feeling and
thought shared by those who pertain to the same trade, it is also
an excellent school for creative activity in preparing socialism.

Considering that the material prerequisites of the future relations of production have to be established already within the
womb of present-day society, the entry of the working class into
the economic organization by means of societies of production and
consumption independent of private capital has become another

phenomenon of at least equal value to industrial concentration. I refer to the co-operatives.

More and more persons believe that in the co-operatives the class-conscious proletariat has found the form of production which combines the social character of production with the social nature of appropriation, that is it resolves the conflict between the modes of production and distribution in modern industrial societies which gave birth to the class struggle of the bourgeoisie and the proletariat. If this be true, if indeed it be possible to build on the foundations of consumers' co-operatives a network of producers' co-operatives which could penetrate into every branch of industrial and agricultural production, and if these co-operatives do not degenerate, as a result of the corruptive influence of the surrounding capitalist enterprises, into mere corporations pursuing nothing but profit, then the co-operatives will have contributed greatly to the arsenal of the class struggle. All the more so because it seems that agricultural enterprise does not keep pace with industry's tendency to concentrate, and there the co-operatives seem uniquely capable of being economic harbingers of socialism. Hence, the co-operatives are significant, both from the point of view of the economic preparation of the final transformation, and from that of mental adjustment.

In addition, of course, all those weapons that the working class has used successfully in the past are still valid: most of all, the weapons in the intellectual struggle. The penetration of modern scientific knowledge into ever widening circles, the constant propagation of socialist principles and of the socialist ideal are and will continue to be the noblest weapons of the working class. In addition, the constant political education of the proletariat, the continuous spread of the knowledge of public affairs, which will prepare it for the development of advanced self-government, are all indispensable ingredients of the class struggle. And if with all this – enlightenment, the raising of the level of public education, the development of political democracy – modern socialism does actually achieve what would, in fact, be the task of liberalism, then we should be allowed to hope that what could be the source of happiness under liberalism would not become the basis for 'demagogy' and for 'the tyranny of the masses', even under the aegis of socialism. For all this is not only the objective means for the realization of socialism but also, and perhaps not in the last instance, for the education of man.

III

This rather sketchy description of the weaponry of socialism should be followed by the description of the final phase in accomplishing the aims of socialism, in other words, I ought to provide a picture of socialist society. I must confess that this is indeed a most difficult issue. Not that socialists would not have more or less sophisticated concepts in this regard. But the contemporary

socialist is imbued with the notion that the political and legal
manifestations of society are determined by the economic structure
to such an extent, that for their visions they do not expect
scientific precision. Throughout this presentation, I have strived
to build the structure of social movement and of socialism from
elements which I am absolutely convinced have a strictly scientific
basis. We can determine the present trends of economic development, as well as the mental motivations which prompt the working
class to strive for socialism. But we cannot determine with scientific precision at what point in evolution and in what form this
yearning will become decisive action. This is impossible not only
because we are dealing with human beings and we are not sufficiently familiar with the laws of our inner life, but also because all
this depends to a great extent on the behaviour of the ruling
classes. All we can say is that modern socialism honestly tries to
make sure that the transformation will be peaceful; yet it is not
in the least deterred by violence, that is by revolution, should
the ruling classes force it to turn in that direction. It is precisely
to head off the violent resistance of the ruling classes that socialism devotes increasing attention to anti-militarist agitation, in
order to deprive the establishment of its most powerful tool of
coercion.

Nor can I say much about the organization of socialist society.
However tempting it may be to paint a picture of socialist society,
we cannot follow Thomas More, Fourier, or Bellamy in this endeavour. Nor is it necessary to do so. Every scientifically inclined
socialist is permeated by the conviction that the scientifically
determined directions of progress do not get lost, but continue to
evolve logically. It is possible that people, as carriers of social
progress, stubbornly close their eyes to the requirements of development, do not promote or even oppose it, hold it up by force.
Two things may then occur: either economic progress proceeds
nevertheless, but at the cost of a tremendous waste of energy, or
social progress comes to a halt, stagnates, and finally perishes
completely. There are plenty of examples of both in world history.

The normal case, however, is that the new forces of production
should burst forth and capture the minds of the greater part of
their representative class and eventually of society at large,
which then will promote a social transformation in the direction of
the development of the new economic relations. The new economic
order and the superstructure - the logical trend of progress in
the state, the law, morality and science - will have an equally
determining effect on the whole social structure. Thus socialist
society is going to be nothing else than the concluding stage of
those trends of progress which we find already in present-day
society, the logical and harmonic elaboration of those objective
and subjective forces the formation of which can be perceived in
our times.

So much is certain that the present direction of economic development, heading as it does towards an ever widening extension of
co-operation, both in the capitalist plants and in voluntary

co-operatives, will define the economic order of the socialist
society as it will be based on the same principle of social production. However, it will destroy that most significant barrier
which hinders the complete unfolding of this new order of economic forces in our own society: the institution of private property.
The fact that the means of production are in the hands of a few
results in free enterprise, an unplanned and wasteful mode of
production and distribution, and in economic crises. This also
makes the complete expansion of the means of production dependent on the speculations of individual entrepreneurs, and para-
lyses the powerful drive inherent in voluntary co-operation, for
only a small fraction of the products of social production will be
enjoyed by the members of the common workforce. Thus private
property can survive only through compulsion: the threat of
misery and government coercion.

Socialism will solve this contradiction between the social character of production and the individual form of expropriation.
Socialist society will convert the means of production into common
property of the community, while all members of society will partake of the fruits of labour according to their work and their
needs; and they will dispose of these goods and advantages as
they please. Thus the socialist economic order will put an end to
class conflicts and struggles deriving from the dissonance between production and distribution by bringing about complete
harmony: it will lead humanity to a free and harmonious social
existence.

As to the form this society will take, and the kind of political
and legal apparatus that will arise on the basis of collective
ownership of the means of production, I am convinced that it will
be in line with the consistent evolution of already existing trends.

Thus it would be a complete mistake to claim that socialism will
be the crudest form of centralism and of the tyranny of the majority in so far as politics and law are concerned. Those who make
this claim discount two factors, namely that the character of the
state will have altered altogether, and that the people's perception
about social needs will be quite different.

The state itself is first of all an organization of domination. In a
class society the state becomes the most powerful tool of the ruling
class or classes in order to maintain and increase their power. In
any case, it is an instrument of compulsion of a minority over the
great majority, appropriate to the greatest expansion of the power
of this minority. In a socialist society, where there will be no
classes, it is first of all this coercive aspect of the state that
withers away in order to make room for its purely administrative
functions. But even this centralized administration will gradually
surrender most of its functions to the lesser organizations of
smaller groups of society.

In the area of economic production this process will also prevail.
The spread of co-operative production will make the voluntary
co-operation of smaller groups the generally accepted form of production, and the central organization will become merely a huge

bureau of statistics, in charge of continually determining the productive needs of society. It will also attend to the division of labour between the innumerable minor centres of production, and will act as a great clearing-house, distributing the produced goods between the smaller groups of producers and consumers.

It is unimaginable that the organization of government should not adapt itself to this organization of production and distribution. This would happen even if we did not observe in present-day society the process of decentralization of the administration, the continuous spread of the principle of autonomy. But even now we may observe everywhere in western Europe a definite tendency which influences every single member of the society to find out and voluntarily carry out the needs of society by continually expanding the area of communal and provincial autonomy. The continuous evolution of economic and administrative autonomy, will foreseeably render the state completely unnecessary, and make room for the free federation of free communities, the central organ of the common economic and administrative interests of all society.

The objection might be raised that this is nothing less than anarchy. Indeed, it is not very different. But while anarchism expects to achieve the same objective by abolishing the state right away, socialism holds that it is not possible to abolish thousand-year-old social formations by fiat and overnight. Like all social change this one, too, can only be the consequence of appropriate economic and intellectual modifications. Hence the words of Engels are entirely accurate: 'The state will not be "abolished", but will die away' ('Anti-Dühring' part III, ch. 27).

So much about the organization of socialist society. Should anyone nevertheless demand a more detailed, more intimate description of social life in the future, I would respond with the query: has there ever been social transformation, the protagonists of which were able to draw an exact picture of the future society in advance? Were the fighters for reforms in the 1840s able to describe in detail the economic and social life of Hungary in the period after the abolition of serfdom and the estates? Of course not! Still, they did bring about, more or less successfully, a bourgeois Hungary. I too will confess without embarrassment that I have no idea who will clean the sewers in a socialist society, and whether these persons will be rewarded in the same way as present-day society rewards certain social functions it deems very important, for instance the public schoolteachers. I hope they will be.

Nevertheless I will have to digress about a reasonable objection. Most of the opponents of socialism argue that it can never be realized, or if so it would be short-lived, because – according to them – it implies the complete annihilation of individual freedom. In their eyes the fact that socialism eliminates individual production constitutes an extreme tyranny, that would kill all individual desire for action, power, or initiative. Socialism, therefore, is seen as opposed to human nature.

On a number of occasions I have had the opportunity to discuss the problem of liberty. I have repeatedly pointed out that the contemporary proletariat's notion of freedom is the direct opposite to that of the bourgeoisie. Also that the inclination to adapt one's actions to the needs of society is constantly growing, hence the need for compulsion is constantly on the decline. Still, the issue of freedom is so important that I cannot bypass it even within my limited time. If the accusation of tyranny were founded, it would undoubtedly constitute the most serious charge against socialism. Indeed, if any social order should exclude the potential for individual initiative, it would find itself condemned to death. The development of society becomes impossible without initiatives taken by individuals or tiny minorities. Thus even the socialists permeated by the great concept of progress, whose greatest ideal is the constant and infinite perfection of society, would recoil from the image of a social order in which there is no freedom, and consequently no progress.

What is freedom? Is it an abolute, an abstract idea, determined once and for all and under all circumstances? Or is freedom, as is any other ideology, relative, defined by the period and the culture? Freedom is a psychological category which refers to that state of mind in which I can bring my personal desires and needs into harmony with the objective conditions for satisfying these desires and needs. In this sense freedom always means the same thing.

But what it is that I desire, what determines my feelings, what are the specific objects of my desire, in other words, what actions provide me with an awareness of freedom, depend on which of my needs are already satisfied, and how much I know regarding the conditions for satisfying further needs. That is it depends on my education, my knowledge, and especially on the constant influence of the environment and the modes of satisfaction of the needs that are guaranteed, that have become reflexes, unconscious acts. It depends also on the extent to which the desires for the satisfaction of certain needs have been relegated to the back of our minds and have ceased to form part of our concept of freedom. Thus our desire for freedom is addressed only to those actions that are aimed at the satisfaction of needs not yet assured. In other words, freedom is but the potential for acting in the direction of satisfying needs that are not guaranteed by society.

Thus freedom is a specific and relative concept, the content and direction of which is always given by the degree of material and intellectual culture of society, by our class position, by our income. If we try to place ourselves into the minds of persons pertaining to different historical periods we will undoubtedly construct concepts of freedom that vary not only according to period and territory, but also according to class position and degree of culture. For the most primitive man, the concept of freedom implied that he be able to eat his weaker fellow human unhampered. His descendants at a somewhat higher level of economic organization no longer felt that their freedom was limited if they were

not able to eat human flesh, for the domestication of animals ensured the satisfaction of their primitive needs. On the other hand,
they would have felt that the prohibition of distinct aesthetic
needs, aroused in them by the attained degree of economic security, for instance the tattooing of the body, would have been an
intolerable imposition. The ideal of freedom for the knight of the
Middle Ages was to be able to raid the merchants travelling in the
valley below, and to rob them whenever he liked; evidently this
was not the concept of freedom for the medieval merchant. And
today, in an economy based on free enterprise, what freedom
means to the bourgeoisie - albeit to an ever decreasing fragment
of it, due to industrial concentration - constitutes but servitude
for the working class, that is for an ever increasing portion of
the population, because it brings about poverty and insecurity.
Thus the so-called tyranny of socialism can, at worst, be in
opposition only to the concept of a small fragment of bourgeois
society, but certainly not to the absolute concept of freedom.

This argument, however, constitutes only a negative proof of
freedom in socialism. We should be able to prove that freedom of
action, corresponding to the concept of freedom in socialism, will
also exist. Hence we must find out what will be the content and
tendency of our desire for freedom in a socialist society.

An examination of the priorities of human needs and particularly
of the development in their quality leads us to the answer. The
development of human culture indicates that, to the extent that
social co-operation has ensured the satisfaction of the purely
vegetative needs of an ever greater portion of humanity, the
greater part of their ability to work, their talent, their creativity
has turned to the production of spiritual goods, to the formation
of spiritual culture. The easier the struggle for animal existence
.(food, drink, clothing, etc.), and the greater the number of
persons liberated from the slavery of a purely vegetative existence, the more the energies inherent in society have sought an
outlet in political, scientific, artistic and literary production, and
in the enjoyment of these products. That is, the concept of freedom has increasingly oriented itself to intellectual areas, and
people have spent less and less of their thinking, time, labour
power on the satisfaction of their economic needs.

This awareness allows us to hope not only that socialism is not
a tyranny, but that it is the first social system since the existence
of private property that truly guarantees human freedom. I am
convinced that even the present degree of development of the
forces of production would suffice, with conscious and planned
co-operation, to ensure not merely the economic needs of all of
humanity, but to free a considerable portion of time and energy
for public life and the production and consumption of intellectual
matters. Instead of the concept of freedom of the contemporary
elite, which is simply success in the economic field, a new concept
of freedom will form in the minds of the members of a socialist
society: the opportunity to work, succeed, excel in the area of
public and intellectual life.

We have no reason to assume that socialism will render this manner of individual success more difficult. Thus socialism will open up infinite perspectives for freedom, hence for human happiness. All our material needs have a limit; beyond a certain degree of satisfaction of these needs we are saturated. But the characteristic of our intellectual needs is that they become more differentiated, more refined, more varied, more extended in depth and breadth the higher their degree of development. They are infinite and boundless. They open up infinite expanses to the achievements of human understanding, desire for action, and will. The opportunity for this kind of achievement will be provided by socialism. Can there be a condition more in harmony with human nature? Is there a social system to which the words of Engels can be more readily applied: 'Socialism is the leap of mankind from the realm of necessity to the realm of freedom' ('Anti-Dühring', part III, ch. 2).

I have reached the end of my task. But I must not relinquish the floor unless I clear a possible misunderstanding. The picture of the future progress and perfection of mankind that I have attempted to sketch here may have led you to believe that I too am prey to that social optimism which, while claiming that human nature is not originally good and spiritual, expects the sudden dawning of this goodness and spirituality from some schematic transformation of social relations. No, honourable Society! I believe that human beings are originally neither good nor bad – after all, good and bad are continually changing and relative social concepts – but, like all creatures of nature, simply want to live and reproduce. The conflict between this powerful instinct and other forces of nature brought about, by means of continuous adaptation, the form and content of the evolution of human society that can be followed through a hundred thousand years of history. A multitude of struggle among men and against nature, the mental and physical force, the tears and blood of several thousands of generations fed the soil from which the admirable material and intellectual culture of present-day bourgeois society emerged. The task is the further organic development of this culture. Much like previous steps of progress which have all been attained at the cost of exhausting, often bloody, and always life-consuming struggles, socialism – the next step in the progress of humanity – will not fall into our laps as ready-made manna, but will require exhausting, perhaps the most exhausting, labour. Who will carry out this work? It follows from what I have said that it will be that class of society which, having filled its soul with the ideal of the next step in the progress of humanity, will accept the great burden of militant solidarity, of self-activity, of self-education, which such a labour requires. This class, which digs the grave of all other classes, and thus builds the foundation for a solidarity embracing the whole great family of humanity, is the working class proclaiming the principles of socialism.

ON EDITING MARX:
A correspondence with Karl Kautsky

Szabó's correspondence with Kautsky began, without their personal meeting, in 1899. Having just returned from Vienna, the young Szabó proposed to report on the congress of the Hungarian Social Democratic Party. Kautsky, not wanting to get entangled into the party intrigues from afar, declined, but encouraged him to write theoretical pieces. Kautsky was very sympathetic to Szabó's plan of a Hungarian Marx-Engels edition, although at first he doubted whether a translation of the 'writings which are not exactly aimed at a mass audience' is at all necessary, considering that Hungarian intellectuals, etc. mostly read German (letter of 21 November 1903). Szabó asked a few questions from Franz Mehring and G. Plekhanov as well, but discussed the general plan with Kautsky, whom he regarded as most competent, although he did not accept all of Kautsky's suggestions. We have selected letters containing theoretically relevant issues.

Fortunately their correspondence has survived completely: Kautsky's letters are in the Archives of the MSzMP Párttörténeti Intézet (Party History Institute) Budapest, Szabó's in the Internationaal Instituut voor Sociale Geschiedenis, Amsterdam. For a complete edition, see Gy. Litván Szabó Ervin nemzetközi kapcsolatai... (International contacts of E. Szabó...), 'Történelmi Szemle', vol. 7 (1964), pp. 30-49 (in original German). The fine nuances in the address (from 'very honoured' to 'dear') have not been translated. 'N.Z.' stands for 'Neue Zeit'.

1 ERVIN SZABÓ TO KARL KAUTSKY

(Budapest) II, Hunfalvygasse 4.
23 November 1903

Dear Comrade,

I am finally at the point that I can send you - enclosed - the plan of our Marx-Engels edition.

As I have already mentioned, the size of the whole work is going to be 1,300 pages (demy 8°) and will include the biographical introduction, explanatory prefaces to the single pieces and finally, if possible, a closing summary and evaluation of Marxism. The text is to be set in Garamond, all editorial matter in Borgis.

It is perhaps necessary that I present briefly the viewpoints that have influenced me in the selection. The first task of the collection is to present as universal and complete a picture of the

intellectual achievements of Marx and Engels as possible. Sociology, philosophy, economics, history and the journals should be
represented. My second aspiration is to have the publication
adjusted to the intellectual level of the greatest possible number
of Hungarian workers.(1) Thirdly, I want to increase the interest
in the book by including all articles which have a special relevance
to Hungary.

These aspects may explain to you why, besides, of course
'Capital', 'Herrn Eugen Dühring' (Revolution of Science) and 'The
Poverty of Philosophy' are missing. Later works of Marx and
Engels, such as 'A Contribution to the Critique of Political Economy' and 'Ludwig Feuerbach', etc. replace them completely and
are more understandable for many readers because they are less
polemically oriented. Even an understanding of 'Dühring' demands
on many counts an acquaintance with the works of Dühring.

The early works are absent as well. I feel that my conscience is
unburdened by the words of Engels: 'What the French and the
English have said already ten, twenty, even forty years ago – and
did so very well, very clearly and in a beautiful language – has
now been finally and gradually in a year assimilated by the Germans, "verhegelt" or, in the best case, once again discovered by
them in a much worse, much more abstract form and was printed
as a new discovery. I do not exclude my own works either.'
(Über Fourier, 'Nachlaß', vol. II, p. 400).

As far as I am concerned, I will certainly miss the 'Critique of
Hegel's Philosophy of Right' and the 'Outlines of a Critique of
Political Economy'; but my feelings should not be decisive. The
advantage of dropping the early works is also that the work can
open with 'The Communist Manifesto'. I could not imagine a more
appropriate and beautiful introduction.

The sequence of the pieces should, I believe, best follow their
original publication. Naturally, Marx and Engels should be inter-
mingled and not separated. The chronological order should only
be broken when (i) an introduction of Engels to Marx has to be
placed before the Marxian texts, or (ii) when articles, as for
example the two speeches of Marx on protectionism and free trade,
would stand among totally heterogeneous (in this case historical)
ones; hence I will put these two next to the 'Critique of Political
Economy', etc.

I have allotted rather more space to the historical pieces; not
only because I hold them to be the most beautiful but also as the
best and the most illuminating ones which offer the most useful
introduction to the spirit of historical materialism.

'Wage, Labour and Capital' has already been translated and
therefore omitted. 'On the Jewish Question' was likewise translated earlier and anyhow, with all its Hegelism, it was not a lucky
shot: so it can be left aside.

I am looking forward to your critique, dear comrade, with great
anticipation and thank you in advance for your trouble taken.

Sincerely devoted,
Erwin Szabó

PS. Please receive my friend, Ludwig Leopold Jr, who is spend-
ing some time in Berlin studying German socialism and will visit
you.(2) I am, in a certain way, an eccentric myself, but he is
even more so. However, he means well, very well indeed: when
he grows older he will even be able to act well. For the time being,
he should write a book about the German working-class movement
for the series in which your 'Marx' has been published.(3)

Tentative Plan for the Selected Works [of Marx and Engels]:(4)
Volume I
Biographical Introduction. Portrait of Marx.
The Communist Manifesto*
'The Fall of Vienna' [Marx, Nov. 1848]
'Hungary' [Engels, 1849]
Democratic Pan-Slavism
The Class Struggles in France
Revolution and Counter-Revolution [in Germany]
The Eighteenth Brumaire [of Louis Bonaparte]**
The Peasant War in Germany**   c. 500 pages
Volume II
Portrait of Engels
A Contribution to the Critique of Political Economy
On Free Trade** [Marx, 1847]
On Protectionism [Engels, 1888]
On Proudhon**
Inaugural Address [of the International Working Men's Assoc.]
The Civil War in France
Critique of the Gotha Programme
Critique of the Erfurt Programme**   c. 360 pages
Volume III
'Soziales aus Russland' [Engels, 1875]
Socialism, Utopian and Scientific
On Historical Materialism
The Origin of the Family [Private Property and the State]
England 1845 and 1885
Ludwig Feuerbach [and The Outcome of Classical German Philos-
ophy]
Preface to 'Capital'
[The role of force...in] the Foundation of the German Empire
The Peasant Question in Germany and France
To the History of Primitive Christianity
Letters
Appreciation of Marxism   c. 470 pages
* With all prefaces of Engels to the Italian, Russian, English, etc.
editions.
** Out of chronological order.

2   KARL KAUTSKY TO ERVIN SZABÓ

24 November 1903

Dear Comrade,

Our letters have crossed each other in the mail and I have just received your plan of the Marx-Engels edition. In general, I am entirely in agreement with it. None the less, I would like to make a few comments on some of the details.

I can very well understand that you want to open with 'The Communist Manifesto'. This is a very suitable beginning in every respect. However, there are some things from the preceding literature which deserve to be included. For example the chapter from 'The Holy Family' about French materialism. I have printed it with an introduction in 'N.Z.' (1885), pp. 385 ff.

In the first volume I note the absence of the treatise of Engels on the uprising in Baden. However, 'The Class Struggles in France' could be dropped since they are adequately covered in 'The Eighteenth Brumaire'. I would only add the Preface by Engels; but only in Volume III as a conclusion to the whole work. If you begin with 'The Communist Manifesto', then the Engelsian Preface would fit very nicely as a closing piece for that course of the development which was opened by the Manifesto.

'The Peasant War in Germany' by Engels could also be left out, as it is essentially only an excerpt from the book by Zimmermann. The work has more propagandistic than scholarly value and is better suited for a separate edition as a pamphlet.

In the second volume you could perhaps include the characterization of Kossuth and Klapka by Marx in 'Herr Vogt' (pp. 121-130, 190) since it is of interest to Hungary.

In the third volume you have to include under all circumstances, an article by Engels about the foreign policy of Tsarism ('N.Z.', 1890, p. 145 ff) and then certainly also his treatiese 'On Protectionism and Free Trade' ('N.Z.', 1888, p. 289). And finally, as a supplement to his Preface to the 'Class Struggles', the article, Socialism in Germany ('N.Z.', 1891-92, pt 1, pp. 580 ff). This article, although it is in parts like a fantasy, does, however, show clearly that the above-mentioned Preface was never meant to be revisionist. The two belong together.

I am very much surprised by the low price. I am afraid that you will not make ends meet this way, but I will be most pleased if I am to be proven wrong. That I wish your enterprise all success is self-evident. With Party greetings, yours,

K. Kautsky

PS. A visit by Mr Leopold is most welcome to me. One more thing: you list an article as the 'Critique of the Erfurt Programme'. I beg you not to commit there the mistake of presenting this critique as if it was addressed to the programme accepted by the Erfurt Party Congress. That programme has been fully approved by Engels; the critique refers to a draft which the Party leadership had prepared and which has been withdrawn in favour of my text, approved by Engels. The draft of the Party leadership has been printed in 'N.Z.' (pt 2, 1890-91, p. 506).

3 ERVIN SZABÓ TO KARL KAUTSKY

Budapest II. Hunfalvygasse 4.
21 January 1904

Dear Comrade,

For some time I have been working on a book which should treat the history of social classes and the theory and practice of class struggle. As I view the matter, it should be a sociological foundation for the modern proletarian struggle based upon the materialistic concept of history. It is far from my wishes to tax your valuable time with sketching the plan for this project. But perhaps it is not too great an imposition if I ask you for your opinion in regard to two details because, to my knowledge, these questions have hitherto not been treated in Marxist literature.

I am at present working on the methodological introduction, where I discuss in detail the so-called psychological sociology (Giddings, Tarde, Fouillée, (5) et al.), the subjective view of history of Lavrov, etc. In opposition to these, I emphasize the position of historical materialism as it has been elaborated in the letters of Engels to Schmidt, etc. and in your writings and those of Labriola.(6). But, in the emphasis of the subjective and psychological side of development, I intend to go further.

1 I find it necessary to establish the role of the individual in history. There, above all, I encounter 'the great man'. Naturally, I am not thinking here of the Leonardos(7) or the Wagners. It was you, in particular, who demonstrated the correct assessment of artistic and philosophical creation. I am asking about the great statesmen.

In a letter to Heinz Starkenburg [of 25 January 1894 – Editors' note] Engels tried to answer this question. He explained the appearance of certain 'great men' as 'pure accidents'. That I believe. 'But', Engels continued, 'if we leave him out, there is a demand for replacement'. Obviously this answer does not go to the root of the issue. The real problem is exactly why is there such a demand? I should like to ask you to reply to this question.

2 Seen from the subjective side, historical materialism explains only short passages in history, primarily those critical moments which we call revolutions, the moments of open class struggle when the shift from one social order to another occurs. Between these lie periods lasting for hundreds of years; what happens during those is not treated appropriately. Still, men and women of many generations lived in these periods who strove and worked for the development of society. Are their contributions to be deemed less valuable just because they did not happen to live in the critical moments? Or was development at a standstill during the 'intermediate' periods?

I remember having read in Saint-Simon (exactly where, I cannot recall momentarily) a categorization of history into 'critical' and 'organic' periods. Those that he called 'critical' periods are adequately explained by historical materialism even in regard to the subjective side, but this is not so for the periods which I too should like to call 'organic'.

As my second question, I should like to have your reply to this matter. Maybe you would like to reply to these in the 'N.Z.' They do not seem to be minor points which I am here addressing.

I would like to take this opportunity to thank you for your friendly suggestions regarding the Hungarian Marx-Engels edition. I have accepted them almost without exception. Only in regard to the uprising in Baden and 'The Peasant War in Germany' do I differ; but this is to be understood from our particular Hungarian point of view. The description of the many small skirmishes and quarrels holds little interest for the Hungarian reader; while the history of the German peasant war sheds so much light on the contemporary (1514) Hungarian one that, even if it is not an original piece, it is extremely valuable for us. The more so as Zimmermann's history is not available to the Hungarian reader, nor is there a materialist history of the Hungarian peasant war (with the exception of a short piece written a couple of years ago in the Party almanac which, however, is no history).

I was surprised that you assumed I would refer Marx's critique of the Social Democratic programme to the Erfurt one.

The work is already proceeding and the first fascicle will be published this 1 September. With the request, honoured comrade, that you will not be forced into answering my questions by any sense of obligation, I thank you in advance for your friendliness.

Very devotedly,
Erwin Szabó

PS. Maybe you will be amused to hear that we are becoming *almost* relatives. My brother is marrying Paula Necas, who, via the Ronspergers, is *almost* a relative of yours.

4   KARL KAUTSKY TO ERVIN SZABÓ

23 February 1904

Dear Comrade,

Your answers demand quite some time. Therefore it is only now that I have a chance to reply to them. You suggest to me that I reply in the 'N.Z.' but if I were to do so, I would have to elaborate upon them in depth and I do not have time for that. Hence, only a few comments.

You find it necessary to establish the role of the individual in history. I have to comment that I do not think much of all these abstract inquiries. The best way to develop historical materialism is to apply it to scholarship. If you investigate a definite historical period, then you will see the role of the individual much clearer than by any speculation about it. We can learn only from experience. All of us Marxists who comprehend historical materialism have reached that stage by historical studies – not by abstract speculations.

In general, one could say the following: the question of the role of the individual in history is identical to that of the role of the individual in society. History is but the presentation of social development. Society, however, is an association of individuals who are in a definite relationship to each other, and this relationship is, in the last analysis, defined by the process of production. The influence of the individual on history is hence the influence of the individual on others. This influence can have its origins in various causes and these have to be specifically investigated in every concrete case. There is no general formula which permits us to explain the role of every single individual in history.

But you are asking about the great individual, in particular, the great statesman. How can he be explained? If a great man is able to act - and that, of course, is true for a woman as well - then he or she needs an arena of action. Let us take a general; what refers to him is true, mutatis mutandis, of the statesman as well. If there is no war, his greatness cannot be acted out. He may be as great as he wants, he still does not exist for history.

An arena of action is, however, necessary not only in developing and acting out greatness: this arena must be a suitable one. Let us take, for example, the time of Louis XIV or the time of the revolution and compare it with the period between them, under Louis XV and XVI. What a great number of talented generals in the former, what a lack of them in the latter! That cannot be mere accident. It can only be explained by the different situations. Louis XIV had to develop absolutism by fierce fights with the nobility and Paris while his position was endangered from abroad as well. Hence he had to appreciate military talent on which his existence depended. The situation was similar, and even more critical, during the revolution. However, under Louis XV, the lord of the army, the monarchy was stabilized both from within and without. Its existence did not depend upon the army. Military commissions were therefore not granted according to talent but rather by preference. Not military ability, but the talents of the courtier were developed in the army. Whether great men appear in war or politics depends entirely on the social conditions.

This, naturally, does not yet answer the question: from whence does the great man come? This has caused a lot of headache to many people; whilst it is indeed very simple: great men - or to put it simply - men, are always around. It is a natural necessity that they are available.

Greatness is, of course, a relative concept; nothing is great in itself. Great men are those who are greater than the average, and since it is a natural law that every individual is different from the other, so it is a necessity of nature that some be greater than others: persons who are more intelligent, more knowledgeable, more energetic than the masses. This fact is often used as an argument against socialism. It explains why there are always great men. Whether their greatness can develop and have an impact on society is decided by the prevailing social conditions. These conditions also decide where this talent will become manifest, that is in which field of social life.

The genius is mostly very versatile and can bring forth magnificent achievements in the most differing fields. The area in which it will become active is by no means prescribed by nature: it will turn in the direction of the most vivid struggles of the greatest general interest, where the individual can have the greatest influence. For instance, during the period of the revolution, we find a great number of political geniuses and a considerable dearth of literary ones in France, while in contemporary Germany the situation was exactly the opposite; thus this cannot be explained any other way. So in this regard as well, it is the social conditions which are decisive. Under different circumstances maybe Lessing and Schiller would have become great parliamentarians and not playwrights, and Goethe an inventor who might have overshadowed Edison.

Perhaps one may state in general that in revolutionary periods the genius will tend towards politics; in times of war, for a nation's life and death he will tend to warfare and in peace to the arts and sciences. But one should be very careful with such formulas as they can never fully encompass the diversity of life.

By this token, you already have a reply to your second question, regarding the view of Marxism in the periods of organic development from the psychological side. Such times have their great men just like those of critical development. Only very rarely – in times of total exhaustion of a nation when everyone lives from one day to the next and nobody has either force or interest for anything beyond survival (as, for example, in Germany after the Thirty Years War) – is the genius restricted in all areas and unable to come to the fore; although most likely there are some even in such times. But otherwise one may say that there are always great men and chances for them to act; but not always in all fields or in the same area of social life. In the sphere of politics, which you have addressed, the great men will probably be unable to overcome the domination of bureaucracy in peaceful times and will turn to other professions so that such an epoch will be rather poor in great statesmen.

I hope that these comments will be of some help to you. I should very much regret it if I had to assume that you want to read into Marxism a subjective and psychological aspect which it does not contain. You would end up in a cul-de-sac where you could not get ahead at all.

The isolated individual – man as an object of natural science – and the social individual are two entirely different things. The knowledge of the isolated individual does not suffice for the knowledge of the social which can only be perceived in and through society. One who wants to understand society and societal processes based on the individual and his relationship to things, à la Böhm-Bawerk,(8) will never achieve a genuine social understanding. Such attempts appear to me like trying to develop the laws of biology from the laws of inorganic chemistry. While, of course, the laws of the latter are valid for living organisms as well, the laws of the former cannot be perceived without a study of life and by the study of inorganic matter alone.

So much for that. As I say, I have not time to expand these

ideas into an article for 'N.Z.', but I have no reason to refrain
from uttering them. If you wish to publish them, even in order
to criticize them, I shall not object.

And now another question. My colleague, Wurm, has accepted
an article of yours about classes. I have read it and I am ready
to print it but I have the feeling that it has a gap: you never
make clear what you regard as a criterion of class, and that is
decisive.

In one passage you point to the distribution of income as the
issue where the conflicting interests of the classes clash. This
can be understood in very different ways, including the common
one which is entirely wrong. There is no conflict of interest between a wage labourer who earns 500 M and another who earns
2,000 M, but there is one between the wage-earning labourer who
makes 500 M and his foreman who may not earn much more. Here
one can immediately see what is the origin of the conflict of
interest: not the sphere of distribution, but that of production.
The form of distribution is derived from the form of production.
The different classes are distinguished by the different roles
which they play in the process of production. I would welcome it
if this were at least to be hinted at. In that case, however, the
critique of Mr Bauer would sound a bit less benevolent. If you
agree with me, please correct the article accordingly, for which
purpose I enclose it herewith.(9)

That we will be *almost* related has amused me very much. I hope
the young couple will not suffer through this dangerous relation.

Best greetings, devotedly yours,
K. Kautsky

5 ERVIN SZABÓ TO KARL KAUTSKY

25 February 1904

Dear Comrade,

I hasten to express my sincere thanks for your extensive
answers to my questions. I would have certainly been pleased had
you used this occasion for an article because it seems to me a
great immodesty, having imposed on your valuable time for myself alone.

The same consideration holds me back from replying to your
exposition of the questions raised. Only in order to avoid a possible misunderstanding do I wish to remark that I stand fully and
entirely on the basis of the materialist conception of history. If I
am given to paying more attention to the psychological side of the
social process of development, this does not mean a sliding over
into the area of individual psychological research but only indicates an emphasis on that subjective aspect which Engels has also
apostrophized in his letters as a relevant moment of development.

The actual topic of this letter, however, is my article about the
classes. This was never meant to be an 'article' proper. I thought
to be relieved of the obligation to expound my views about the

question of classes by having formulated my words in the frame of a modest review. And I did this for good reasons. I am presently engaged in a work directly connected with the classes. Naturally, I am most anxious to collect as much inductive material as possible from prehistory, history and the description of the economies. This work is now approaching completion and I am now finally near to formulating my own views. Nevertheless, I would prefer not to anticipate my results.

So, if you wish to publish my writing as a review or an announcement of a book, let it be at your disposal. I will then make a few minor corrections as you have suggested. Right now, however, I could not agree to an extensive elaboration of my views. Rather some time later.

With repeated thanks for your most valuable explanations of which I will certainly make use, and for your attention, I remain,

Yours very obliged,

Erwin Szabó

PS. Still one more question. How do you stand to the works of Max Zetterbaum and Max Adler?(10) Their articles, especially those of the former, are, indeed, nothing else but psychological foundations of historical materialism.

6   KARL KAUTSKY TO ERVIN SZABÓ

Berlin-Friedenau
17 September 1904

Dear Comrade,

I did not read the manuscript of your review on Asturaro,(11) and saw it only today in the proofs; I have a few requests or rather doubts.

1 Arturo Labriola cannot very well be called a pupil of Antonio. The latter has always protested against being connected with Arturo.(12)

2 According to you, Asturaro maintains that Marxian materialism explains only one period of society, the capitalist one. This is false. A Marxist perception of history is valid for the entire course of social development, beginning with the archaic society. This should be noted unequivocally in the review.

3 Asturaro's amplification of historical materialism is, to my mind, only that he subdivides the 'superstructure' into different tiers and assigns a place to its single forms in this sytem. I think that it is impossible to establish such an order. Asturaro's statement that economy is the earliest and simplest social feature and the only one that existed in archaic society is entirely wrong. War, family and kinship, social instincts (ethics) can be found even in the animal kingdom. Social phenomena are very closely interrelated so that it is impossible to say which of them is stronger. The task of a conception of history is not to set an order among social phenomena but to discover that moving force which transforms this intricate process and changes the connections and interrelations

of the complex social features. This force was found by Marx in technology, the change of which transformed the economic - and in consequence all other - relations among men. Hence technical development is in the last resort the motive force of the whole development of society. If A[sturaro] wants to transcend this by creating some kind of sequence among social phenomena, he is neither expanding nor improving on historical materialism but is reducing the method of perceiving social life in all its many sides to a scheme into which he tries to force the realities of life.

The statement about an economy's development being independent of other social institutions and existing autonomously is also erroneous. Technical development is in the last analysis the motive force of social development, but technical development is itself a function of other social features such as war, politics or science. The way in which technology transforms the economy depends, in turn, again on the prevailing forms of law, politics, ethics, family, etc.

Technology is essentially the most active, revolutionary force in social development; the other social factors are in comparison conservative and passive, and become revolutionary only occasionally under the impact of changed technology. This is their relationship; hence it is not permissible to say that an economy exists independently of all other features.

I leave it, of course, to you, to decide how far you wish to accept and utilize these comments. But I should like to avoid any misunderstanding in the 'N.Z.' about our often misunderstood concept of history. I should appreciate it if you would find an opportunity to take a second look at the theses of A[sturaro].

With cordial greetings,
K. Kautsky

PS. Urgent dispatch would be appreciated.

7 ERVIN SZABÓ TO KARL KAUTSKY

Budapest II. Hunfalvygasse 4
26 September 1904

Dear Comrade,

I have been unwell for a few days and then I had to catch up. Hence I was not able to answer your letter as quickly as I would have wished. Unfortunately, the quality shall not be quite to my liking either. On the 8th, I shall leave for a holiday to Basel, Brussels, Paris and Cologne. If I were to consider the state of my health, I should have left long ago.

Therefore, please be content with these very few corrections or else leave the whole thing aside. 1 Arturo Labriola can go without loss. 2 With regard to the validity of historical materialism I have always shared your views. 3 Has caused me great joy. In the book on which I am working at present, I shall make an attempt to reduce human society to two instincts: survival and *mutual aid* [English in the original - Editors' note], and then the

original differentiation of the classes immediately to the development of technology. These sections are already done. I want to
give them a last polishing in Paris. But to develop this in opposition to Asturaro - I have neither the inclination nor the leisure
and now, not even the ability.

This week I have completed the introduction to Engel's Hungarian Revolution and Marx's Kossuth. I believe I have developed
a few new points of view for the understanding of Hungarian
history. Maybe it will be possible to find someone who could
translate this into German.

I should like to correct the article about professional statistics
myself: with tables mistakes creep in too easily.

Yours very devotedly,
Erwin Szabó

PS. Maybe you could give me a recommendation to Guesde and
Lafargue? That could save me boring introductions and small talk.
Many thanks in advance.

NOTES

1   This sentence may have been Szabó's implicit reply to Kautsky's doubts about the need for a translation. [Editors' note]
2   Lajos (Lewis) Leopold (1879-1948) was a Hungarian sociologist
interested in social psychology, sociology of religion and the
agrarian question. His book, 'Prestige: A Psychological Study
of Social Estimates' (London, New York, 1913) was acclaimed
internationally. [Editors' note]
3   Kautsky's book on the economic teachings of Marx was published in E. Garami's translation in 1903 in the 'Sociological
Library'. [Editors' note]
4   The plan enclosed with the letter also contained information
on the translators, the technical and financial arrangements
and a table showing the contributions of Marx and Engels
separately. Some of the titles refer to selections from articles
and letters of Marx and Engels on the topic. All additions are
ours. [Editors' note]
5   Franklin H. Giddings (1855-1931) was an American sociologist,
see 'Int. Enc. of the Soc. Sc.', vol. 6, pp. 175-7; Gabriel
Tarde (1843-1904) was a French sociologist, see ibid., vol.
15, pp. 513-14; Alfred J.-E. Fouillée (1838-1921) was a French
sociologist, see 'Enc. of the Soc. Sc.', vol. 6 (1963), pp. 401.
[Editors' note]
6   Antonio Labriola (1843-1904), a leading Italian Socialist theoretician, was 'the first professor of philosophy in a European
university to expound historical materialism' (P. Mondolfo,
'Enc. of Soc. Sc.', vol. 9 (1964), pp. 7-8). [Editors' note]
7   I wrote down Leonardo's name without reflections, but it is
perhaps his impressive personality that can be best explained
by the circumstances. [Author's note]
8   Eugen von Böhm-Bawerk (1851-1914) was an Austrian

economist and politician; see 'Neue österreichische Biographie 1815-1918', vol. 2 (1925), pp. 63-80. [Editors' note]

9 Szabó's review of Arthur Bauer, 'Les classes sociales' appeared in 'Neue Zeit', pt 2 (1903-4), pp. 62-4. [Editors' note]

10 Szabó may have read Max Adler's first major work 'Kausalität und Telelogie &c.', published in his 'Marx-Studien' in 1904; on Adler, see 'Neue österreichische Biographie ab 1815', vol. 18 (1972), pp. 83-99. [Editors' note]

11 Szabó's review of A. Asturaro's 'Il materialismo storico e la sociologia generale' (Genoa, 1904) appeared in 'N.Z.', vol. 1 (1905-5), pp. 61-2. [Editors' note]

12 Arturo Labriola (1875-1959) was an Italian syndicalist. [Editors' note]

BACK TO MARX!
Editor's preface to vol. I, the 'Selected Works of Marx and Engels'

The first Hungarian translation of a major selection of Marx's
and Engels's writing was planned by Szabó in co-operation
with the Social Democratic Party towards the end of 1903.
Utilizing Kautsky's suggestions, the plan was soon adopted
and the first volume published in 1905. Szabó intended to
produce a collection that would address the learned social
scientist unfamiliar with Marx as well as the interested, but
uneducated worker. It was for the latter that he had the volumes published in inexpensive pamphlet form in instalments.
Owing to the editor's illness, only two of the projected three
volumes were completed, the second only four years after the
first. The selection - and Szabó's reasons for it (see above,
Letters to Kautsky 1 and 3) - reflect the editor's historical
and economic orientation. Every selection was introduced by
Szabó with an essay, many of which (see below, pp. 74-92,
139-49) not only explain the place in the oeuvre of the classics but also add much of Szabó's own thinking to it. The
fate of Hungarian socialism was such that no similar extensive
publication of Marxist classics appeared in Hungary until
after 1945, hence Szabó's two volumes remained the main
source of Marxian thought for several generations of sociologists, social scientists and socialists.

Few of the writings of Marx and Engels can be found among the
socialist works translated into Hungarian, and even these are not
their best pieces. They were published in rather poor translations,
and are rarely still available. On the other hand, the number of
Hungarian readers of socialist literature has increased considerably in recent years. These were our main reasons for publishing
a collection such as this one.
 It is a rather courageous and thorny enterprise to play the
censor's role with the works of great authors, to select some and
reject others, especially if there is - like here - only space for a
tenth of their literary output. The main work of Marx, 'Capital',
together with the recently published volume on the theories of
surplus value, is in itself larger than the three volumes of our
collections. A whole series of writings had to be excluded for lack
of space in this, unfortunately, severely limited collection. I wonder whether it is not too great a responsibility to present, as we
do, a selection motivated by our subjective preferences and thus
force the Hungarian reader to judge the work of these great men

not from the totality of their writings, which alone would guarantee their complete knowledge and a well-based judgment of their value, but from a small part of it.

I am very well aware of this responsibility toward the two men to whom I am more indebted than anyone else, when I launch their writings in this, my selection. But I do so in the conviction that due devotion did not suffer from the necessary practical limitations. In order to demonstrate that this collection is capable of presenting the whole of Marxism in an objective manner, I should like to explain the points of view that led me in the selection and organization of these volumes.

The main purpose of this collection is to introduce to the Hungarian public the system of socialism inaugurated by Marx and Engels: Marxism. My primary aim was to include the best and most characteristic of those writings which demonstrate their new and specific contributions to sociology, philosophy, economics, and to historical and political studies. My second consideration was to present all aspects of Marxism through such works that demand the least prior knowledge. I reckoned that the majority of the readers of this collection would - either because they lack previous schooling or because of the miserable conditions that exist in this country for reading learned publications - not be able to study difficult scholarly texts. The inevitable gaps caused by this procedure in the system of Marxism had to be filled by my humble words: that is the purpose of the editorial introductions placed at the head of every piece.

Whether I have succeeded in these tasks, will be decided by scholarly critique, unimpeded by class or party prejudice. I shall, however, have to bear the full burden of fault for having left out, for example, Engels's main work, the 'Anti-Dühring', this veritable encyclopedia of Marxist sociology, philosophy and economics. Or that not a single piece represents that stage of the authors' mental development which preceded 'The Communist Manifesto', although these early writings would be most helpful in judging Marxism's specific contribution and particular merits in the development of socialism's theory and practice. Maybe it would have been better to replace the 'Contribution to the Critique of Political Economy' by a few chapters from 'Capital' or the second part of 'Anti-Dühring', which contain more complete and mature formulations of the basic economic views of Marx. It could also be argued that the popular treatment of the German peasant war by Engels takes away too much valuable space from more important pieces.

Nevertheless, I am convinced that the collection will be no worse than any other Hungarian editor would have produced. I agree that the character of a scholarly work - just as that of a natural phenomenon - can be best understood by the observance of its genesis and development. Still, I had to omit 'The Holy Family', 'The Condition of the Working Class in England', 'The Poverty of Philosophy' and all other pre-1848 writings. They are, to my mind, too difficult to understand, owing to their polemical character, or would demand such detailed treatment of the age, the authors and

early nineteenth-century currents of thought that they could not
be offered in the necessarily limited introductory essays. Some of
them are only of historical interest anyway. Similarly, the inclu-
sion of 'Anti-Dühring' seemed unwise because it is a polemic
against Eugen Dühring, hardly known to anyone in this country.
But I did not want to include chapters of it or of 'Capital': a
selection from the work of great men is arbitrary enough, and I
did not wish to commit the unpardonable sin of an outright assault
on the totality and beauty of their mental product by tearing
passages out of context and thus mutilating their writings.

On the other hand, I took the liberty to include a few pieces of
minor importance to the body of Marxism, not because of their
scholarly value but because this collection is designed for Hungarian readers: such as Engels's writings on the German peasant
war and the Hungarian Revolution and Marx's comments on Kossuth
and Klapka. Most of us are naturally more interested in topics that
touch upon our lives, our traditions, emotions, on issues especially relevant to us. It may therefore not be a mistake but rather
a useful service to the memory of Marx and Engels, to try through
these selections to bring their more difficult writings on less familiar topics nearer to the Hungarian reader, to the rural workers
who will be interested in these works, and to the general public
who cherish the traditions, even though in quite distorted form,
of the revolution of 1848. I am convinced that there is not a single
piece in the collection that an intelligent worker could not understand and read with enjoyment and mental profit, even if he has
to skip one or two foreign expressions or far too abstract reason-
ing. And if the editorial introductions will in any way enhance
this reading experience, I shall be most pleased with the results.

I can already hear the objection of those whose total knowledge of
Marxism is that it has already received its coup de grace by that
St George of revisionism – Eduard Bernstein. I hear the 'but' of
the sociologists who believe they are the guardians of objective
and progressive science by detesting the dogmatic Marxists: 'But,
what is the point of the whole exercise?' Would it not be better –
if it is good for anything at all – to introduce the Hungarian public to more modern, advanced and more 'pluralist' socialist authors?
Why these unshaven and unkempt fellows and why not those
whose names are welcome in the salons of Parisian 'haute finance'
as well as their persons in the ministerial chambers and the rows
of the senate? Those who are not so ruthless as to be unable to
reconcile old, say national, ideologies with new subversive ideas?
Those who do not entrench themselves behind the one-sided ram-
parts of a class theory? Why extend the slow agony of the hapless
authors of the theory on impoverishment, the 'Zusammenbruchstheorie' or the theory of 'Mehrwert'?

What would these gentlemen say, if they knew, that besides
Bernstein, there are French authors who not only refute Marxism,
but demonstrate that there is nothing at all to be refuted, because
Marx and Engels had plagiarized everything from different French –

mind you, only French! - socialists.(1) The university professors
of Jaurèsism will soon build a national tradition for their brand of
nationalist socialism by proving that in formulating the evolution-
ary theory Condorcet preceded Hegel, that internationalism began
with Saint-Simon and Proudhon, the teachings about proletarization
come from Vidal, historical materialism from Pecqueur and Proudhon, the concept of class struggle from Saint-Just, Babeuf,
Pecqueur and Proudhon and the socialization of the means of production was Proudhon's idea; all before Marx and Engels. Marxism
is not only today not a science, but it never was one!

Detailed replies do not belong in such a preface. If those, who,
disregarding my advance warnings about the uselessness and
worthlessness of reading these volumes, spend their time and
energy on studying Marx and Engels and even read my introductions - which do not lack critical comments - with some attention, find the answers to the charges of the French reform-
socialists, they need not become Marxists for it. Muslims hold that
the Koran, and Jews that the Talmud contains all wisdom, even if
certain things are only in nucleus. We, too, hold that every
scientific system, every theory exists, at least in germ, in preceding theories. This holds true no less for Marxism. Still, it can
be new and special. Its novelty and originality lies not only in the
details, of which Marxism certainly abounds, but in the composition, in the novel structure, in original conclusions and - what is
significant with a social and political theory - in its modern applications. Even if all that which, following Anton Menger, Georg
Adler, et al. has recently been said by Charles Andler, Eugène
Fournière, etc.(2) should be as extensively and comprehensively
true as they would wish, it still would not touch upon the originality and special character of Marxism. The mere fact that Marx
and Engels alone were able to foresee the modern working-class
movement and even more, to unite it by a theory applicable to
three continents, elevates Marxism above all other socialist theories and systems. For this reason alone, it is not only worthwhile,
but mandatory to know it.

I cannot say anything else to the sociologists either. Do not
satisfy yourself with a third-hand acquaintance with Marxism, not
even with one received from its so-called official interpreters.
Karl Kautsky, Antonio Labriola and Paul Lafargue are certainly
good Marxists, but Marx and Engels were better. And the best
interpreters are we ourselves, because we can fertilize and elaborate the old theory by our more recent and personal views.
Everyone can do so with his own.

While repeatedly studying Marx and Engels I have been convinced that nothing is more alien and opposed to the method and
essence of Marxism than blind dogmatic belief in any theory, including, of course, any theoretical tenet of Marxism itself. Nothing
is constant; everything changes and develops. This Hegelian (or,
if you please, Condorcetian) thought, which constitutes the basis
of Marxism, cannot be invalidated with regard to Marxism itself.
Dogmatic Marxism is as much a nonsense as conservative

evolutionism would be. I dare to say this, because if I am a Marxist, in my particular way I do not exclude in a dogmatic narrow-
mindedness the results of new scientific insights, but, while
admitting these, my scientific thinking is essentially oriented on
Marxism. And what is true about myself, is true of many others,
mainly younger people, who have absorbed modern scholarship as
eagerly, and have still become Marxists.

Wherever we look, we witness the renaissance of Marxism all
over Europe - if it is permissible to speak of the rebirth of something that has been alive and vivid ever since its inception. 'Back
to Marx!' is a slogan resounding in an increasingly general and
clearly focused tone. Just before this Hungarian collection of Marx
and Engels was launched, a French edition of the complete 'Capital'
and several other important works were published; simultaneously
with our selection, an Italian translation of the entire oeuvre of
Marx and Engels is in progress. It is hardly by chance that the
working-class movement of these two great civilized countries is
being nourished by this mental diet. It is not mere chance that in
France Georges Sorel and the circle of the 'Mouvement Socialiste',
in Italy the Sorelists, Arturo Labriola and others are most successful in returning the movement to the bases of the glorious age of
the Marxian International. And it is no coincidence that the specific workers' organizations in these countries, the trade unions
and their militant leaders, the syndicalists, are about to follow
that road which had been theoretically mapped out in the most
manly years of Marxism. Maybe the time is not too far, when Germany, the country of Marxism par excellence, will also realize the
need for a rejuvenated, strong Marxism, unhampered by the
fetters of political considerations.

But, who knows whether our predictions are correct? Still, miracles happen. Who would have believed only a few years ago that
such a thing as a three-volume Marx and Engels is possible in
Hungary? Who would not be stunned hearing that this project is
going to be published in more copies than any other scholarly book
in Hungary? Indeed, such signs permit me to quote the great
Florentine: 'Segui il tuo corso, e lascia dir le genti!'(3)

NOTES

1   Szabó refers to the reformists of the Parti Socialiste Français
    as 'Jaurèsists'. François Vidal (1814-72) was an adherent of
    Louis Blanc; Charles-Constantine Pecqueur (1801-87) was
    another economist, utopian socialist, who wanted to abolish
    the unequal distribution of the means of production through
    nationalization by the existing, bourgeois state. [Editors' note]
2   Anton Menger (1841-1906) was an Austrian jurist and politician,
    brother of the economist Karl (see above p. 19, n. 5), author
    of 'Neue Sittenlehre' (1903), 'Neu Staatslehre' (1905); Georg
    Adler (1863-1908) was a German bourgeois economist; Charles
    Andler (1866-1933) was a French university professor, philo-

sopher, translator of 'The Communist Manifesto'; Joseph Eugène
Fournière (1857–1914) was a French 'petty-bourgeois' socialist.
[Editors' note]
3 Correctly: 'Vien dietro a me e lascia dir le genti,' Dante,
'Divina Commedia. Purgatorio', Canto V: 13. [Editors' note]

MARX AND BAKUNIN
(Introduction to Marx's 'Inaugural Address to the International Working Men's Association')

Szabó edited the second volume of the Marx-Engels collection after his definite break with the Social Democratic Party, as an avowed syndicalist. In the Preface to the volume (1909) he wrote:

> If someone is able to develop, then four years have to leave traces in his mental development, knowledge and judgment. My convictions did not remain untouched by time. While in the first volume I thought to fulfil my editorial task best by not emphasizing my budding doubts and objections to the official school of Marxism, now, four years later, when I take up the uncompleted task, I feel it my duty to express clearly and decisively that new direction in Marxism which I follow and which I regard as correct and true.

Minor changes from the original plan reflect this change of heart, and even more the introductions to a few crucial texts. In the editorial preface to 'The Peasant War in Germany' Szabó underlined the role of force in history; in the rather extensive introduction to the 'Inaugural Address' he not only rejects the accusations of Social Democracy against anarchism but attempts to harmonize Bakunin's views with Marxist theory and in the Foreword to the 'Gotha Programme' (below, pp. 139-49) expounds his views on the political party.

Every nation and every generation has its favourite legendary epoch into which they project their yearnings and their ideals in the form of extremely enlarged realities; enlarged and exaggerated, because only such unconscious self-delusion can ever compensate for the misery of the present - a present upon which desires get shipwrecked, in which the most beautiful principles shrivel into commonplace facts.

What the heroic age was for warlike peoples and the era of the martyrs for the Christians, that is the era of the International for the socialists of western Europe. That was the legendary age when the bourgeoisie and the rulers of all Europe were trembling at the sight of this international spectre, which was in high fever burning and consuming itself in the rivalry of the titans, Marx and Bakunin. The Inaugural Address was the first public document issued by the first international organization of the working class.

Today we know that the International Working Men's Association was far from being the awe-inspiring power the bourgeoisie imagined it to be, terror-stricken as it was by revolutions and counter-revolutions, and as it still is in the less developed countries. The workers of any minor country today could throw larger masses and greater force into the struggle than the entire international camp that the International would have been able to muster. It could hardly have been otherwise: the working class was much less developed in some countries, much less conscious in others. It was not its actual power that rendered the International truly great and awe-inspiring, but rather its clear understanding of basic principles and the guidance it was able to provide the workers' movement. This guidance was precisely what was least appreciated at the time, by the working and by the ruling classes alike. The attention of contemporaries was drawn to immediate goals, occasional tactics, devices meant to shock, and very few were able to recognize the essence, the great principles of liberation.

Perhaps today we are better able to appreciate the true significance of the International, that it emphasized certain principles more clearly and more consciously than any of its predecessors: 'that the liberation of the working class can be accomplished only by the working class itself'; 'that every kind of servitude is social misery'; 'that in consequence the economic liberation of the working class is the major goal, and all political movements must be subordinated to it'; and 'that the liberation of work is not a local or national problem, but a social one, which extends to every modernized county'. All this is eminently up to date, relevant and weighty even now, and it includes what we recognize as the basic principles of the contemporary socialist movement. In fact, many wordy party programmes say no more, but take longer to say it less well.

Since we have embarked on the right path to the evaluation of the theoretical and practical significance of the International, I would like to deal with a superstition derived from its internal struggles and which still has an impact on socialist movements in certain countries. In those countries where 'German Marxism' prevails, that is mainly in the German Empire itself, in Austria, Hungary, Russia and the Balkans, Social Democrats are stubbornly convinced that the International was destroyed not because it came before its time, but because of personality clashes, particularly the disruptive activity of Bakunin. In other words, that Bakunin, the true father of anarchism, was the enemy of every kind of organization, and the true objective of anarchism to this day is disorganization. Consequently, there can be no more irreconcilable contradiction than the one between anarchism and socialism; anarchists and socialists are not brothers, but enemies.

> Every improvement in the organization of the proletariat is a step towards its liberation, and every obstacle to its organization is a step backwards. Those friends of the proletariat

who would weaken its solidarity for its own alleged benefit
are actually much more dangerous enemies than the opponents who would destroy the proletarian organizations by
force. No tendency has advanced further along this line
than that of Bakunin. This is why the Marxists are waging
a merciless war against it.

Thus wrote Karl Kautsky, the leading theoretician of the so-called
orthodox revolutionary Marxism, only a few years ago. The dec-
laration of a Dutch Social Democrat at the 1904 international congress in Amsterdam, that 'the anarchists are our greatest enemies',
likewise went unchallenged. Furthermore, in the above-mentioned
countries, the anarchists are frequently accused of being spies
for the police, or 'agents provocateurs'.
   The history of the International sheds light on the origin of
these arguments and accusations. The roots can be found particularly in the polemical writings with which Marx fought against
the growing influence of Bakunin and which ultimately led to the
latter's exclusion from the International. These writings not only
distort Bakunin's theoretical statements to the point where they
appear totally muddled or absurd, but include grave accusations
against his personal and political integrity. Even Kautsky admits
that these charges were entirely without foundation: 'It is impossible to deny', he wrote in the twentieth volume of 'Neue Zeit'
(1902), 'that in the heat of the struggle against Bakunin and his
followers Marx and his friends overshot their mark and resorted
to any number of baseless accusations.' Nevertheless, only two
years later, a German Social Democrat wrote a rather successful
book about the International in which the followers of Bakunin
were, in the words of Kautsky, 'labelled liars, demagogues, and
even criminals'. Another Social Democrat has distorted the teachings of Bakunin in utter bad faith in a pamphlet that has been
translated into every European language. The party newspapers
and agitators make sure that the poison of libel spreads everywhere.
   On the other hand, certain anarchists seem to believe that they
can best serve their cause by raising similar charges against Marx,
Engels and Social Democracy in general, in the same bad faith.
   Under these circumstances it seems necessary to head off a
possible attempt to embitter the already acute objective contradictions with further myths invented in our own country. Hence I
will do my best, in so far as that be possible within the framework
of an introduction, to make an objective comparison of the theories of Marx and Bakunin, and determine their mutual relationship.

I BAKUNIN'S THEORY AND MARXISM

It cannot be claimed that Bakunin was one of the great masters of
style. Predisposed to oral agitation and to action, engaged in constant and almost superhuman activity, Bakunin could not possibly

have taken up the pen with the serenity and objectivity which lucid writing requires. With few exceptions, his writings are occasional pieces about the initiation or justification of some action, or else polemical writings. We know how easily a writer becomes dominated by his temperament in such cases, how he stresses certain points which might otherwise have remained in the background, and how he sharpens certain arguments to harm his adversary rather than to serve the cause of justice. All of Bakunin's works are of this nature, created in the heat of combat. No wonder his opponents have had no difficulty culling contradictions from them, or pointing out his many sloppy formulations in order to demonstrate his ignorance and confusion.

Should someone approach his works not with a view to detecting contradictions at all cost, but rather with the realization that the work of the agitator must be single-minded to exert deep influence on countries and generations - such a person is bound to discover something altogether different in the works of Bakunin. He is bound to conclude that the father of anarchism was far from being a representative of idealistic philosophical speculations or of the fantastic individualism of the post-Hegelian period. Rather, Bakunin was, in every respect, the disciple of the nineteenth-century school of positive sociology. So how could he possibly be cast as the theoretical opponent of Marx?

Bakunin himself claimed to be a disciple of Marx. 'I am your disciple', he wrote to him in one of his letters, 'and I am proud of it'. And he declared this much to others as well. When Herzen urged him to resort to reprisals even against Marx, for those rumours which purported to his being a paid agent of the Russian government, Bakunin replied:

> As far as Marx is concerned, I know as well as you do that he is guilty towards us like so many others; what more, that he is the author of the ignominies attributed to us. Why have I praised him, then? For two reasons. First, because of my love of justice. No matter how despicably he behaved towards us, I for one will not pass over his outstanding merits regarding socialism; he has been serving the cause for almost twenty-five years intelligently, dynamically, and faithfully, and he is undoubtedly worth more than any of us.... Second, for political reasons. Marx is one of the surest, most influential, and most intelligent pillars of socialism in the International, and one of the most solid dams against penetration by any kind of bourgeois tendency. And I would never forgive myself were I to annihilate or diminish his unquestionably beneficial influence for the sake of the satisfaction of my personal desire for vengeance ('Sozialpolitischer Briefwechsel', pp. 174-5).

Bakunin had not spoken in such glowing terms of any of his predecessors or contemporaries even though, like most persons with an impulsive character, he was inclined to exaggerate the virtues and merits of others. Still, he does not mention Proudhon in such favourable colours, though he was the only truly significant theoretician of socialism next to Marx, and undoubtedly shared some of Bakunin's ideas. Even less does Bakunin praise the person who is sometimes described as the true father of anarchism (although his influence was quite limited), Max Stirner. Or anybody else, for that matter. Actually Bakunin felt himself closest to Marx, both in theory and in practice. Bakunin was the first to translate 'The Communist Manifesto' into Russian, and he began to translate 'Capital' as well, while it never occurred to him to translate the works of any other west European socialist.

Nevertheless, we cannot refer to him as simply a disciple of Marx or as a Marxist. Even if we mean no more by Marxism than a method of research - historical materialism - and the concomitant principle of action - class struggle - and exclude from it everything that is not a generally valid sociological thesis but merely an observation applicable to a specific period such as capitalism, or to a specific field, such as political economy, even then we would still have to concede that the basic theories of Bakunin and Marx are not completely identical. Not because Bakunin rejected historical materialism, nor because he did not proclaim and practise class struggle, but because, in his reading of these Marxist notions, alien elements had crept in which often interfered with their consistent application.

Even his general views on social philosophy predisposed Bakunin to Marxism. Some of its opponents like to pretend that anarchism is an extension of bourgeois liberalism, the cult of ultimate individualism and of absolute personal freedom. I hardly need to discuss the truth of these assertions; but I can marshal any number of quotations to demonstrate that Bakunin was not an individualist. He was far from interpreting historical progress as the work of arbitrary individual will, or to consider social existence as the death of, or even a barrier to, individual liberty. He was far from satisfied with the vapid and superficial formulations of the principle of individual liberty which states that the only limit to the freedom of the individual is the freedom of other individuals. This was the principle upon which the most typical and most outstanding master of the liberal school of sociology, Herbert Spencer, would have based the society of the future. This definition matches almost word for word the principle of liberty enunciated by Rousseau, and that was precisely the target of Bakunin's sharpest attacks. For him social life is as much determined by implacable laws as nature is. The universal law of causality reigns in one domain just as in the other; the same unseverable connection and fateful ineluctability prevails in one sphere as in the other. It is impossible to revolt against the natural laws, because they are the base and condition of our existence, they surround us and penetrate our every movement, our every thought, regulate our every action; even when we think we are disobeying the laws of nature we do no more than proclaim their omnipotence. With respect to these laws man can have but

one freedom: to recognize them and use them increasingly along
the road to collective and individual liberation and humanization,
on which he is advancing (L'Empire Knouto-germanique et la
Révolution Sociale, 'Oeuvres', vol. III, pp. 49-59).

Man has reached this road thanks to his understanding, thanks
to his capacity for abstraction. But does this mean that abstract-
ions and ideas are the springs of historical development? According to the idealists, yes. They claim that certain ideas and feelings
are innate in humans. Nothing can be further from the truth.
What humans bring with themselves at the moment of their birth -
at various stages of their evolution and to different degrees - is
nothing but the material or formal capacity to feel, think, shape
and develop ideas. These capacities are strictly formal. What gives
them content? Society does.

How did the first concepts or ideas come about in history? The
only thing we can say about this is that they were not created
autonomously, in isolation, by the miraculously enlightened mind
of certain inspired individuals. They were the outcome of collective effort, something that passed mostly unnoticed by sections of
society and by the minds of individuals. The geniuses, the outstanding individuals of a given society, are only the most fortun-
ate spokesmen of this collective effort. Every person of genius is
pretty much like Voltaire: 'He took the best wherever he found
it.' In other words, it was the collective mind of primitive society
that created the first ideas (Dieu et l'État, 'Oeuvres', vol. I,
pp. 289-90).

Thus man is a social being both physically and intellectually.
To the idealists à la Rousseau man was free and immortal at the
beginning, and became mortal and a slave only in society. He surrenders the freedom of his immortal and infinite soul in order to
satisfy the needs of his finite and imperfect body. Social life,
therefore, is the surrender of the infinite and of freedom.

The concept of freedom held by materialists, realists and
collectivists is precisely the opposite. Human beings become
human only within society, and it is only by the collective
action of all society that they attain the consciousness and
realization of their humanity. Only social or collective work
is able to convert the surface of the earth into an area con-
ducible to human development and liberate them from the
yoke of nature. Without this material liberation, moral and
intellectual liberation would remain impossible. Nor is it
possible to free oneself from the yoke of one's own inner
nature; that is one cannot subordinate the instincts and
movements of one's body to the direction of a more developed
intellect except by education and culture. Both processes of
liberation are social manifestations par excellence. Outside of
society man would have forever remained a wild animal....
The isolated individual would not even have awoken to the
realization of his freedom. To be free means that others, all
humans, recognize one as free, and deal with one accordingly.

Thus freedom is not a factor of isolation, but mutual
reflections; not of exclusion, but of contact. The freedom
of every individual is nothing but the reflection of his
humanity and his human rights in the consciousness of
others. It is only in the presence of others, and vis-à-vis
others that one can claim to be and actually be free (ibid.,
pp. 276-8).

The progress of society amounts to the widening of the sphere
of human liberty. What does this widening mean? It means that
man learns the laws of nature better and better, and thereby
becomes master over them. The road to civilization and to freedom
is one and the same.
A thinker who made individual freedom and will thus be dependent on the social environment can certainly not be accused of
individualism. When Bakunin emphasizes, as he often did, that
'one must look for the freedom of man not at the beginning of
history, but at its end', because 'the true, great and final goal
of history is the actual and complete freedom of every person',
he is merely saying something all Marxists can subscribe to, and
which has been expressed by Engels in this sentence: 'Socialism
is the leap of humanity from the realm of necessity into the realm
of freedom' ('Anti-Dühring', pt III, ch. 2).
We have seen that Bakunin places the origin of ideas in society
and makes freedom dependent on social progress. Only one step
separates this interpretation from historical materialism. And
Bakunin took this final step. In the pamphlet aimed at the German
school of socialism ('Sophismes Historiques de l'École Doctrinaire
des Communistes Allemands'), he once again contrasts the idealists
with the materialists:

While they derive all aspects of history, including material
progress and the development of various sectors of economic
organization from ideas, the German communists, on the
contrary, see in all history, in the most ideal manifestations
of collective and individual life, in the intellectual, moral,
religious, metaphysical, scientific, artistic, political, legal
and social changes in the past and at the present, nothing
but the reflections of economic factors, or necessary reactions
to them. While the idealists claim that ideas precede facts
and even create them, the communists... on the other hand,
claim that facts give birth to ideas, and that the latter are
nothing but the ideal expression of discrete events. The communists claim that the economic, the material world are the
facts par excellence; these are the ones that create the main
base, the essential foundation, while all other factors, intellectual or moral, political or social, are merely inevitable
consequences...
Who is right: the idealists or the materialists? Once the
question has been formulated in this manner, our answers
cannot be hesitant. Without a doubt the idealists are mistaken,

only the materialists are right. Yes, the facts do precede
ideas. Yes, the ideal, as Proudhon stated, is but a flower,
the material conditions for the existence of which are the
roots. Yes, the entire intellectual, moral, political and
social history of mankind is the reflection of its economic
history. Every branch of serious and self-aware modern
science can be cited to support this great, decisive truth.
(L'Empire Knouto-germanique et la Révolution Sociale,
'Oeuvres', vol. III, pp. 14-19).

We can see that Bakunin not only felt free to explain historical
materialism, but actually accepted it in its full expanse, though
he himself proceeded to limit its applicability right away. Given
the gaps in his training in economics one could hardly expect that
at times he should not perceive other factors as dominant; the
objective view of things, the consistent derivation of the facts of
psychological life from the objectified outside world was incompatible with his active fighting spirit. Thus Bakunin easily forgot
what he had often argued regarding the social origin of ideas;
next to the economic factor he placed two bio-psychological factors
– the ability to think, and the capacity and need to revolt – as
complementary aspects of social evolution. He refers to these two
capacities as the negative factors of progress, whereas the economic is the positive one.
Obviously Bakunin has cited two elemental and general factors
of the organic world in one breath with a specifically social factor.
For the capacity to think and revolt is not an exclusively human
trait, but merely the psychological expression and subjective
reflection of that great elemental force to which all living creatures
owe their life: the struggle for survival. Every revolt is a struggle for life, for survival, hence every struggle is a revolt; the
same for the tiger, the caterpillar, the fir tree, the moss as it is
for man. Historical materialism does not deny this in the least.
But the person who uses social science as a method of research
has to restrict himself to social facts and seek nothing more than
the specific means humanity uses in its social struggle, and hence
will find that the existence of humanity is shaped by the development and forms of its economic activities. In other words, the
complex manifestations of society are to be reduced to the most
basic social activity. That this basic social activity is founded on
even more basic natural conditions is not a matter for the social
scientist but pertains to the domain of the natural sciences.
We would be inordinately strict with Bakunin, however, if we
were to bar him from the ranks of the adepts of historical materialism simply on the grounds that he has mixed biological and psychological factors into the basic factors accounting for social
development, or because at moments he attributed greater importance to ideas. Any number of thinkers who had no greater familiarity with the true essence of historical materialism than Bakunin
were counted as true Marxists to the end of their life. A whole
school of thinkers have identified the examination of economic

factors, that is the derivation of social manifestations from the means of production, simply with economic interest; that is they have reduced it to a purely psychological category. Engels himself – after Marx's death – made rather significant allowances to the subjective tendency. Others have confused historical with philosophical materialism. True enough, the problem of historical materialism is not simple, and Bakunin is not the only Marxist who used the concept mistakenly.

It is undeniable, however, that Bakunin never fell into extremes; when examining specific social problems he perceived, along with the basic economic aspect, the concomitant intellectual, moral, religious and other factors; nevertheless, in the critique of ideologies and the struggle against them he never neglected the social bases of ideas.

Among his most deeply rooted tendencies were his antagonism to religion and to the church. In each one of his works he ends up by discussing God and religion. Nevertheless, he writes about the propaganda activity of free thinkers.

> Only social revolution, and not the propaganda of free thinkers, will be able to extirpate religion from the bosom of the people. To be sure, that propaganda is quite useful. It is even indispensable as a means of converting the more progressive individuals; but it cannot affect the masses, because religion is not simply a slip or dislocation of the mind, but rather and particularly the protest of the live and active character of the masses against the miseries of actual existence. The people go to church for the same reason as they go to the tavern – to be drugged, to forget their misery, and to think of themselves, at least for brief moments, as equal, free and happy. Let him have a human life and he will no longer go to either pub or church. This human existence can and will be provided for him only by social revolution. ('Il socialismo e Mazzini', p. 50).

Some Marxists claim that to attribute decisive significance to human understanding in social development or to attempt the transformation of society by means of legislation is compatible with the economic perception of society. Bakunin's reply to these social scientists is completely in accord with the spirit of historical materialism.

> Society is ruled by morals and customs, never by laws. Individual initiatives, rather than the thought or will of the legislator, drive it slowly along the road of progress. There are laws which govern it unconsciously, but these are natural laws, inherent to the social body, just as physical laws are inherent to material bodies. The better part of these laws are unknown to this day, and yet they have ruled society since its beginnings, independent of the thought and will of the persons constituting it; from which

it follows that we must not confuse them with political and
juridical laws. ('Federalisme, socialisme et anti-theologisme',
vol. I, pp. 141-2).

II BAKUNIN'S PRAXIS AND MARX

Thus far I have endeavoured to show the proximity between the
general social philosophy of Bakunin and Marx. I have placed
greater stress on this than I will on the next section, in which I
compare their political and tactical views, their praxis. Yet it was
not about theories that they clashed in the International but
rather about questions of tactics and organization. Admittedly
these matters are much more important than theories. They mean
action, life, actual history; at most, theories provide an account
of the extent to which historical events have registered in the
heads of individual persons. If I have dealt at length with theories, it was because, while the writings of Marx and of the Social
Democrats, most of which were in German, are easily accessible,
the works of Bakunin and the anarchists, mostly in French and
Italian, remain largely inaccessible to Hungarian readers. The
inevitable consequence of this has been that our working class
has gained a totally one-sided view of the significance of both
tendencies of the socialist movement, and accepts uncritically all
the bona or mala fide errors of the German Social Democrats.

I believe the passages from Bakunin quoted above should make
everyone more cautious in regard to the usual accusations; and
it should no longer be easy to pretend that the contradiction between Bakunin and Marx is like the one between the working class
and the bourgeoisie; moreover, it will not be possible to deny that
Bakunin and Marx are related by close theoretical ties.

This kinship seems even closer when it comes to the politics of
the working class and the socialist movement. While studying
objectively the history of the International, one is bound to feel
that the mutual accusations, in so far as they had some basis in
reality, were either eminently premature, or simply pretended or
far-fetched conflicts. There was but one serious source of conflict: whether the organization of the International should be
centralized or federalized; whether the General Council sitting in
London should be an organization controlling the local sections, or
merely a correspondence office transmitting their communications?
Because of his temperament, his inclination to authoritarianism,
and his personal vanity, Marx was inclined to centralism; whereas
Bakunin was swept towards the opposite point of view by his
temperament and his unbridled desire for action.

Yet all this relates solely to the internal organization of the
International. Not a word was said about applying the principles
of organization of the International to either the workers' movement on the whole, or to its national, political and economic sub-
divisions. After all, every section and, what is more, every single
member belonged to the Association not via some central national

organ, but directly. However, as today, almost forty years after
the Hague congress at which Bakunin was excluded from the
organization, the central organ of the international Social Democratic movement, the 'Bureau Socialiste Internationale' in Brussels,
is simply that – a bureau, an office, rather than a higher forum –
we must conclude that time has vindicated Bakunin.

As to the basic points of the programme of the International,
Bakunin was in total agreement with Marx. What were these points?
The programme specified: class organization and politics of the
working class in total independence from other classes and of
bourgeois parties; a halt to the monopoly of the means of production as a basic condition of the liberation of the working class;
hence the subordination of the political movement to the economic
struggle; finally, the assertion of the international nature of the
workers' movement.

The contradictions that have arisen in these matters do not
refer to the essence, but to inconsequential details or to conclusions that were not at all relevant to the primitive stage of the
working-class movement at the time: such as parliamentarism and
participation in government, or to the problematic of the organization of future society – all of which were entirely academic
matters at the time. It is fairly obvious, however, that it was
precisely the Bakuninians who stuck rigidly to the basic principles of the International – which, as we know, were formulated
by Marx – whereas those who stood by Marx during the controv-
ersies (it is not possible to refer to them invariably as Marxists)
were often mere politicians who made concessions to the early
times and the as yet undeveloped conditions out of political oppor-
tunism. That is they have acted much the same way as Bakunin
had been justly accused of acting in his Russian policy. The
economic and social conditions in Russia were incomparably more
primitive than those of western Europe at the time, for industry
and an industrial working class simply did not exist, hence the
only possible politics were aristocratic or liberal; in western
Europe, on the contrary, it was not possible to do anything
except pure working-class politics. This was all Marx insisted on,
as is clearly stated in the programme of the International. Bakunin
and his disciples wanted the same; and so it happened that each
time Marx opposed Bakunin, he ended up by opposing himself.
Mutual recriminations are mostly what we get in these matters.

We can see this immediately in the issue of class consciousness.
Bakunin was accused of being petit bourgeois; Bakunin says the
same about the Socialists and workers in Germany:

> In Germany though the socialist paper kept insisting on
> awakening within the proletariat a feeling and consciousness
> of its necessary contradiction vis-à-vis the bourgeois
> ('Klassenbewusstsein, Klassenkampf'), the workers and
> peasants remain part of the network of the bourgeoisie
> whose culture surrounds them completely, and whose spirit
> permeates the masses. And these same socialist writers, who

are thundering against the bourgeoisie, are themselves
bourgeois from top to bottom; they are the propagandists
and apostles of the bourgeoisie and, although unwittingly
for the most part, they have become the defenders of bourgeois interests against the proletariat. (Lettres à un français,
'Oeuvres', vol. II, p. 167).

Accordingly, Bakunin took the most determined stand against
the bourgeoisie, as well as against the so-called bourgeois socialists or reform socialists, who are intent on purely political reform
by means of charity, moral preaching, or state assistance: helping
the lower classes, but only through initiatives taken by the upper
class. He fought them particularly in Italy, where he had most
room for practical action, but in other countries as well. In this
regard Bakunin's attitude was not a bit less determined than that
of Marx. In general he claimed that the bourgeoisie, 'this class
which at one time was so powerful, enlightened and flourishing
and which today slowly but inevitably heads towards decline is
already dead as regards its reason and morals. It no longer has
faith, or ideas, or any spirit of endeavour. It does not want to
and cannot turn back, yet it dares not look forward either'. ('Il
Socialismo e Mazzini', p. 39). 'The character of contemporary
bourgeoisie is to appreciate the beautiful only in the past, and to
adore in the present only that which is profitable and useful.'
(Les ours de Berne, 'Oeuvres', vol. II, p. 29). Hence Bakunin
kept reiterating that the working class should not count on the
bourgeoisie. No one could have expressed more clearly and point-
edly the contradiction separating the concept of the two classes
regarding the means of progress. One of the two classes, having
developed its economic forces, can increase its power only by
means of political power, whereas the other can develop the
forces latent in its social situation only through the struggle
against this power.

> The bourgeois see and understand nothing that is not part
> of the state or of the means regulated by the state. The
> maximum of their ideal, of their imagination, and of their
> heroism is the revolutionary exaggeration of the power and
> function of the state in the name of general interest. But I
> have already shown that the activity of the state cannot
> save... France.... I am the absolute enemy of 'revolution
> par decrets', the consequence and application of the prin-
> ciple of the revolutionary state; that is of the kind of
> revolution which bears only the outward appearance of
> revolution. I confront the system of revolutionary decrees
> with the system of revolutionary acts, the only truly effect-
> ive, consistent and true one. (Lettres à un français,
> 'Oeuvres', vol. II, pp. 87, 95)

Let no one think, however, that Bakunin naively believed it
would be sufficient to make a revolution and a collective society

would be ready. He often stressed that the bourgeois world still has more material means and organized and educated government forces at its disposal than we would wish. In the sequence of historical periods in which cannibalism was replaced by slavery, slavery by serfdom, and serfdom by wage-labour 'there will come the terrible day of judgment which in turn will be followed, much, much later, by the era of brotherhood'. Bakunin claimed, however, that society cannot be shaken by words and resolutions: actions are needed, but an act deserves the name of action only if it changes the world in some way. Undeniably he was inclined to overestimate the value of violent revolts and to greet every violent uprising as an action; but no one can pretend that he felt that individual action was the only possible one, or that the organization of the masses was superfluous. In some Italian cities where Bakuninism was especially strong he had thousands of adherents organized by trade, in accordance with his principle that it is not enough 'to be merely conscious of the truth; it is necessary to organize the forces of the proletariat... because without prior organization even the most powerful elements remain impotent and nil' ('Il socialismo e Mazzini', pp. 31, 52). The first congress of Bakuninists was to decide to this effect: it proposed to all its members the establishment of trade unions and of strike funds.

In fact, this was not what separated the two nuances of the International. It was not a matter of whether organization was necessary or not, but rather whether the basis of socialist organization should be unions by trade or purely political organizations. One of Marx's most faithful disciples, Jung, in an official letter addressed to one of the leaders of the Swiss Bakuninists, James Guillaume, on behalf of the General Council of the International, wrote:

> You believe that the trade unions will be the ones to obtain the liberation of the workers? You are wrong. We use trade unions as one kind of tool among many, but not as an end in themselves. The trade union organizes the workers; it divides society into two enemy camps: that of the workers, and that of the employers. In today's society the trade unions are the expression of economic struggle. They will never transform society, however; they may initiate social revolution, but could never finish it. In order to change society, in order to complete the social revolution, the workers will be obliged to seize political power. (Quoted in the 'Mémoire presenté par la Fédération Jurassienne de L'Association Internationale des Travailleurs', Sonvillier, 1873, p. 136)

It is also an unquestionable fact that all the Social Democratic parties, and especially those that consider themselves the bastions of orthodox Marxism, remained for a long while completely indifferent towards the trade union movement, and credited it with little or uncertain value. The force of reality, the tremendous

growth and impact of economic organizations as compared to the
political movement was necessary to convince finally some contemporary Marxists that the economic movement was at least as
important as the political one in the struggle for the liberation of
the working class. On the other hand, the International had proclaimed the great significance of the economic organizations some
forty years ago, while still under the influence of Marx. As early
as in 1864, the first congress held in Geneva, stated that:

> The trade unions had unconsciously become organizational
> centres for the working class, just as towns and cities had
> been for the bourgeoisie during the Middle Ages. If the
> trade unions are indispensable in the daily struggle of
> capital and labour, in what might be called true guerrilla
> warfare; they are even more important as the organized
> vehicles of the abolition of wage-labour and the reign of
> capital.

It is the International itself that describes trade unions as the
organized vehicles against wage-labour and capital. Hence, when
the Bakuninists were stressing the economic movement at whatever cost, surely they could not be accused of acting against the
spirit of Marx.

Therefore, the Bakuninists and the Marxists clashed not about
matters of organization, but rather whether it was the seizure of
political power or economic struggle that would lead to socialism
in the long run. In the early period of the workers' organizations
this question was undoubtedly premature; theoretically speaking,
as far as it refers to their teachings about the state, the issue
did not imply any fundamental difference between Marx and
Bakunin.

True, anti-statism was Bakunin's most pronounced tendency. It
is hardly necessary to quote him to prove the point. We can see
it as a red thread running through each and every one of his
writings and actions. The state, everything that is referred to as
political power, must be destroyed, both in theory and in practice.
As long as there is political power there will be rulers and subjects, masters and servants, exploiters and exploited. 'Once
political power has been destroyed, it has to be replaced by organizations of the forces of production and economic institutions.'
(Les Ours de Berne, 'Oeuvres', vol. II, p. 39). Each of his arguments was directed against the claim that the democratic state and
its prerequisite, universal suffrage, could, if it only tried, change
the economic and social predicament of the working class. The
state is necessarily a class-state, under all circumstances, because when it is not the propertied classes that use it as their
tool of exploitation, then it is those interested in the maintenance
of political power: the state officials, the bureaucracy. Consequently the state is the natural enemy of every truly revolutionary
act, because it trusts only in itself, and feels insecure in face of
the free movements and spontaneous actions of the masses as they

turn against the state at any moment. But because the free collective society can emerge only from the free and spontaneous
action of the masses, any participation in politics is detrimental,
since it enhances the confidence in the state and contributes to
its strength. The state has to be eradicated and society liberated.

But those who would resort to these tenets to construct an
unbridgeable gap between Bakunin and Marx neglect the fact that
while Marx made all kinds of concessions to the state and to democracy in practice, he was just as anti-state in theory as Bakunin
was and did not imagine the political organization of future society
in different terms. In a hundred places in his works Marx con-
demns with ruthless irony those who see in the state the organization of public interest, an impartial, unprejudiced, and ethical
power above class or group interests. The state is the powerful
weapon of the ruling classes by which they violently ensure their
power; the state is a class-state; and will remain so, as long as
there are classes. Since the objective of the struggle of the working class is the elimination of classes, the state must perish along
with class society. In 1847 Marx asked:

> Does this mean that after the fall of the old society there will
> be a new class domination culminating in a new political power?
> No.
>   The condition for the emancipation of the working class is
> the abolition of all classes, just as the condition for the
> emancipation of the third estate, of the bourgeois order, was
> the abolition of all estates and all orders.
>   The working class, in the course of its development, will
> substitute for the old civil society an association which will
> exclude classes and their antagonism, and there will be no
> more political power properly so-called, since political power
> is precisely the official expression of antagonism in civil
> society. (Marx, The Poverty of Philosophy, 'Collected Works',
> vol. 6. (1976), p. 212)

And thirty years later, in his critique of the German party's Gotha
programme, he speaks with sharp irony of state-socialistic tendencies in the programme.

> the German workers' party strives for 'the free state'.
>   Free state - what is this?
>   It is by no means the aim of the workers, who have got
> rid of the narrow mentality of humble subjects, to set the
> state free. In the German Empire the 'state' is almost as
> 'free' as in Russia...
>   The German workers' party... shows that its socialist
> ideas are not even skin-deep... it treats the state rather
> as an independent entity that possesses its own autonomous
> intellectual and ethical bases...
>   But the whole programme, for all its democratic clang, is
> tainted through and through by the Lassallean sect's servile

belief in the state, or, what is no better, by a democratic
belief in miracles, or rather it is a compromise between these
two kinds of belief in miracles, both equally remote from
socialism. (Marx, 'Critique of the Gotha Programme', ch. IV)

After all this, it is not surprising that Marx came to the defence
of anarchy itself in the face of Bakunin, and gave the concept a
broadly socialist interpretation.

All socialists see anarchy as the following program. Once
the aim of the proletarian movement, i.e., abolition of classes,
is attained, the power of the state, which serves to keep the
great majority of producers in bondage to a very small ex-
ploiter minority, disappears, and the functions of government
become simple administrative functions. (K. Marx, Fictitious
Splits in the International, 'On the First International', ed.
Padover (New York, 1973), p. 222)

In comparison with these quotes, which we could continue ad
infinitum, the debate between the followers of Bakunin and the
followers of Marx on whether the organization of future society
should be collectivist or communist, pales into insignificance. How
insignificant these distinctions were is clearly demonstrated by
the fact that in those times it was the disciples of Bakunin who
referred to themselves as collectivists, and Marx's friends as communists; whereas nowadays it is mostly the anarchists who call
themselves communist, and collectivism is the social ideal of the
Social Democrats. In any case, we are still far from the day when
the different principles of organization of socialist society will be
on the agenda of the struggling working class.
The struggle of the working class will continue for a long time
to come within the framework of the present state, and the immediate problem facing it is not the philosophy of the present or,
if you prefer, the future state, but whether the power of the
state can be used in its everyday struggle. While this issue could
hardly have been brought up at the time of Marx and Bakunin,
because of the embryonic development and organization of the
working class, today, as a result of its strong representation in
parliament, this has become the most burning issue among those
which played a role in the contest of the two leaders of the International.
It seems to be that the best guideline on this issue is to be
sought in a synthesis of the views of Marx and Bakunin. Although
Marx believed in parliamentary action, he was far from enthusiastic
about it. He followed the activity of bourgeois as well as social
democratic parliamentary parties with sarcasm and never ceased
reminding the workers that truly constructive action takes place
not in parliament, but in society, in the economy and in the movement of the masses. He [rather, Engels - Editors' note] referred
to this involvement with parliaments as *parliamentary cretinism*:

a disorder which penetrates its unfortunate victims with
the solemn conviction that the whole world, its history and
future, are governed and determined by a majority of votes
in that particular representative body which has the honour
to count them among its members, and that all and everything going on outside the walls of their house – wars, revolutions, railway-constructing, colonizing of whole new continents, Californian gold discoveries, Central American
canals, Russian armies, and whatever else may have some
little claim to influence upon the destinies of mankind – is
nothing compared to the incommensurable events hinging
upon the important question, whatever it may be, just at
that moment occupying the attention of the honourable
House. (Engels, Revolution and Counter-Revolution in
Germany, 'Collected Works', vol. 11, (1979), p. 79)

Bakunin, on the other hand, argues that even in the most democratic states such as the United States and Switzerland, while the
people may appear to be omnipotent, self-government by the
masses is pure fiction, and it is a minority who rules. Nevertheless, he comes down in favour of democracy.

Let no one think that when we criticize democratic government we are speaking out in favour of monarchy. We are
firmly convinced that the most imperfect republic is worth
a thousand times more than the most enlightened monarchy,
because in a republic there are at least moments when the
people, although continuously exploited, are not oppressed,
whereas in a monarchy the oppression is continuous too.
Moreover, a republican government educates the masses
little by little to gain an understanding of public affairs,
which the monarchy never does. But though we prefer a
republic, it must be admitted and announced that no matter
what the form of government, as long as human society is
divided into classes as a result of the inequality of professions and trades, of fortune, of culture, and of rights, it
shall always remain in the hands of the few, and a minority
will inevitably exploit the majority. (Federalism, Socialisme
et Antithéologisme, 'Oeuvres', vol. I, pp. 173-4)

My description of the internal struggles of the International, of
the battles fought with poisoned arrows, in which I attempted to
stop short of evoking the insults exchanged, might be concluded
at this point. I deliberately allowed the two antagonists to speak
for themselves more and more and let them stand next to each
other in order to let everyone acquire a direct view of them.
Nevertheless, as we well know, this view cannot be complete. My
chief endeavour was to show the similarities between these two
leaders, and I had to relegate into the background other traits
which might have underlined the differences. Yet, in the face of

so much intentional or unintentional falsification, in the face of all the malevolent and fanatical distortions obfuscating the true history of the International Working Men's Organization, perhaps I am justified in emphasizing the similarities for once. From these everyone can see that both Bakunin and Marx served enthusiastically and unselfishly the great cause of the working class, albeit with differing temperaments, with differing estimates of the real and practical opportunities. Undoubtedly, the differences between them were profound. But my presentation should make it clear that the distinctions must be sought not so much in their teachings, but in that they each represented different types of human being. One was a thinker, the other a doer; one a scientist, the other a fighter. The conditions of the emerging and undifferentiated workers' organizations particularly demanded the unity of theory and practice - not as if a person could ever be a whole without this unity. Under these circumstances two such different characters yet equally born leaders were bound to clash: their whole personality made it impossible for them to express the needs of the parturient movement of the working class in the same terms, though they were certainly its most outstanding representatives.

From the passages quoted it should be obvious that the unbridgeable gap which certain Social Democrats perceive between anarchism and socialism exists only as a figment of their imagination, not in reality. Even less is this gap to be found in the writings of Marx and Bakunin, although they were cited most often by the disciples of each tendency. Anarchism is one species of socialism, as is social democracy itself. Socialism and social democracy are by no means identical. The essence of socialism is the common ownership of the means of production, and the achievement of this community through the struggle of the organized forces of the working class. All the anarchist leaders agree with this, except for a few individualistic anarchists who have never found roots among the workers. And this is all that matters. Everything else is but a means to an end, and not the end in itself. It cannot be denied that the advocates of revolutionary action have at least as much right to refer to Marx for the justification of the means as the fanatics of parliamentarism and peaceful transformation. It is not the advocates of revolutionary action who are attempting to free themselves from the heritage of Marx today, but rather those who advocate parliamentary action. And those whom the advocates of parliamentary action would so lightly label anarchists are increasingly sounding off the old slogan: back to Marx!

Those who continue to feel, even after the death of the two leaders, that they should fight with the selfsame poisoned pens against the memory of these men as well as against their heirs and disciples, might like to read and assimilate what may have been Bakunin's last pronouncement before his death.

Try to introduce into your contacts with new people with whom you want to establish closer relationships as much justice, sincerity and kindness as your nature allows. You must understand that it is not possible to construct anything live and solid on jesuitic mischief, that the success of revolutionary activity must not reside in base and low passions and that no revolution will triumph without higher ideals. It is in this direction and in this sense that I sincerely bid you success.

MARX

This article, the last major writing of Szabó, was published
for 5 May 1918, the hundredth anniversary of Marx's birth,
in 'Huszadik Század', pt I (1918), pp. 280-6, that is in a
sociological, not a socialist journal. It reflects the feelings
of Szabó in the fourth year of that war which 'relieved'
Social Democracy of Marxism as a revolutionary teaching on
class - not parliamentary party - struggle. It is also a
retrospective summary of two decades' study on Marx and
propagation of Marxism. He surveys with fine irony (and it
is worth noting the development of his style from the early
schoolmasterish precision to this sharp and elegant essay!)
the fate of Marxism from science, 'its original sphere' into
politics, where it became prostituted. Though somewhat
ambivalent, Szabó does not come down for an 'abstract
Marxist scholarship', but rather demands a Marxian science
that is genuinely praxis-oriented but subscribes to the tenets of primacy of class, that is of immediate working-class
action. Still, he closes on an elegiac note, claiming for Marx
above all the place of an exemplary heroic life - and wishes
no more than this be seen by 'educated men' and masses
alike.

What an unfortunate moment for celebrating the one hundredth
anniversary of the birth of Marx! Seventy years ago he proclaimed
in his manifesto what at the time, in its historical context, and
within the context of the evolution of his own mind, was a bold,
revolutionary slogan: workers of the world, unite! Indeed, Marx
became the most influential theoretician and leader of international
socialism. Yet now, at his jubilee, his disciples can do no better
than wonder and debate whether they ought to commemorate Marx
at all. In Russia, Lenin's government has declared an amnesty for
the occasion; but in the country where Marx's son-in-law, grand-
child and closest disciples have been leaders for decades, in
France, where at one time he was proclaimed their redeemer, it
seemed, until the very last minute, that his disciples would deny
him.
  But where his birthday will be celebrated without fail on 5 May
with triumphant speeches amidst red banners - how many there
will truly consider Marx as their redeemer, as the philosopher
through whose eyes they scan and perceive the secrets of the
universe, as the man whose life is a model for their lives and

whose actions were the beginning and the model for their actions? But how many more will have chosen him as their hero, the great man, the redeemer, merely because their everyday souls and brains conceive of him in their own image? Or else because they have recreated him in their own image like an anthropomorphic god to serve as the right trademark for their own commonplace goals and have appropriated him as a slogan, as a cover, have transformed him, deformed him.

Who, then, is the real Marx, and what is Marxism – the Marxism that lives in the consciousness of the masses and of the so-called 'educated men'? To find the answer to our question, we must consider how and through whom did the present generation become acquainted with Marx. After all, how many are there who have taken the trouble to read more than a handful of his historical and propagandistic works? And how many have read even these with the pure desire and ability to assimilate? The reading of Marx's major works is arduous indeed. Few of the great minds in world history have shown such scant courtesy, one might say, so little sense of democracy towards their reading public; and few have done what Marx did: neglect to the very end the task of organizing systematically his basic philosophical and sociological views which determine his economic theory in its entirety. What he has done was to scatter his views in the form of incidental and brief observations through hefty volumes which contain innumerable elaborate, often sarcastic, even satirical and sometimes hypothetical deductions, frequently failing to divulge his premises.

We humans are made in such a way that we are only capable of understanding, our intellect only becomes fertilized, our will, feeling and actions can only be permeated by that which harmonizes with our inborn abilities and tendencies. All other impressions roll off us without leaving any lasting intellectual or emotional trace, much as drops of water roll off the back of the waterfowl. You can understand the character of a person if you know who were his or her guides, teachers, or preceptors; not in the 'schoolish' sense but in regard to life experience, in actual thoughts and even more so in actual behaviour. Who were the minds who fertilized his mind. Who were the great men and women, the heroes, who became his ideals, whose life was the model for his life? Whom does he depend on, not for daydreaming, but for establishing real and lasting relationships by means of conscious daily actions? The person from whose life not a single thread leads to the majestuous current of the past is indeed a poor, miserable, forlorn person, separated from the leading minds of humanity who have, from time immemorial, been charting the course of future tasks, objectives and principles of mankind.

What sublime pleasure is there when a young person starting out into the world of the mind with a mysterious yearning for a leader, a guide to the secrets of the universe who will become his model for a congenial life, discovers talents and inclinations the existence of which he had only suspected; when this seeker finds that great mind whose every word seems a magic key which opens

every secret lock, whose every action fills him with invincible
strength and gives him power to undertake heroic tasks, as if by
the touch of the magician's wand! Even if the critical side of the
mind should enter into action later and temper the passion of the
initial discovery by objective cognition and life experience – still,
those who have never experienced such a meeting with an intellectual leader of mankind, and have not lived through the excite-
ment of a first spiritual and intellectual love, its enthusiasm, its
despair, will remain incapable, I think, even later on, of real
knowledge related to their inner needs; they will not be capable
of a life in harmony with their awareness and ideal goals.

Throughout Europe thousands upon thousands will claim Marx
as their teacher, their guide, their hero on 5 May. Was he really
their guide? Was he really their teacher? Is he truly their leader?

At the present stage of European culture a system of thought or
a personality can become the actual content of the thoughts and
feelings of the masses in two cases only: if the thinker is on the
intellectual and moral level of the masses to begin with, or if he
is brought down to that level. Two significant factors have contributed to dragging the intellectual creation of Marx down to the
level of the masses.

One of these is the brand of economics taught at the universities.
The 'Universitätsökonomik' has become, almost everywhere, the
worthy counterpart of Schopenhauer's 'Universitätsphilosophie'.
More precisely, it has become political economy in the literal
sense, truly the ancilla politicae. Since the dawn of classical
economics, we can count on our fingers the professional economists who have dealt with economics as a science, without bias,
with no other motive than to discover the prevailing laws which
control man's economic acts and economic relations. These included
the founders of the theory of marginal profit, Jevons, Menger and
Walras; the Italian mathematical school of Pantaleoni and Pareto;
the more recent Austrian school, the Americans and a few Germans; most recently the two Webers. And a few more here and
there. The majority of the university economists have a different
conception of the function of their science: they want to raise
good citizens. Their economics is more like economic politics, and
what they teach is simply politics wrapped in the garb of science:
whether they be advocates of free trade or of protective tariffs,
agrarians or mercantilists, partisans of artisanry or of heavy
industry, capitalist or state socialist (or even just plain socialist).
Whatever it may be, it is always politics. Who could expect from
this kind of economics to deal in a methodologically adequate way
with the new Marxist ideas that have revived the traditions of the
classical school? It took them decades to even take cognizance of
these ideas. Once these ideas have turned into a battle-cry, once
they have become the banner of political parties, then these economists began to deal with it – now making up for the time lost,
but with an enthusiasm nurtured by bias. One cannot expect this
kind of critique to have joined the fray of the battle with all the
elements necessary for scientific debate: that is with a feeling of

respect for the adversary, with utter respect for his mode of thought, and with the expectation that the reward of the struggle be nothing but truth itself. They did not seek to defend the truth, but rather the social order, the fatherland and property against the perturbers of the social order, against the enemies of the fatherland and of property, against the people whose theoretician and leader was none other than Marx. The kind of Marxism which the hosts of students came to learn about from these economists' lectures was a simplification shaped by their mental capacity and by their limited knowledge, a pale plaster copy of the bright original, a skeleton without flesh and blood. This was what the students have come to know as Marxism, this is the Marxism of the so-called 'educated men' who, in fact, merely constitute a mass of their own. But is the other one any superior: the Marxism of the so-called unlearned masses? That of the believers standing on the foundations of historical materialism, of class struggle, of internationalism?

The inheritance of every truly great mind is inexhaustible; it constantly yields interest. Even if the thought of humanity was to take a different turn and conditions were to change radically from those in the context of which Marx had constructed the edifice of his thought; as long as the spirit of humanity in general is aflame, he will never cease to provide future generations with new visions, a new awarenes, new spiritual satisfaction. Everybody may discover something different in him, but everybody is bound to find the truth; because everybody finds himself or herself, that which is eternal and universal, in this great ancestor.

For who can deny the greatness of Marx? Even now Marx will be feted as not only a great innovator and pathfinder, but as the legendary prophet of certain sciences and movements. Does Jesus become any less great for having given rise, over the last two thousand years, to the most contradictory tendencies tó save the world? To be sure, his innumerable disciples have all interpreted his personality in a hundred different historical ways. Are not Plato and Kant among the all-time great men of the human race, for having provided answers even to questions they themselves never asked?

We should not reproach the disciples, commentators, or glossators of Marx for seeking the answer to every problem in the writings of Marx; what we do reproach them is that they have limited their search to Marx, and still have found what they sought.

What a misunderstanding of the nature and purpose of science! What a humiliation of the truth! It is understandable that the splendour of the master has blinded some of his disciples; it is also understandable that the neglect of academic science, and all kinds of malevolent deprecations and misinterpretations have endowed him with the glory of a martyr of science; that no matter how great he actually was, he is still overestimated by some who see in him the source of all wisdom, who find in him the solution to all mysteries. The disciples have often claimed: he is a circle starting from himself and ending in himself, a work without ante-

cedents yet definitive, valid for ever, Such an occurrence is
rather common in the history of science, but usually ephemeral:
it lasts hardly longer than the generation which lives under the
spell of the master's personal influence.

But the case of Marxism is different. Here we are dealing with a
phenomenon in which a system of thought has been transferred
from its original sphere to another sphere. Marxism is a system of
philosophical, sociological and economic truths; it is a science,
hence the laws of scientific life and scientific progress apply to it.
It lives and evolves only as long as it remains in this sphere. But
Marxism did not remain within its sphere. It became politics, it
became the profession of faith of political parties, of practical
mass movements. Thus it came under the rule of the laws which
prevail in politics, whereby it lost the bases of life and progress
appropriate to its original character.

Far be it from me to argue that science and politics have nothing
to do with one another. Since we agree with Marx that the most
positive proof of the theoretical tenets of real science lies in its
application, in real life, we desire nothing more than that ordinary
contemporary politics, this mixture of the most primitive empiricism and of improvised twenty-four hour solutions, may find
inspiration in the general truths of philosophy, and their long-
range perspectives. Had Marxism entered the sphere of politics in
this sense - in the interest of human progress (which, by the
same token, is scientific progress) we could but feel pleased.

However, the connection between Marxism and politics is altogether different. From a science which inspires, it turned into
the programme of a political party; and at the expense of both
science and politics, as Christianity has hurt the church, and the
church has, in turn, hurt the teachings of Christ. As science,
Marxism could live no longer; as a party - inasmuch as it conceives
of itself as based on eternal truth (and because of the true believers it has to believe and proclaim this) - it has come into conflict with the eternal principle of science, the principle of disinterested research, of critique, of cognition and of change.

Let us imagine what might have happened had Lassalle not been
slain by the bullet fired by Janko Rakovitza, had this general
agitator remained the inspirer and leader of the 'Allgemeiner Deut-
scher Arbeiterverein', and Marx and Engels had been forced to
remain satisfied with what they had actually done: to express their
indignation, from far-away London and Manchester, at the incom-
prehension of their own disciples and at their continuous falling
into Lassallian heresies. Undoubtedly the brilliance of Marxian
theory would still have affected the German labour movement; but
it is equally certain that Lassalle would have been the leader of the
unified German Social Democracy, and the programme of this party
would not have been Marxism mixed with a certain degree of Lassallism, but would have been Lassallism modified to some extent by
Marxism.

What is the implication of all this? Nothing more than that the
programme and theory of the German Social Democracy would have

coincided with what it actually was: a political party which strived to realize its state socialist objectives through legislation and to attain success in parliament by means of universal suffrage. This was what it had actually been doing for fifty years; and this was indeed Lassalle's concept of the tasks and objectives of the German labour movement.

Had Lassalle prevailed, German Social Democracy would have been spared the fact that, instead of consciously pursuing realistic objectives, it used up its strength for half a century in an attempt to solve a contradiction: the contradiction between its theory and its nature as a political party, together with the practice which followed from this nature. And science would have been spared one of its greatest, most glorious achievements being dragged body and soul into the arena of politics, and continually raped in the name of party interest. Then Marxism, remaining in the domain of ideas, obeying only its own laws, would freely and organically interrelate with the great work of science, the soil from which it had grown in the first place; and into which it could have extended fresh roots, as long as it appeared in its own sphere cleansed of all foreign matter.

As far as the Social Democratic parties inspired by Marx are concerned – the German one and others, particularly the Austrian and the French – the war has more or less freed them from the ballast of Marxism, and they have been shown for what they really are: parliamentary political parties sans phrase. Though they have now decided to celebrate Marx, they no longer don the tiger-skin of Marxism. Provided, of course, that the war does not continue until the final social contradictions are simplified and polarized in the same way in western Europe as they were in Russia.

We should do what we cannot possibly do on this occasion: systematically contrast the key issues of Marxian theory with Social Democratic praxis, and demonstrate in what area lies the contradiction between Marxist theory and so-called Marxist party politics. Then it would become evident why this contradiction cannot be reconciled, without doing violence either to science or to politics.

The key issue lies in the difference between the concepts of class and of party. The basic tenet of Marx's philosophy is the illusionary nature of individual consciousness. His entire methodology in economics is based on this tenet. For he, much like the classics, researches the abstract economic categories: but whereas the classics saw eternally valid concepts, he recognizes historical categories according to different social relations. These different relationships are primarily the relations of people to each other, spiritual relations. In order to know these, instead of the illusion of individual consciousness, we must seek other relations that can be objectively determined, that are constant and subject to rational laws. According to Marx, only classes have these properties. Thus in Marxist economics the subject of economic relations are not the entire population, nor the individual, but social classes; and the categories of economics are derived from the economic relations between classes.

Thus classes become the basic factors - by way of historical materialism - of Marxist sociology. On the other hand, the political party bases its fate on the individual removed from his class determination. The essence of parliamentarianism is majority rule: every party must strive for majority to achieve its end. It cannot base its politics on class consciousness, for that would not result in a majority even in the simplest of modern societies.

The party can, for the time being, rely only on minorities differentiated in a number of ways. Thus parties necessarily turn to the individual, regardless of the fact that his or her consciousness is illusory and unreliable; for turning to the individual is the only way the parties can attain majority. The 'Marxist' Bebel spoke from the very depth of the soul of a political party when he told the French anti-militarists: wait until, out of the eight million, not three but five million vote for us. This war has demonstrated the true value of a majority that had never been raised to a real unified consciousness by economic conditions.

But if - still according to Marx - classes are the carriers of social struggle and transformation, and a class is defined by consciousness (and this consciousness brings together, of necessity, only minorities, both because of the economic structure and because of the psychology of society), then legislation would be inappropriate to solve even those situations in which 'the material forces of social production conflict with the relations of production or, to use a legal expression: with property relations'. By elections or majority votes, no class was ever forced to change property relations; the majority principle becomes unworkable even in such situations as it contradicts the concept of Marxist sociology about the dynamics of social change. But if majority cannot be the appropriate means, it follows that legislation and political parties cannot be either. What remains is the minority's political method: violence. Hence the Social Democratic Party - inasmuch as it wants to exist and exist in its own way - cannot arrive at the logical conclusion of Marxist theory, because that can only be reached over its own dead body.

All these incompatibilities stem simply from the basic differences between Marxist sociology and the nature of the parliamentary principle. Beyond these there are many contradictions in the details which we cannot even begin to discuss here. Since I am compelled to limit my statement to noting the basic contradiction between Marxist theory and political practice, it cannot be my intention to aver the correctness of Marxist theory in such a gingerly fashion. True enough, the theory has to a large extent freed itself from the unnatural relationship which so far has hampered it from resorting to the only methodology appropriate to the critique and development of science; yet the present circumstances are hardly the right ones for an examination or for the establishment of social theories. But this need not worry us.

That today Marx would have been a hundred years old, that a few weeks ago it was the thirty-fifth anniversary of his death; all these dates of the calendar mean little in comparison with his life's work, in comparison with his scientific and practical influence. Yet I am convinced that the full impact of his influence will be felt only in the future. So let us wait until that time and be satisfied, on his personal anniversary, with the maximum the memory of a great man can leave to his heirs: the example of his heroic life. He, too, had to be satisfied until his very death with the awareness with which Schopenhauer's hero had to comfort himself:

> A happy life is impossible; the most one can attain is a heroic life. This is the life of a person who in some way and in some undertaking struggles against superhuman difficulties in the pursuit of general good, and finally triumphs; yet his reward remains small or nil. Then he finally stops, like the prince in Gozzi's 'Re corvo', converted into stone, but with a noble bearing and a magnanimous gesture. His memory remains and he is revered as a hero; his will, gradually extinguished by fatigue and hard work, by failures and by the ingratitude of the world, sleeps away in Nirvana. ['Parerga und Paralipomena', vol. 2 (Leipzig s.d.), p. 337 – Editors' note]

Part II
ON THE SOCIALIST
MOVEMENT

MASSES OR INDIVIDUALS

This early journalistic piece, originally published in the
24 April 1902 issue of 'Volksstimme', the Hungarian Social
Democratic Party's German-language newpaper (written for
the still unassimilated German craftsmen and skilled workers)
is one of Szabó's attempts to find a common ground between
the heroic Russian revolutionaries, whom he admired since
his youth, and the socialist mass party. Szabó seems to have
been 'in charge of Russia' in the Social Democratic press in
those years, and used the occasion of the assassination of
Sipiagin to present not only his admiration for the Russian
students but also raise, however moderately, his objections
against the strict discipline and centralized command of
German-type Social Democracy that did not encourage
individual initiative and heroism. Szabó's image of an organized mass led by courageous individuals who remain closely
enmeshed in the struggle of the masses is one of his best
passages, in parts because the subject helped him to overcome his alienation towards a dialectical approach. That he
had serious theoretical quandaries in this matter is clear
from his letters to Kautsky (see above pp. 55-66), and
finally he opted in terms of political struggle also for the
more individualist-anarchist position, of course, always
insisting on the primacy of the class as the main actor in
history and revolution.

Last week the revolutionary movement in Russia brought about an
event that calls to mind the wildly agitated times of terrorist
propaganda. Sipiagin, the Minister of Police, was assassinated by
a student from Kiev. We denounce murder as a means of revolutionary propaganda. However, the entirely exceptional conditions
of the Russian revolutionary movement have to be accepted as a
perfect excuse by every freedom-loving and upright person who
has blood and not milk in his veins.
    For nearly a hundred years the Russian intelligentsia has been
fighting an unprecedented courageous and self-sacrificing struggle against Tsarism. Tens of thousands of human lives have been
sacrificed in the struggle. Every year hundreds and thousands are
sent to gaol or banished to Siberia where they suffer all the horrors that thoroughly inhuman gaolers and judges can dream up.
In Siberia they have to face the dread of loneliness and of complete isolation from western civilization or the company of the

worst dredge of society, robbers and murderers. None the less
the number of revolutionaries is increasing. In the greatest war
there could not be so many casualties as only those revolutionaries whose names are known and mentioned by their successors
with devoted awe. And there are the uncounted nameless who
have been fighting, alone or in groups, with deed or word for
freedom and have faced the horrors of gaol, of torture, of banish-
ment without any hope, fully aware of the fact that the moment
they leave the battlefield of revolutionary struggle their name will
be forgotten and nobody will mention them in devout memory.
What an incredible heroism!

Still, the Tsarist regime does not seem to have changed. Is it
then surprising that under such circumstances, the Russian revolutionaries are driven to extremes? Is it surprising that they see
no other way but to terrify the representatives of the regime, the
ministers, the governors, the high officers and bureaucrats of
the Tsar through murder and thus force them to grant concessions?
Particularly under a Tsar like Nicholas II who upon his accession
was praised and acclaimed by so many as a 'European' and a
humane man. What did his reign bring for Russian freedom? If at
all possible, further restrictions, more brutal attacks on the revolutionaries and much more horrible persecution. The revolutionaries have documented that, in the first four years of the rule of
the 'European spirit' and 'humanity', more upright men and
women were gaoled and banned to Siberia than in the fifteen years
of Alexander III's 'Asiatic' and 'terrible' reign. In the last two
years we again had daily to bury in spirit more workers and students who lost their lives for the love of freedom.

Under such conditions it is easy to understand that the Russian
revolutionaries cannot help but turn to the weapons of murder,
and take revenge on those who caused so much suffering; revenge
that may act as a deterrent. It would be rather surprising if they
did not act in this way, if they were to remain unaffected in the
face of daily human sacrifice from among their comrades and to
hold on to the forms of western European revolutionary methods.

We know, however, that the Russian revolutionaries of today do
not belong any more to the old school that subscribed to the dogma
according to which the unshakeable faith of gifted individuals and
the unselfish courage of a handful of revolutionaries are sufficient
to achieve victory. Today's revolutionaries have accepted the
principle which guides socialist propaganda in the western countries: mass violence is to be opposed by the masses, by the organized people – by the class. Class against class! On the one side,
the proprietors who control all economic and social power, and
their tools: the state, the army, the bureaucracy – on the other,
the masses, every one of them aware of its situation, burning with
the same fire of hope and fighting spirit, acting in united solidarity. Since it is on the shoulders of the masses that the whole of
society rests and it is on their necks that the privileged and the
slaveholders are dancing, therefore the people, all the people,
have to be made aware of their condition, be organized and armed
for the common struggle.

The Russian revolutionaries have also been turning their attention to winning the masses. The events of the last few years have
shown that wide strata of the working people were indeed won for
the struggle, as the students do not fight alone any more, but
side by side with tens of thousands of workers.

Still, the Russian revolutionaries are not content with mobilizing
the masses. When and where they believe that the deeds of individuals can advance the cause of freedom, then and there individuals – at one in spirit with their brethren, at one in spirit with
the masses – will step forward from the ranks to perform a deed
by their own will, their own force and their own conviction. Without condoning terrorist acts and without justifying them with
anything but the particular Russian conditions, we cannot hide
our sincere admiration for the Russian revolutionaries.

The struggle of the masses should not mean that everyone has
to suppress his courage, reduce his energy and adapt his actions
to the strength of his weaker neighbour just to keep the masses
together, shoulder to shoulder. This is a very schematic interpretation, convenient, nay, cowardly for the stronger and better
educated ones. To fight in and with the masses means rather that
every single person striving to the one common goal gives the
best and the greatest of what his strength and energy can afford;
it means that every individual should endeavour to equal with all
force and energy the stronger comrades fighting ahead of him.
Mass struggle demands the greatest courage, the greatest energy
and the greatest deeds from everyone.

Those whose heart and soul feel with their comrades-in-arms,
who feel and indeed are united with the masses and whose actions
reflect fully the will of the masses, but are more able to combat
than their comrades and hence fight not in the ranks but in the
front line – or, if it is possible and necessary, even a step or
more ahead of it – they should be the radiant examples for the
others, for the weaker ones. To close ranks with them, to catch
up and fight together with them should be the ideal of all, even
of the weakest!

Thank you, Russian students, young heroes, for this lesson!
You have shown us that you can feel not only with your selves but
also with the masses for whom you have for so many years sacrificed the best of your goods, your knowledge, your hopes, your
lives. You have shown us how to carry the seed of enlightenment
in the most inclement weather into the darkest, most barren fields.
You are showing us that you know how to unite for a common
struggle, abandoning personal advantage and individual wishes,
for the sake of the joint fight with the masses.

We admire you, Russian brothers!

PARTY DISCIPLINE AND THE FREEDOM OF THE INDIVIDUAL

This article, one of the most important and most differentiated writings of the young Szabó, was published in the
short-lived paper of the inner-party opposition, 'Világosság'
(Light) in 1904. Its immediate purpose was to justify the
existence and the theoretical position of the opposition, but
Szabó went far beyond this practical aim in sketching an out-
line of his philosophy of history and politics. He explores,
once more, the relationship between the consciously acting
individual and objective social development in order to argue
for the guarantees of liberty within the socialist movement -
and without - and the respect of minority will by the majority.
It is in this article that Szabó contrasts most clearly the
'army discipline' of the Social Democratic parties with the
self-motivated discipline and courage of the Boer and Japan-
ese fighters, so much admired in those days, and concludes
that a party that is unable to build its tactics on the development of 'class consciousness' deserves 'to be burned!'
    The last chapters of the article were reprinted under the
title 'How to Change the Organizational Statutes?' (under
the 'pseudonym' Ernő Szontágh) for the preparation of the
party's congress in 1905 - where the opposition was defeated
by the leadership to which even some of their friends also
changed over.

The materialist doctrine that men are products of circumstances
and upbringing and that, therefore, changed men are products
of other circumstances and changed upbringing, forgets the
fact that it is men who change circumstances and that it is
essential to educate the educator himself. Hence, this doctrine
necessarily arrives at dividing society into two parts, one of
which is superior to society. (Marx, 'Theses on Feuerbach', 3)

I

The issue of democracy and party discipline has been almost constantly on the agenda of socialist parties around the world in the
past few years. This is most amazing. One might think that the
party which claims to be the sole legitimate heir to liberal

democracy would have solved the problem of democratic organization and the democratic process within its own ranks long ago;
and would have solved it in accordance with the discipline and
unity of will needed to carry on the struggle successfully. Yet
these issues are still debated; and the debate happens to be most
lively in those countries where the so-called revisionist or reformist current of socialism is critically reappraising practically all
basic problems of socialism: in Germany, France and Italy.

Can it be that those who argue that democracy is an unattain-
able illusion are correct? Was Ostrogorsky correct, for instance,
when, not so long ago, he endeavoured to prove that true democracy has never existed?(1) And should we attenuate the rigidly
negative evaluation of those who deduced from Darwinism that the
only possible order of society is an aristocratic one?

The subject debated by the socialist parties is not whether the
continued existence of social classes is desirable, whether the
rights of individuals should differ accordingly to their social
function, or whether people should retain privileges according to
their capacity to rule. On these issues there appears to be complete agreement. Nevertheless, it seems to me that the debate in
progress radically affects the basic issues pertaining to the organization of society.

What is the debate about? Apparently the debate is about
whether a minority within the party should be accorded the right
to act independently, even if this were to result in the dissolution
of old and presumably democratic processes. Would such a right
be compatible with party discipline? Should a minority within the
party be allowed to publicize its dissent, and even to act according to its dissenting views? Or, on the contrary, is it the clear
duty of the minority to subject itself unconditionally to the will of
the majority?

In fact, however, the question has not been properly formulated.
To formulate the question in this manner among socialists would be
all right if they were convinced that the consensus of the majority
has been arrived at with the same degree of consciousness as that
with which the minority is struggling for the truth, or for what it
believes to be the truth. For this, in my opinion, is the sole point
of view of socialist democracy, I repeat, of socialist democracy,
which differs essentially from the vulgar form of democracy, the
bourgeois democracy. Political democracy pays no attention to
subtleties such as consciousness, conscious will, consensus, etc.
Democracy, according to the interpretation of these democrats, is
simply the opposite of aristocracy: there, a minority is ruling over
a majority; here, the minority is subjecting itself to the will of the
majority. Democracy is this and nothing else.

The kind of democracy the socialists are striving for goes beyond this formal difference between these two principles of social
organization. The aim of socialism is to bring about the greatest
possible happiness to the greatest number. But this happiness
does not coincide with the complete satisfaction of the intellectual,
moral and physical needs of present humanity. According to the

most prominent socialist thinkers this happiness can become perfect only when the intellectual, moral and physical aspirations of
every single individual are in concert with the ideal of the integral human being which advanced science allows us to regard as
attainable. This new man has been described in such glowing
terms by Kautsky:

> A new type of person will emerge who will surpass the highest
> types produced by civilization up to now. We can truly say:
> a superhuman person, not as an exception, but as a rule; a
> person who will be superhuman as compared to his predeces-
> sors, but not as compared to his contemporaries; a man who
> will not derive joy from being a giant among miserable dwarfs,
> but who will be great among the great, happy among the happy.
> A man who does not derive his strength and stature by step-
> ping on trampled bodies, but rather from the fact that he has
> undertaken to solve, in unison with the aspirations of his
> fellow men, the most difficult problems.(2)

Indeed, we cannot know what kind of social and political organization these true 'Übermenschen' will create for themselves. Will
it be democracy, or something we cannot as yet foresee? One thing
is sure nevertheless: any social and political order which the
socialists attempt to bring about must serve but one end, namely
to educate human beings in order to allow them to develop intellectually and emotionally, and to become ever more consciously
close to the ideal in their physical and spiritual needs. We should
have individuals serving the highest purpose of humanity with
their every word, their every deed.

If the overwhelming majority of socialists believe - and it seems
they do - that democracy is the most appropriate social and political form for realizing their immediate objectives, then this democracy cannot be identical with bourgeois democracy. It cannot
simply be the rule of the majority. It has to be a kind of democracy
where the will of the majority is composed of the personal wills of
individuals who think independently, who have clear ideas about
their goals - goals which agree with the ideals of human society -
and who respect all the conditions required by this development.
All minorities, members of which share these characteristics, will
obey the will of such a majority gladly, without complaint.

We know full well, however, that for the moment there are only
very few persons of this type: and therefore, such a democracy
would be impossible today. Hence no socialist democracy exists as
yet. On the other hand, this is the only kind of democracy that
can be meaningful for socialists. But since it does not exist,
neither the reformists, nor the revolutionaries formulate the
question properly when they argue about whether their procedures
are democratic or not.

Today the problem is not democracy. The problem is the organization of society and of the socialist parties in such a way as to
ensure the education of individuals capable of bringing about the

above-mentioned kind of socialist democracy, and realizing the highest human and social ideal. And this is simply a matter of laws determining the progress and development of society.

II

Hence, when we talk about condemning or judging the behaviour of disobedient minorities, we must not view the issue from the point of view of whether the minority has trespassed against the principles of democracy, but from a much higher point of view: whether those allegedly democratic party organizations are in harmony with the requirements of social development or not, and whether the behaviour of those minorities serves the progress of society or not?

Of course, it cannot be my aim to provide comprehensive answers to these questions here. Such an undertaking would not only go beyond the narrow confines of this article but would also, I am afraid, exceed my potentials. After all, devising such a theory or philosophy of society is tantamount to creating a complete sociological system. I only wish to consider a part of the problem, a part which, in my opinion, has been handled rather step-motherly by socialist theory. I simply wish to attempt to answer the question: what is the role of the individual in the development of society?

Two concepts of society stand in contrast to one another. One is objective sociology, which deals with external circumstances: according to this concept the development of society is determined by the natural environment, by changes in the economic organization. The other is subjective sociology, which regards the individual as the only factor in all social progress.

Historical materialism, the concept of society commonly accepted by socialists, is generally classified under the category of objective sociology. We have become used to interpretations according to which no individual work or individual effort is necessary for the realization of socialism; that the automatic development of the economic structure towards the concentration of industry and the centralization of capital will, in time, necessarily bring about conditions which will make the organization of society on a socialist basis mandatory. Thus, even if we should not budge an inch, the economic conditions will automatically bring about socialism.

It is hardly necessary to insist that such a one-sided interpretation of historical materialism, an interpretation which neglects entirely the role of man, the role of the individual in the development of society, has nothing to do with the ideas of its creators, Marx and Engels. This interpretation is nothing but a one-sided exaggeration by those disciples whom Engels himself has described in the following terms.

Unfortunately very often people believe that they have completely understood a new theory and can even apply it as

soon as they have learned its principal theses, and even
those not always correctly. And I cannot spare even some
of the newer 'Marxists' from this criticism, as they have
discovered many an oddity along these lines.(3)

Historical materialism, if correctly interpreted and especially if
reconstructed from the later writings of Engels, means just the
reverse: it is an analysis of social development that starts from
man himself, and explains social changes by the conscious acts of
the individual. The difference between this and the so-called subjective concepts of society is that the latter operate on the basis
of a human will that purports to be independent of social conditions and institutions, whereas historical materialism remains
conscious of all those interrelations which make up the inner world
of man: interrelations between his thoughts, his feelings and his
will, on the one hand, and the economic, social and cultural
structures, on the other.
It follows from this that, according to the teachings of historical
materialism, the life of society is a continuous interaction between
feeling, thinking and wanting human beings, and the objective
elements of society. If we draw a picture of society from which the
feeling, thinking, wanting and, consequently, the acting person
is absent, the picture will remain incomplete because it represents
only one element of society. This is only natural. Historical materialism, if it is to become what its creators intended, that is the
method for the scientific study of society, can only be considered
scientific if it is able to give an explanation of social phenomena
in such a way as to build a series in which each element necessarily follows from the preceding one. In other words, it should
present an interrelationship of all factors of society in such a way
that they follow from what precedes, and are necessarily the
cause of what follows: a complete chain of causation.
An example will make my argument clearer. Here is a sentence:
I throw this ball, the ball describes an elliptical trajectory in the
air, and then falls to the ground. Behind this sentence we find
the following scientific explanations. 1 I communicated to a body
at rest a force opposite to the pull of gravity of the earth (cause).
2 As a result of this force, and overcoming the pull of gravity
and other obstacles, the ball rose into the air (a consequence and,
at the same time, a cause of what follows). 3 The moving body
fought with the help of the force I had communicated to it against
the pull of gravity and other obstacles and, as a result of this
struggle, described an elliptical trajectory in the air (consequence
and the cause of what follows). 4 In this struggle the force communicated to the body became consumed and the body fell back to
earth (final consequence).
In this process every single element – the rise of the ball into
the air, its elliptical trajectory, its falling back to earth – was
necessary, and forms a chain in which every element is a necessary consequence of what precedes and a necessary cause of what
follows. If I do not communicate force to the ball, it will not rise.

If it does not rise with this force and does not struggle with the pull of gravity and other obstacles, it will not describe an elliptical trajectory. If the pull of gravity and other obstacles do not triumph, it will not fall back to earth. In other words, everything follows from what precedes: a complete series of causation.

We must present a similar series of causes regarding society if we want to attempt a scientific explanation of it. It is easy to do so in the natural sciences. There we deal with quantities that can be determined with mathematical precision: the weight of the ball, the strength of the pull of gravity, the amount of friction caused by air, etc. Cause and causation can be known with mathematical precision. But the object of social science is human society. The elements of human society are economy, the state, the family, ideologies, etc. All these have come about as a result of human interaction.(4)

Such interaction results from conscious acts of the will. Hence it is of a psychological nature. Here it is impossible to present an accurate quantitative analysis, as in the case of the natural sciences. It is impossible to express with mathematical precision the weight or strength of psychological relations. But if social interaction can be analysed only on the basis of psychological relations between the persons involved, then the series of causation in the social sciences must consist in part of relations which produce psychological phenomena, and in part of purely psychological phenomena. Only in this case can we obtain a complete picture of society. The first are the objective factors of society. As for the carrier of purely psychological factors, who else can it be but human beings, the subjective factor.

So far I have merely meant to prove that the social sciences (and the social scientific method of most socialists, that is, historical materialism) can only be truly scientific, if it studies the objective as well as the subjective elements of society: in other words, if it assembles the chain of causation necessary for the understanding of society from external circumstances as well as from man in action. After this digression, I embark on my actual task, which is to determine the role of the individual acting consciously for the development of society. I hope to find the answer to the question posed in our title on this basis.

III

We know full well that the two extreme interpretations of society are equally defective. Objective sociology omits human beings from its calculations, although society is an interrelationship not of things, but of people, and all changes in society necessarily go through human brains. As for subjective sociology, since it does not take into consideration the extent to which people's feelings and thoughts are shaped by objective external circumstances, it can present but one aspect of this development. We have to draw the exact boundaries of both approaches if we want to determine the role of the individual. The following notions will help us in this procedure.

1 Historical idealism, which considers historical development a consequence of ideas, is not a subjective explanation of history. This thesis, although it may seem surprising at first sight, requires no lengthy commentary. In my opinion, a subjective explanation of society is that which assigns the ultimate cause of social change to feeling and thinking man. Historical idealism, on the other hand, finds the prime cause in ideas which remain outside and above man. This is quite obvious in ancient and in theological history writing: interpretations were based on the will of God, that is an objective factor quite apart from man. And other idealistic interpretations are just as objective. Whether we regard history as the increasingly perfect manifestation of the Hegelian absolute spirit, or whether we consider ideas of a lesser order as the moving force – nationalism, patriotism, aggression, truth, or justice – in any case, it would be a factor standing above human will and the human power of conceptualization, and which exists in the individual only in part, but determines his behaviour with all its weight. It is not the individual who feels, thinks, and acts accordingly, but the idea; the idea which, disregarding physical and spiritual potentials, geographical environment, economic and social conditions, and cultural levels, compels man to put it into practice. The individual exists without an independent will, he is a slave subjected to a power outside himself.

2 The objective environment in itself is not always a factor affecting development. This statement is equally valid for the natural, the economic and the social environment. How else can one explain the fact that we find the most divergent cultures in identical environments? Even in varying parts of Hungary there are differences of a hundred years in the level of culture. The ethnic group living in Greece had at one time brought about a culture which, even today, cannot be surpassed in some of its achievements. Today the half-barbarian Turkish people and the weak little Greek nation live a precarious existence in this same area. How can one explain that a nation relatively well developed from the economic point of view stops developing at a certain level without the intervention of any outside force. A thousand years ago the economic organization of China was at a level with that of the nations of western Europe; and how far did the latter develop, whereas China remained at the same level? How can one explain the fact that Japan, which twenty years ago was a textbook example of feudal conditions, leaped into the social order characteristic of western Europe with a sudden break, without gradual development, and is now engaged in a victorious war against the Russians?

It seems likely that in all these cases one cannot explain either progress or stagnation merely by environment. Various cultures can originate in the same environment. One finds progressive, then stagnating cultures, or centuries of stagnation, and then, all of a sudden, development without transition, in the same environment. Under these circumstances, even the theory of the milieu has to resort to other explanations.

3 The striving of the individual can have no effect, unless it is consonant with the general direction of social progress. This is a logical consequence of the previous statement. Though the environment is not always a factor for progress, it does not follow that it never is. It puts its stamp on everyone, it determines their way of thinking, it provides them with the means of action. In other words, the environment is always the basic element of development because it provides its external circumstances. And the external circumstances determine the life content, the world of feeling and of thought of the overwhelming majority of mankind. The individual who rises above what exists, who attempts to alter society in some way, can only be effective if his attempts lie in the direction of the tendencies of social development. If the tendency of economic development is towards mechanization, towards the introduction of more machinery, it would be useless to make a discovery or proposal that would favour, for instance, the reintroduction of artisanry; if the dominating tendency of political organization is democracy, that is the participation of the so-called lower classes in political power, it would be hopeless to attempt to resurrect ancient oligarchy. The obstacle is always the dominating force among the masses. This is the reason why those plans to save the world we meet with several times a year, the planners of which speak with greater or lesser eloquence, but invariably with indomitable conviction, always burst without effect. It is possible that all indigence would cease if every one of us would put a penny, or whatever amount, in a savings bank, or if the increase in population were well under control, etc. The only difficulty is that people are not inclined to do so. They do not want and they cannot want to accomplish things that are not in accord with outer circumstances and with the direction of objective development.

4 The environment is a passive factor, whereas the active, reflective and effective factor can only be man. The environment itself does not accomplish any change in society. Human intervention is necessary for any change, even for the slightest modification. This does not contradict the correct observation that society is not made, but grows. Societies grow, but they are made to grow by man. The misunderstanding stems from the fact that it is often assumed that the action which produces change has always been consciously planned or designed to achieve that change. This seldom is the case. People do something new, discover some technological improvement by chance or by speculation, discover some new principle of social organization by accident, and adjust to it out of habit, without ever thinking about the consequences of the innovation, without accounting to themselves about its impact. But all progress in society is due to some human intervention.

Naturally, as I have demonstrated in connection with the previous assertion, those inventions which do not fall upon receptive soil perish without effect. Every period produced extremely able

men whose genius was recognized only by persons belonging to a
much later generation. There have been inventors of genius in
engineering, innovators of genius in the social and political fields;
but their ideas went far beyond the degree of development of the
objective environment, and beyond the capacity of their contemporaries to understand. The fire of genius often became ashes of
the pyre under the stake - due to those whose happiness might
have been based on his invention.

Another reason why the role of man in effecting social change
has been misunderstood is that the result is usually - one might
even say always - different from the consciously expected one.
Therefore one may be inclined to believe that will has little or
nothing to do with the results obtained. And yet these results
were brought about by human will. Not the will of one man, but
rather the will of a hundred or a thousand, of innumerable wills,
which have collaborated in bringing about the result. Hence the
result is a combination of many forces, something that no one had
foreseen, and could only have foreseen if he had been able to
calculate beforehand the effect of each of the forces involved. The
social result is similar to the vector of divergent forces in physics,
a vector that differs from the direction of each of its component
parts. Is there a physicist who would assert that the direction of
individual forces and their magnitude is irrelevant to the overall
vector? Only a few sociologists arrogate the privilege of asserting
such a thing.

5 The better we see the direction of objective social development the surer and quicker progress can be. If the prerequisite
of any innovation in society is that the new concept must adjust
to the general direction of progress and to the general will of men,
it is probably that the innovators can count on a more rapid, a
more assured success if they are aware of these directions, and
of the ideas of men as determined by them. This is valid whether
the innovator is a single individual or there are several of them;
and the more there are, the better they should ·be aware of the
possibilities, so that their wills should not dissipate by heading
in several directions. Everyone must want something that can be
realized, and it would be a sheer waste of potential to want something that does not have a base for development in the outside
circumstances and in the mind of men. From this it follows that a
study of the laws governing the development of society and teaching of these laws in ever wider circles are the most important
means for the rapid and certain progress of society. Thus culture,
the development of the mental culture of the individual and of the
masses, becomes the most important moving force in society.

6 All social progress is the merit of critically thinking individuals. This fundamental thesis of Lavrov's philosophy of history is
also the final conclusion of my thesis. I would not, however, make
of it such a general law valid for all times as Lavrov had done.
Progress has always been due to the more intelligent individuals,
the inventors, the innovators; but the further back in time we
look, we find that change was less the outcome of their conscious

goal. Even today we cannot say that all social change has been foreseen and forewilled. Undoubtedly, however, social progress would never have been possible without the above-average intelligence of certain individuals. And it is likewise certain that the better we understand the laws governing society, the more directly we can apply discoveries made in any area of science to the service of the conscious change of society. Thus Lavrov's thesis becomes indeed an increasingly valid law of social development. The number of those who analyse existing society critically, its wants, its defects, its sins, is ever increasing. They seek the cure for the ills, the possible changes, and the best way to carry out these changes. The more numerous these critically thinking individuals become, the less will social progress be the uncertain result of unconscious mass forces, the less difficulty there will be in carrying out decisions, the more the best possible society of the present will fall within the general direction of the ideal society. Thus all those who want social progress, all those who have chosen as their life-goal to work towards the ideal order of society - or a society which ensures the greatest possible happiness of the greatest possible number - all those will consider the development and education of thinking individuals as their most sacred duty, as the leading principle of all their political activity. They have to attempt to bring about an economic, social and political organization which makes it possible for the greatest possible number, and educates the greatest possible number, to consciously participate in the development of society; and, furthermore, that this conscious participation be ever deeper, ever more integrated, ever more critical. The organization of a socialist party can be properly evaluated only from this point of view.

IV

What is the principle of organization, therefore, which ensures the effectiveness of the critically thinking individuals, and enables them to work in the direction of social progress? This is one of the most difficult problems of political science. It is identical with the question, how do we reconcile strict social discipline with the notion of maximum freedom for all members of society? It is identical with the problem of liberty.

The memory of millennia of bitter struggle comes to mind. We may recall Greek democracy, whose destructive class struggles so often prepared the ground for tyrants. We recall the struggle of the Roman plebs against the patricians. We think of the innumerable forms of government, of monarchy and republic, of oligarchy, of democracy, which alternated with such frequency in the history of peoples, cutting their path with blood and iron, without any one of them ever satisfying the yearnings of those who hoped for freedom.

The struggles for liberty have taught us an important truth: that no kind of formal principle of social organization is sufficient in itself to guarantee freedom. The most extreme political democracy, universal suffrage, complete freedom of assembly, complete freedom of the press, a republic, and other such, are all totally inadequate to guarantee the freedom of the individual.

Two conditions have to be satisfied in order that extreme political democracy does not become an instrument of oppression. One of these conditions has been recognized for the first time in all of its clarity by the socialists of the last century. Democracy, and other forms of government, are not primary social factors, are not causes, but results and secondary developments, which can only have secondary significance in the solution of the most important issues of social policy. As long as the basic structural organization of society forces one part of society, with a force greater than any outward compulsion, to serve the interests of another part of society, the general principle of social organization is almost a matter of indifference. Neither monarchy nor republic, neither aristocracy nor a democratic form of state can alter the basic fact that the economic order, if predicated on the existence of the haves and the have-nots, is a much stronger limitation on the individual freedom of the dispossessed than could be remedied by the most beautiful principles of political organization. Thus the most important guarantee of political liberty is economic liberty, that is a social order in which there would be no economically weak and strong, but where everyone was equal.

For modern man this is such an obvious truth that it almost counts as a tautology. Everyone knows that in contemporary society, based as it is on the existence of classes, one can only speak of relative freedom. It is possible, however, to attempt to move further out the barriers limiting the freedom of political movement as determined by the economic order. And if today it appears that democracy is the political form which gives the greatest play to individual forces, we struggle to achieve political democracy without deluding ourselves as to its true value.

But even that kind of political democracy which is based on complete economic democracy, a democracy which as yet is only a mirage in the future, is not a guarantee of individual freedom in and of itself. This is not due to political antagonism of the minority and the majority. The basic principle of democracy remains that the will of the majority prevails, and the minority must subject itself to that will: and this is a correct principle. But the principle of the dynamic state of society and of the static state of society are contradictory. The origins of every conscious social change can be traced to an individual or a small group of determined people: in contrast, however, the rule of a minority has always resulted in oppression and stagnation. (5)

Thus, as long as the absolute freedom of the individual, in the sense of individualistic anarchy, cannot become a principle of social organization, the rule of the majority will constitute the liberty of the greatest number of people.

Liberty in the most extreme democracy runs against the same obstacle that diverts all creations of man from their true purpose.

Society is not merely the relationship of objects. Things are
organically connected by much finer, much more subtle strands;
by strands that can be bent, entangled, by strands that can lose
their way. Society is a relationship of people, hence also of spiritual relations. No matter how well the basic objective elements of
society have been constructed, no matter how beautifully the
economic mould has been poured, or the constitution devised in
the most harmonic way, or the laws the most numerous, the most
just, the clearest, the most purposeful: all this is worth but little
if the spirit ruling those who execute the laws is not in accord
with the spirit of the laws and of the institutions. The intention
of the best legislation can be vitiated by ignorance, prejudice,
love of comfort, love of power. A good government is worth more
than the best of laws.

Because of these facts, because institutions alone are not sufficient guarantees of freedom, and even the best laws do not
preserve us from rulers who might abuse their power - whether
they be a single person or any number - we can only truly guarantee freedom in an extreme form of democracy, that is in a
socialist democracy, if we reduce to the minimum the tendencies
to abuse power, both in the objective institutions and in the
hearts of men.

Institutional guarantees should be in the direction of the greatest division and diffusion of power. One must concentrate only
that much power in the hands of a single individual as is absolutely necessary to achieve the desired objective. Self-government
must be generalized to such an extent, within the limits prescribed
by the desirability of a communal existence, that everyone be his
own law-giver and executive arm. Representation must be eliminated as much as possible both in the law-making and in the
executive. Controls must be active and effective. Such are the
objective means which can prevent democracy from degenerating
into bureaucracy, dictatorship, or tyranny of the masses.

Institutions can inculcate the feeling and respect of true freedom in men; we must, however, take care to provide mental safe-
guards well in advance. The leaders and rulers could never reach
the point where they abuse their power if they did not find support in the ignorance, weakness and subservience of the masses.
The brains of men must be cleaned. Men must be made to understand that the objective towards which they strive is not some
outside institution, but their own happiness, greatness and
strength. Therefore, even if they submit to the instructions of
their leaders for the sake of attaining some immediate goal, it is
their utmost responsibility not to lose sight of the ultimate end.
And this ultimate end is higher and more valuable than any decision, organization, or justice of the moment. Hence we must leave
the way open to every attempt which, while in opposition to the
prevailing institutions or dogmas, would nevertheless find the
path leading to new truths, indicate a new way. The second main
guarantee of individual freedom within a democracy is the respect
shown towards new opinions that are in contradiction to established

authorities. At the same time this would be a guarantee of the effectiveness of critically thinking individuals.

V

It remains for us to apply the principles of democracy – a democ-racy in accord with the requirements of social progress – to political parties, including the socialist party. There is only one worthwhile objection to applying all this to political parties as well.

It can be said, and it is being said by those who constitute the majority within the socialist parties, that the party is not a de-bating society. The party is an instrument of struggle which, much like an army, requires a tight organization, strict and un-conditional discipline, a united and unwavering leadership.

This objection would certainly be correct if it were applied to the army. The majority of socialists are of the same opinion, amaz-ingly enough, as the officers of the general staff, the cadres who torture enlisted men, the parade marshals and martinets, that is precisely those individuals who have been looked down upon, mocked and whipped by the socialists.

It was precisely the socialist who never tired of pointing, dur-ing the recent wars, to the superiority of the free, light and individually trained Boer troops over the British, who were sup-posed to be at the pinnacle of European military science. It was again the socialist who did not tire of emphasizing that the Japan-ese owe the triumph of their arms not only to their superior leadership and equipment, but also to the superior intelligence from a military point of view and the higher morale of the Japan-ese soldier. Thus, when it comes to the army, they condemn everything that implies a 'tight organization', a 'strict and uncon-ditional discipline', etc. and praise to the skies everything that constitutes a conscious 'infraction of discipline', initiative, or individual ingenuity in pursuance of the common end. Why do they not apply these same correct observations to the party, 'which is like some military force', as well? We cannot find the explanation of this incoherent logic.

Until we receive such an explanation, we must conclude that in our socialist party we find symptoms of the same disease as in other democratic institutions, viz. that the leadership wants to perpetuate its rule. The leaders may indeed be entirely well-intentioned: they persist in their thinking as a matter of sub-conscious conservatism, of perseverance in traditional party principles, of philistinism which instinctively abhors all innovation, all departure from accepted ideas. On the other hand, this persis-tence may also be the result of a plain selfish striving for power. But, in any case, it is a symptom of disease, against which we must fight. The indicated antidote is nothing but the remedy of the weakness of democracy.

The party is a party, true enough: an organization of struggle. By its nature it cannot tolerate in its midst anything that does not

agree with its goal and with the means of struggle which derive
from those basic principles which are determined by that goal.
But should agreement result from automatic assent to the words
of the leaders, out of some servile respect for authority, out of
some bewitched submission, or should it, on the contrary, develop
out of a conscious, well-thought-out individual decision?

'No development without parties: no progress without parting'. (6)
The socialist party is rightly proud of the fact that its programme
is based on the findings of the social sciences; can it ever forget
that its development becomes impossible from the moment it gives
greater weight to the party creed and the party truths endorsed
like a uniform at the behest of the leaders, than to the consensus
that develops naturally and individually?

Finally, can the socialist party ever forget that it has claimed
to be the only party which is seeking to realize in its struggle not
merely the class interest of a particular class, but something far
higher, far greater: the emancipation of man from the confinement,
humiliation and diminishing he suffered in the course of millenary
class rule? And who can be the liberator but man himself? We have
had enough of the Judeo-Christian teachings which have promised
or brought a saviour from the sky. Nor do we need earthly saviours who 'divide society into two parts, because they stand above
society'. The working class and, by the same token, humanity will
be emancipated only by the individual workers who have evolved
in their knowledge, who have increased in feeling, in effort, in
greatness and in their yearning for beauty.

The most successful tactic of the socialist parties is to develop
the consciousness of the working class. This was how they have
attained their greatest victories to date. This is how it must be
done in the future as well. This tactic may clash with certain
individual interests, it may jeopardize certain traditional positions,
it may lower the prestige of certain accepted authorities by a few
notches. Yet it remains the only party principle which is unquestionably in agreement with the higher laws of social development.
Whatever party deviates from this road, either has a defective
organization, or a false spirit, or both. In any case, it only
deserves to be burned!

NOTES

1   M. Ostrogorsky, 'La démocratie et l'organisation des partis
    politiques', 2 vols. (Paris, 1903). [Editors' note]
2   K. Kautsky, 'Die soziale Revolution' (Berlin, 1903) vol. 2
    (Am Tage nach der socialen Revolution), p. 48. [Author's note]
3   Letter to Heinz Starkenburg, 25 January 1897, in E. Bernstein
    (ed.) 'Dokumente des Sozialismus', vol. 2 (1905), p. 72.
    [Author's note]
4   Marx states this in the following terms: 'History does nothing,
    it "possesses no immense wealth", it "wages no battles". It is
    man, real living man who does all that, who possesses and

fights; history is not, as it were, a person apart using man as a means to achieve its own aims; history is nothing but the activity of man pursuing his aims.' (The Holy Family, 'Collected Works', vol. 4 (London, 1975), p. 93) [Author's note]

5   This is an apparent contradiction. If progress is the achievement of minorities, why could the rule of minorities not likewise be the instrument of progress? We do not have the space to discuss this issue here; we merely wish to point out that (a) minorities have only been a force for progress when their reforms were accepted by the large majority, (b) progress allows us to learn new truths which may be in opposition even to the most recently accepted truths, and (c) all rules have a tendency to perpetuate themselves. [Author's note]

6   Ohne Parteien keine Entwicklung, ohne Scheidung kein Fortschritt, 'Neue Rheinische Zeitung' (1842), p. 172. [Author's note]

SYNDICALISM AND SOCIAL DEMOCRACY

Written originally for 'Mouvement Socialiste', where it was published in 1908 (vol. 1, pp. 108-29), Szabó published this personal credo of his later years, in the translation of his friend Gyula Mérő also in Hungarian ('Huszadik Század', pt II (1908), pp. 273-92, and separately in 'Huszadik Század könyvtára', (Budapest, 1908), no. 35. It shows, among other things, Szabó's familiarity with the many directions of the working-class movement in Europe and America - about which he wrote several reviews in the early 1900s - and his awareness of the special problems facing socialists in central and eastern Europe. While he offers a socio-economic analysis of capitalist development as the basis for his argument on economic and 'educational' class struggle, in opposition to 'active work' in bourgeois states and parliaments, he admits that in countries where the bourgeoisie did not fully acquire political hegemony, such as Hungary, the struggle for democracy and civil liberties may be the task of the workers. In the differentiation of these aims from the genuinely class-oriented target of socialism, Szabó adumbrated many an issue that became particularly relevant in the decades after his death with regard to the 'underdeveloped' countries' road to socialism. Even though his expectations from the syndicalist movement may have proved wrong, much of the programmatic ideas included here are theoretically valuable in our own days.

This essay was originally meant for the 'Mouvement Socialiste', and I had not intended to publish it in Hungarian. The economic and political conditions in Hungary are not as yet propitious terrain for the teachings of syndicalism; nor do I believe that this tendency of the labour movement will be driven by more favourable winds in the near future, even though, in my opinion, it points the way to the future reformulation of the socialist movement. It seems to me that the particular political and social relations which predominate in Hungary will, for a long time to come, drive the working class into one of two extremes: either a purely parliamentary and political struggle, or violent economic ones. It will be a long time before the unhealthy and lopsided economic development in this country will cease torturing our political life with cramps or nervous ticks, only to repress time and again the seeds of a new order which have been so difficult to sow. In this confused, inchoate country wallowing in the throws of the past there is no one to whom syndicalism might appeal: after all, is syndicalism not the expression of the social needs of the most developed countries? If, nevertheless, I decide to have my essay published in Hungarian, the reason is as follows: it seems that a storm of severe trials is threatening the Hungarian labour movement in the near future. In the wake of serious struggles some theoretical clarification becomes necessary. For this purpose we must take the most recent theoretical developments into consideration. Although theory has but little impact on practice and on life itself, it nevertheless seems indispensable; I am led to believe that it is not entirely useless, in fact, it may even be my duty, as long as I have the ability, not to hamper the already difficult penetration of socialist ideas into the circles of the Hungarian working class with the barrier of a foreign language. Should I fail, then, at worst, my sin would have been the same as that of so many other Hungarian writers in the past and, foreseeably, in the future: I too will have written something for which no one here has any use, and which, had it remained unwritten, would merely have hurt the paper, ink and printing industries.

I hardly need explain that this article is not in the least the expression of some official school of thought. Some have mocked Marxism - perhaps not entirely unfairly - arguing that, much like the official science and theories sponsored by the establishment, it too has official doctrines and ex-cathedra pronouncements. Syndicalism has not reached this point. It is still very young and, let us admit, very weak. It has no armies, no masses protecting - or, as the case may be, constraining - its theoreticians. Everyone is responsible for his own words. Thus my writing is but my personal opinion, and it differs in many respects from the opinions of foreign representatives of the movement, who also differ amongst themselves. I have to say this much in defence of syndicalism: the criticism which my article may elicit should not claim to have defeated syndicalism. The kind of criticism which expects to have an impact by exacerbating personal differences should always bear Marx's principle in mind: it is never theory that decides, but practice. Syndicalist theory may still be at a primitive stage, and even its practice may be shaky at the beginning, but in terms of actual achievement, in terms of economic and political impact, it need not defer to other movements which may be much better founded or more smoothly polished. All this is not to say, of course, that I would not stand behind every word I say.

I

It is no more possible to judge the trade union movement of any country on the basis of statistical tables, as to gain a basic orientation about its socialist movement from the programme of its party. The programmes of practically all socialist parties are similar - yet what considerable differences we find in their theories! Conversely, how different the most popular slogans, the most effective calls to arm – and yet how monotonous the practice, how uniform the actions! The situation in the trade union movement is very much the same. The neutrality of the Germans differs from the neutrality of the Americans; the 'action directe' of the French differs from the direct action of the Italians, etc.

In order to be able to evaluate properly the labour movement of a given country it is necessary to free ourselves from slogans, to withstand the temptation to generalize. A true revolutionary syndicalist from France would see only chaos and contradiction in the fact that Arturo Labriola has become a candidate for parliament, that Michels is upset because the Germans refuse to fight more dynamically for civil liberties, or that Krichevsky can take part in the struggle against absolutism. A French syndicalist would not understand how socialists in certain countries might resort to direct action in a struggle for parliamentary political objectives such as universal suffrage, without being even aware of the apparent contradiction; or how some large trade unions can fight, with the selfsame organization, at times for purely political, at times for purely economic goals; or that while they do not neglect the economic objectives, they likewise make no concessions about the political ones. All these are contradictions which do not seem to promote much the general perception of all phenomena of the labour movement.

Yet, if we expect a uniform appraisal of these trends and concrete manifestations, we cannot avoid the questions: what might be the lot of specific trends within the labour movement? The big issue which has dominated the socialist and trade union congresses for years, and which will keep their theoreticians busy for many years to come – namely the problem of the party and of the trade union – is undoubtedly also the basic problem of socialism. If we can find the answer to this question we have also found the right point of view for the appraisal and evaluation of the actions of parties and trade unions: if the answer does not work out, then we invariably fall into either crude empiricism, or unscientific generalizations.

What is socialism? According to the Marxist perception – and at the present stage of socialist thinking we might as well omit all other schools – socialism is the theoretical expression (or ideology) of the wage-earning proletariat, the necessary goal towards which it is driven by the contradictions of economic production and distribution. Since all class struggle is political struggle, the class struggle of the modern workers' movement is likewise a political struggle. The organization by which it attempts to reach this goal is a political party. The name of this political party is Social Democracy. Thus, in contemporary society, Social Democracy is the visible carrier of the struggle for socialism, a necessary political organ; the objective of Social Democracy, the demands couched in the programme of the party, constitute socialism.

If this definition were correct, if Social Democracy would indeed be identical with socialism and represent it, then there would have to be a Social Democratic Party in every industrial state.

Socialism is the only solution to economic contradictions, hence it is the necessary ideology of that class which must strive towards the solution of these contradictions because of its relationship to the organs of production of goods and their distribution: the class struggle of the proletariat must everywhere bring about the kind of organization which alone is capable of realizing this solution. The more developed the country, the more powerful industrial capitalism, the more numerous the wage-earners, the stronger this organization would have to be, the more powerful the Social Democracy of the country concerned.

We know, however – and this is an argument used by numerous opponents of socialism and Marxism – that the facts of the history of socialism in the civilized world do not jibe with this concept. In England, the classical home of capitalism, the great field of experimentation used by Marx, there has hardly been a significant socialist movement until quite recently; there has been no movement that had an impact on the working class and could have led it on the path to independent political action. In the United States, an even more classical case of a capitalist country inasmuch as capitalism was able to evolve there free of any form of ethical constraint and traditional sentimentalism, one might say that even now there is nothing comparable to European socialism. What is more, even France, the original home of revolution, is also without the standard form of Social Democracy, because the party – whether united or once again split – is so far from reflecting the homogeneity of the situation of the modern working class. On the other hand, Germany already had an extremely well-organized Social Democratic Party well before it had become a serious competitor of England and America on the world market; the party had hundreds of thousands of voters and dozens of legislators. Austria has the largest parliamentary faction, whereas in Italy, social democracy often plays the role of the most dedicated supporter of the state. How do we explain this phenomenon?

We know there is an answer. As regards the United States it has been argued time and again that the land available for homesteading contributed to the exodus of the reserve army of labour from the city, hence any revolutionary stirrings got squashed from their very beginning. Yet there was no Social Democracy in England either, even though free land had not been available there for a very long time. As regards England the explanation has been sought in the monopoly its industry enjoys on the world market, something that allowed or even compelled its capitalists to make far-reaching concessions to the working class in order to avoid any revolutionary disruption, as a matter of the most elementary precaution. As regards France, at least on the surface, the lack of a pure unified Social Democracy was ascribed to the fact that the French are individualists, and do not tolerate any form of party discipline. I do not believe that any of these explanations hit the nail on the head, although there is some truth in them. But much too often it is overlooked that the two Anglo-Saxon nations, while not socialist, nevertheless already had a huge trade union

movement when in Germany the value that trade unions might have
for the working class was still being hotly debated. And the sup-
posedly individualistic French were shackled for centuries by the
same chains of church and state as other countries during the
feudal period, and that even today, we witness in France the
most rigid form of centralization in the administration of the
country. Could its character have changed all that suddenly?
Furthermore, can we disregard the fact that free land was also
available to the reserve army of German workers? Two decades
ago it was almost as easy to reach North America as it is today,
and there were times when emigration was quite considerable.
Yet Social Democracy flourished in spite of emigration and, even
today, now that Germany has become the most formidable competitor of the United Kingdom and the United States on the world
market, the number of party members has not diminished.

From all these cases we can see that large countries have gone
through identical economic stages, yet the social superstructure
that evolved in each was not identical, and political development
did not follow the same direction. From this we should conclude
that the supposed parallel of economics and politics does not exist,
that the thesis which avers that similar economic circumstances
necessarily breed similar political forms is incorrect. However,
this is only apparently so. For very rarely has there been a period in the economic development of a nation when an economic
model has reached perfect fruition by completely superseding the
remants of the previous model, and by precluding even the seeds
of a subsequent system from germinating. Still, there have been
such periods. There were times when feudal estates had been the
exclusive and unlimited system over immense territories; and at
another, albeit brief period, the bourgeoisie did consistently construct a new economic order on the ruins of an old one. We used
to say that certain political forms, such as the organization of the
state, of administration, of legislation are the typical expressions
of particular economic conditions and the typical forms of the political rule of a given class. At such times these political forms
break through neatly and consistently, and present us with the
objectified appearance of the ideas of these political forms in rare
purity.

We must be careful, though: we are only dealing with form. And
since it is merely form, much too often it becomes filled by an
alien content and, while the economic and social contents depart,
the form becomes a false cover. Contraband may be sailing under
foreign flags.

This happens every time diverse economic models coexist within
the same society. And since almost every European country is in
this situation, since in addition to the predominant capitalist mode
of industrial production remnants of feudalism also survive,
whereas the seeds of a future system have already been planted,
we can safely claim that this is the normal state. Conditions in
which a pure economic type would determine the interaction of the
social and political superstructure with the economic base in the

form of complete harmony would be the end or the very beginning of development, hence a contradiction in adjecto, because it is not possible to imagine a beginning or an end to development. Such exceptional conditions are so rare that they might be called idealizations. None the less it is necessary to make this assumption, without which it would not be possible to find a scientific interpretation of the relationship of various social formations. The conditions described above, which exist in reality, display a very different parallelism of politics and economy. Since no mode of production prevails exclusively, different classes share political power and therefore we see the struggle of the highly differing political, ethical and legal ideologies. Since scientific insight into the motives and goals of social struggle is still rather limited – and practically non-existent among the masses – one can also observe the most varied classes serving alien interests and fighting struggles inimical to themselves. Political traditions, and the historical peculiarities of the class struggle of those which have attained power either permanently or temporarily, influence the struggle of all the other classes and impress it with the stamp of their alien character, mislead it and constrain it into unfitting moulds.

Thus the law of parallelism in political economy obtains a different concept or, if you prefer, a different interpretation: every class struggles for social success, for political power, but the form of the struggle and the political objectives it selects do not allow us to draw immediate conclusions regarding the essence of the struggle itself. The struggle for political rights, for the democratic transformation of the state, does not necessarily signify the struggle of the working class itself, or socialism; similarly, the lack of a political organization or political struggle among the working class does not signify that an actual movement of the working class does not exist, or that the preparation for its specific social order for socialism is not taking place.

If we examine the historical progress of Social Democracy and trade unions among the great nations from such a point of view, the following becomes evident. In all those countries where the bourgeoisie itself exerts a guiding influence in government, a working-class movement concerned with parliamentary politics has developed only ephemerally, or hardly at all; everywhere, however, where the feudal estates and the administrative bureaucracy dominate, a more or less powerful Social Democracy has had a chance to develop.

More precisely: wherever the bourgeoisie had itself created the political tools for its economic interests and social success, socialism did not have a chance to flourish. In these countries the working class, for the time being, had to emerge and act only as an economic class. The political rights extended to all citizens of the state made this role possible. A specific vital ideology derived from the economic situation could only develop when the workers had formed a separate economic class, strictly distinguished from other classes by its economic and social circumstances, and which has attained a consciousness of the conflict of economic interests.

On the other hand, wherever the bourgeoisie did not create its own political organization, a political democracy - either because it had failed in the struggle against feudal absolutism and the bureaucracy, or because its own development had taken place at such a late date that the struggle between the bourgeoisie and the working class in the more developed countries had served as a discouraging example - in those countries the working class, partly because of economic backwardness, or because of the lack of civil liberties, has been prevented from developing as an independent economic class. In these countries the working class took over the strife for the achievement of the political calling of the bourgeoisie, and has endeavoured to carry out the bourgeoisie's ideology: the working class thus became the executor of the political testament of the bourgeoisie.

The programmes of all Social Democratic parties are ample evidence of all this. But even more than the programmes, which also contain a fair amount of genuine socialist demands, this can be seen in their practice; and, after all, it is practice that really counts. Not what people think, nor how reality is reflected in their consciousness is essential, but how they actually act - as Marx so clearly pointed out. The essential is practice, action. They may diverge considerably in the interpretation of the doctrines of socialism and the theoretical justification of specific tactical decisions; but in matters of parliamentary politics, in the demands for the so-called minimal programme, they all agree - Guesde and Jaurès, Bebel and Vollmar, Ferri and Turati, and all the rest. The action of the Social Democratic parties finds fulfilment in the struggle for parliamentary and political democracy.

This explains why the political movement of Social Democracy is the stronger the more backward the country is in matters of social and political democracy. The Social Democratic Party in Germany was the strongest member of the International even at a time when the German Empire's economic development could hardly have accounted for this strength; on the other hand, the boundless cowardice of the German bourgeoisie, the suffocating feudal bureaucracy, militarism, and the medieval spirit of caste and class pride could very well have provided an incentive for this development. The situation is not much different in Italy, Austria, or Hungary. As far as France is concerned, the regime has oscillated between democracy and bureaucracy for the past century or so, between the absolutism of the caesars and that of high finance. No wonder, then, that the French working-class movement is so halting; sometimes it blossoms, sometimes it wanes, sometimes it pursues exclusively political, and sometimes exclusively economic objectives. Here too Social Democracy has become the vanguard of bourgeois democracy - as the events of the past decade have clearly shown - or the powerful rearguard of a tiny group of intellectuals and petit bourgeois, the Millerands, the Vivianis, the Briands, or the Gerault-Richards.

II

The question is: what should be the stand of those socialists who arrived at a clear understanding of the essence of present-day Social Democracy vis-à-vis parliamentary politics?

I believe the Marxist would answer this question as follows. He would first of all take the economic conditions into account. Not because he considers everything dependent exclusively on economic factors, on technology, on the relations of production, or the automatic development of the economic structure. He knows that in order for a superstructure to develop that is appropriate to the economic base, the will, the conscious action of the masses is absolutely necessary. But he also knows that economic development is subject to immutable laws. It is his conviction that socialism can only be realized if the productivity of labour has reached a point where forced labour becomes superfluous, and if the industrial plants can assume forms which correspond to the socialist mode of production. It is the task of the industrial bourgeoisie to achieve this degree of production. The road to socialism leads through the bourgeois regime.

Hence he must argue: if there is no capitalism there can be no socialism. The perfect productivity of labour cannot evolve without capitalism, nor can there be socialized production. Without capitalism there is no industrial wage-earning proletariat either. Socialism cannot be carried out by the peasants, the artisans, or the intellectuals. It is not their business. It is the business of the industrial wage labourer.

From this insight it follows that the proletariat must adapt its stand to contemporary issues and to politics in general to the degree of economic development of the country concerned. The proletariat cannot remain indifferent to the symptoms of capitalist economic development and to the incidents of the bourgeois regime. Since capitalism is the precursor of socialism, the working class is of necessity interested in everything that even now, in capitalist society, seems to have a bearing on the development toward socialism. These can be divided into three groups: economic order, political order and intellectual matters.

First, with regard to economic order, rapid industrial development is the prime interest of the proletariat in all countries. First and foremost because, as already mentioned, socialist social order is only possible if socialized work has attained a high degree of productivity, and this cannot be achieved solely through agriculture, even less by means of pre-capitalist small-scale production. The rate of industrial development is also an important factor, not only because it may bring us closer to the realization of our yearning: to see our immediate progeny, and perhaps even ourselves, live under better conditions (as a consequence of which the desire for struggle and the willingness to bring sacrifices must rise), but mostly because, as can be universally observed, the periods of economic boom and advanced industrial development are accompanied by the increase of the revolutionary spirit of the working class and most active class struggles. A rather essential mental precondition of socialism is that the working class receive and retain a spiritual training in a revolutionary frame of mind and that it be inoculated by a spirit of permanent rebellion which could, under no circumstance, be extinguished by a spirit of submissiveness.

This, of course, does not mean at all that the working class should adopt a programme of industrialization for the sake of a more rapid development, or that it should support subsidies and bonuses, colonization or incentives for export. Nor does it mean that the weak industry should be granted periods of grace, or that for the sake of unimpeded development the working class should enter into temporary truce with the capitalists – as has been suggested to them by some socialists (albeit often in euphemistic terms), particularly in France, Italy, Hungary and other industrially underdeveloped countries. My arguments are by no means intended to contribute to industrial peace, a slogan we hear nowadays not only from strictly bourgeois sources.

Quite to the contrary. If struggle – whether individual or group struggle – is the motive force of natural evolution, then it must also be the mainspring of social evolution. 'The history of all hitherto existing societies is the history of class struggle' (The Communist Manifesto', ch. I). Wherever the economic classes believe that their struggle can be substituted by mutual favours, economic and political deals, or state protection we cannot find a prosperous economy. Let us take a look at industrial development in those countries where the bourgeoisie did not have the courage to seriously challenge the feudal latifundia. Even such an extensive system of regulations as protective tariffs – the panacea the land-owning class has offered to share with industry in its own interests – cannot help them. Up to this moment it is highly questionable whether protective tariffs have ever succeeded in bringing about any sort of industry. The experience of the nations of eastern Europe certainly does not confirm such a hypothesis. It is certain, however, that protective tariffs have a rather withering impact on already existing industries, because they exempt the entrepreneurs from the need to foster their branch of manufacturing by broad vision and an ever-fresh spirit of enterprise; France may serve as an example here. This is even more true about bonuses and subsidies which are barely more than presents to groups of influential powerful industrialists, or even to individuals. These gifts may allow them to deal with their workers more effectively, or to compensate for the losses which have hurt them as a result of the workers' movement but, on the other hand, they definitely prevent them from compensating for the losses by improving the production process. As far as strikes are concerned, while the increase of strikes, as of the spirit of liberty and independence, is the subjective reflection of economic boom, strikes themselves are the inevitable symptoms of a vivid industrial development.

Strikes do not ruin industry, as some socialists are prone to argue; on the contrary, the lack of strikes implies the decline of industry. Thus the workers have absolutely no reason to conduct economic struggle under so-called 'more peaceful' forms. Quite to the contrary: their main objective should be to heighten the struggle, to conduct it with utmost ardour and ruthlessness, not only because of its direct relevance, but also for the sake of economic development, the acceleration of which carries society more rapidly towards a superior order. The workers must prevent, with all the means at their disposal, the employers from slowing down this process of development or even stifling it with government protection – for their own comfort and to the direct and indirect detriment of the working class.

Second, with regard to political order, the daily political interests of the workers are less important than their involvement in the economic development of capitalist society. If socialists and others in western Europe speak of politics in connection with the workers' movement they mean but one thing: parliamentary action. I believe it is unnecessary to demonstrate that parliamentarism by no means exhausts the concept of politics. Parliamentary action is but one part of politics. By politics we mean the ensemble of those activities which aim at influencing the state and its organs. For the sake of definition it is entirely incidental whether this impact is direct or indirect, regards positive or negative measures; the main thing is that it always pertains to public authority, the state, the organs of legislation and the executive.

The definition of these concepts is not splitting hairs. I believe that syndicalism would have been preserved from many errors – errors which have often led it into ambiguous positions – if some of its advocates had not so crudely identified parliamentarism with politics and with the state. The anarchist model, which does not deal with politics as a matter of principle, because parliamentarism is part and parcel of politics, amounts to nothing more than a refusal to take cognizance of reality. Yet it is more than a refusal, because their practice is something else again: the state itself, unfortunately, is very much a reality, and the only workers' movement that could avoid constant conflict with the state would have to be a movement that itself is not real.

Two kinds of important concerns relate the working class to government. The working and operation of every mass movement requires a certain freedom of movement. Such freedom is necessary even if the objectives of the movement are purely negative, destructive, and much more so if the objectives are positive, such as the creation of its own specific institutions. If the movement is harassed on all sides, if objects and persons are perpetually insecure, if it is continuously forced to tread on the seeds of its own creations, then there is but one choice for individuals and groups alike: revolt.

Modern working-class movement aspires to more. Its objective is not just to destroy, but to build as well. It is convinced that the cells of a new social order must begin to grow in the womb of the old. The economic elements of a socialist system – socialized production, machines that supplant human labour, etc. - are already developing without the active or direct contribution of the working class. On the other hand, it is the task of the working class to exploit this trend for its own benefit, and to adjust to it. This is achieved through its economic organization which, on the one hand, are its own kind of public authority used for obtaining the economic advantages of the improved forms and conditions of production, and on the other, the great educational institutions for the future where active solidarity of action, unselfishness, willingness to subject oneself to the public will are taught, and in which the organs for the different social functions are selected by natural differentiation from the working class itself. The organs of the contemporary working-class movement are not mere gatherings of those who rebel against sheer misery, but are the examples of a future socialist order, as indeed they should be. It would be impossible to imagine the creation and existence of such organs of the working class under the system of feudal absolutism which exists only in memory in western Europe, but which is still predominant in the eastern part. Without basic political rights such as freedom of opinion, the right to unite and assemble, etc. a constructive working-class movement is hardly possible, because all its energies would be consumed in warding off persecution by the state.

These political freedoms are the basic ingredients of a so-called political democracy. Democracy has extorted them from feudal absolutism. From the point of view of political power, these freedoms mean no more than that part of it that has been transformed from the bureaucracy to the subjects; it means the limitation of state power. Hence it is in the very interest of the proletariat to ensure these democratic liberties for itself. Some may argue: how seriously do the ruling classes take the laws, the constitutions, the guaranteed rights? It is true that the ruling classes do not respect these very much; every class, and particularly the class of the oppressed, acts this way once it becomes conscious of its power. We are talking not of classes but of the state, and a state in which the feudal-aristocratic bureaucracy rules is certainly worse than the bourgeois state. Let them just ask the Russian workers why they are willing to sacrifice their lives for the struggle against bureaucratic absolutism. Because the feudal-absolutist state, unmindful of the consequences, ruthlessly represses every minute manifestation of the working class; whereas bourgeois absolutism cannot exist without certain political rights which serve to defend its interests against the bureaucracy. This derives from the nature of contemporary industry and commerce.

The bourgeoisie, as a result of the same opposition of interests which makes it relatively favour certain political liberties, considers every representative system superior to bureaucratic absolutism. At this moment, the parliament is the most appropriate organ of control over the finances of the state, a matter of major interest to the bourgeois. The expenditures of the modern state are increasing at a considerable pace, as are its incomes. These

incomes come from basically two sources: loans and taxes. The
financing of loans is almost exclusively the concern of the bourgeoisie, and the more powerful the political influence of the
feudal landholders, the greater the tax burden the bourgeoisie
has to bear. Hence the bourgeoisie has to find ways and means of
controlling and influencing the utilization of public funds. It does
this through parliament.

We have started from the premise that capitalism is the prerequisite of socialism, and that the full flowering of capitalism can
only take place if the bourgeoisie is in control. Since the bourgeoisie cannot attain power without exerting a controlling influence over the power of the state, and since, on the other hand,
the absolute state in which the feudal bureaucracy rules pre-
cludes the possibility of conditions for the organization of the
working class - it cannot be denied that the working class is tied
to the public authority by certain interests, that is it also has
political interest.

We would, however, overestimate political power if we were to
grant it decisive influence over social developments. We have
shown above that the political evolution of the most diverse
countries has not kept pace with the evolution of their economic
structure, and that any kind of political form can become the
adequate expression of the power and interests of a given class.

No matter how important the question is of what kind of social
and political superstructure the working class will erect over its
own economic order - indeed, this is the basic issue of socialism -
the political organization of contemporary society will not touch
the essence of its economic organization. Here again it is simply
a matter of accelerating and ensuring progress.

On the other hand, we would be equally mistaken in assuming
that the working class, if it were to take on the political mission
of the bourgeoisie, would be able to quicken the pace of progress.
As with political economy, here too struggle engenders everything. The bourgeoisie grew politically strong in the struggle
against the nobility and the state. Germany is the classical example of this. Here a 'Junker' - Bismarck - introduced universal
suffrage and a parliamentary system long before the bourgeoisie
or the working class could have compelled him to do so. Yet can
one imagine a more shameful parody of a parliament than the
German 'Reichstag'? Or a more ridiculous constitutionalism? Can
one imagine a more pitiful parliamentary and political debility of
all social classes in the face of the feudal agrarians and the
bureaucracy? I believe there is no better example of the principle that every social class must take care of its own business.
(As we know, in Germany government takes place outside parliament.)

Thus the working class can derive a political advantage from
action directed at influencing state power only if it does not tarry
further in the veneration of political forms, and liberates itself
from the fantasy that particular forms of state or government are
indispensable conditions for its victory. It should consider with

favour every serious attempt of the bourgeoisie to strengthen its
political organization, and may even actively support them under
certain circumstances, but it must never compromise by even a
hair's breadth its economic interests for the sake of a political
principle. The working class must never demur from any actions
aimed at influencing the government merely for the sake of not
potentially harming some political ideal of the bourgeoisie. In all
cases it is in the direct interest of the working class, as well as
in the interest of general social progress, to insist on its class
position in the most rigorous way.

There is no need to spend much time on the third group of
concerns of the working class, which we have classified under
the term intellectual interests. By this term we mean all those
attempts which aim at the raising of the intellectual level of the
masses, their liberation from superstition and obsolete notions
and the spread of modern science.

It is not necessary to discuss at length the importance of improving the intellectual preparation of the working class for the
sake of its struggle. We all know that the nucleus of any working-
class organization consists of the better educated workers who
are immune to the prejudices of dogmatic religions, and have a
thirst for knowledge.

It is not necessary to stress to the readers of 'Mouvement
Socialiste' the importance and value of that education which has
made it possible for workers to conquer certain intellectual functions even in our time. It cannot be expected, for the time being,
that all intellectual functions become compatible with manual labour,
and we know that these functions cannot as yet be filled by persons not trained specifically for the purpose; we cannot assume,
for the time being, that intellectuals from a working-class background should radically alter the relationship between the masses
and the intellectual leaders; still, we can never stress sufficiently
the symptomatic significance of the fact that the working class is
indeed capable of selecting its leadership from within its own
ranks. This means that the struggle and victory of the working
class does not in the least constitute a threat to the survival of
civilization.

Of course, we must not assume that everything which is commonly known as culture or civilization also means civilization to
the working class. Far from it. There are but very few absolute
cultural values which would continue to play a role in the social
life of all future periods. Certain biological and physiological
tendencies determined by man's social existence will continue to
exist, certain general ethical principles will be adhered to in the
future as well, at least theoretically, certain scientific cognitions
will preserve their validity, but the greater part of our scientific,
sociological, philosophical, ethical and aesthetic knowledge and
culture is very much subject to the law of relativity of social
values. As every ideology, which is the accompaniment of a particular economic form, the expression of certain social forces and
the tool of particular social goals, has arisen and disappeared a

hundred times, in the same way, what the bourgeois society regards as its own culture, yet at the same time as something that
is universally and eternally valid, will have to make room for a
newer civilization.

It is, however, necessary that everyone who wants to work for
a better future should be familiar with man's position within nature and with the laws of social movement as far as the present
stage of human knowledge permits.

III

We have attempted to determine those contemporary social interests of the working class which transcend the direct striving for
better wages and better working conditions. In the area of economics it is the quickest possible development of capitalism, in the
political arena it is the conquest of the state by the bourgeoisie;
in the intellectual arena it is the spread of modern science. We
have shown that the proletariat serves these interests best if it
lets the bourgeoisie take care of them, for this is its specific task.
We have shown that the working class should not shield the bourgeoisie in its struggle either against its predecessors, feudalism
and bureaucracy, or against its heir, the working class itself.
The working class should support these struggles only if it does
not have to sacrifice any economic interests in exchange, but
should concentrate on building up its own organizations and def-
ending these against all attackers. And now the question remains:
by what means and in what manner does the working class represent these interests in specific instances?

One of the most characteristic manifestations of contemporary
societies is the outstanding role played by the state. This fact
has been noted innumerable times. While some see in this manifestation the product of a healthy and natural development, and
cannot imagine the future on any other terms than in the form of
a state regulating all aspects of the life of the individual and of
society, others refuse to admit that there can be a more dangerous enemy of humanity and its future than the power of the state.

Since we are dealing here with the contemporary interests of
the working class we need not enter into a debate with either one
extreme or the other. We do not conceal the fact that we are not
favourably inclined to statism. Nevertheless, we must limit ourselves to noting the influence exercised by the state in capitalist
society on the preconditions and organization of the workers'
movement, and find rules applicable to the present struggle of the
movement, rules which have immediate application.

In its present form the state appears as the organized violence
of the ruling class, as an enormously developed organ which
reaches into all aspects of social existence, which regulates all
extant and would-be institutions, and forces them into a permissible mould. The very basis of the state's existence, the process
of production and the economic struggle appears to us through the

medium of the state, inasmuch as the ruling classes are not at all reluctant to use the centralized power of society for purposes of economic organization and economic techniques.

Thus the working class, in its movement, is confronted at each step by the state. Even while remaining within the rigidly delineated boundaries of its present-day economic interests, the movement cannot take one step without clashing with the laws. Even if the workers simply want to set up a mutual-aid organization, they have to subject themselves to legal forms, and submit to the right of the authorities to supervise them; if they want to make propaganda for the most peaceful economic purposes, the laws determine the forms, the tone, the means and the limits this activity will take; if they have claims based on private law against the entrepreneur, the rights and means are defined by law; and if they want to initiate an open struggle for the improvement of working conditions, they soon find out that the circle within which they can resort to freely selected means is very precisely marked by rifles and bayonets.

Yet in all these it is strictly a matter of economic interests. The state responds even more aggressively when other matters come on the agenda: economic policy in general, issues of taxes, tariffs, and commerce, the extension of secular as opposed to ecclesiastical authority, or matters of education and culture!

All this, however, as already mentioned, pertains to the bourgeoisie. What does not pertain to the bourgeoisie, but solely to the working class is the freedom of action for its organizations. This freedom is defined for the moment by the organized power of the working class, but in the long run by the government. Those freedoms that have already been secured are constantly endangered by enemies; only the government is capable of ensuring the rights already obtained. For this, however, the working class must exercise some influence over legislation and administration.

Precisely because parliamentarism, the modern form of legislation, is the form of the bourgeoisie's rule, it has a certain force of suggestion: the bourgeoisie, attributes a far greater importance to what is merely a superficial manifestation, namely the number of parties represented in parliament. The bourgeoisie is continually worried lest its organization become enlisted in the service of inimical interests. This worry of the bourgeoisie - in which the individual representatives' fear of losing their mandate also plays a considerable role - serves as a guarantee that working-class representation in parliament can prevent the denial of political liberties.

This reason, and this reason alone, can justify the participation of the workers in parliamentary life. Representation in parliament results in continuous pressure. It is as if the workers were saying: you must allow our organs to thrive in peace, otherwise we will show you how we can destroy your prized possessions! Within the larger, integral working-class movement this is the role of the parliamentary-political action. Everything that goes beyond this leads to so-called positive work, that is to carrying out the tasks of the bourgeoisie; and everything that falls short of this role forces the working class to fight continually for the most basic preconditions of its organs. This is not an arbitrary construct, nor a carefully defined middle way meant to satisfy all nuances between par excellence parliamentary action and direct action. We do not express wishes, but state objective developmental tendencies on the basis of objective data.

Let us consider that in the era of primitive capitalism the working class everywhere organized political movements and, what is more, the working class itself fought for parliamentarism in those countries where the bourgeoisie had failed to do so. In the developed capitalist countries, where the bourgeoisie is completely in charge and the parliamentary-political regime has been achieved by the bourgeoisie itself, we note that at a certain point the working class which, until then, has limited itself to economic struggle and the organization of trade unions, launches itself into the parliamentary-political struggle. This is the case in Great Britain and in the United States where, as we know, a Social Democratic movement has come into existence of late. The circumstances which have elicited the change in these two countries are well known. In both bourgeois states the government has resorted to force and repression in the economic struggle between the bourgeoisie and the workers' organizations.

We conclude from this that the working class, wherever the legal possibilities for organization have been limited or suppressed, much like in those countries where these possibilities have to be created for the first time, has engaged in a political struggle. It seems that the preservation of political rights will always be a social necessity, whether we like it or not. Thus, whatever our subjective desires or convictions may be, we cannot avoid certain social necessities which derive from the economic and political character of the environment in which the labour movement of the country functions.

In the semi-feudal countries even the bourgeoisie has not developed full class consciousness, let alone reached the stage where it can fight for the democratic transformation of the state. In these countries we cannot stop the working class, in spite of the fact that it is already involved in an economic struggle with the bourgeoisie, from getting excited about democracy and parliamentarism, organizing a party of Social Democracy and in it expending the great part of its energies and often its ultimate weapons for demands which, on the whole, are of little value for the workers, such as universal suffrage. In such countries the social revolutionary trade union movement - syndicalism - can hardly function other than in a politically revolutionary way. In these countries there is not much we can do except foster the trade union movement with all our strength as the seed of the future revolutionary organization, without disturbing the process of development, though constantly pointing out the rather relative and limited value of parliamentarism and of political movement in general.

The situation is entirely different in those countries where the bourgeoisie has taken the defence of its political class interests into its own hands either without democratic institutions, having secured the place it deserves in government as a consequence of its economic power - as seems to be the case in Germany - or else by fighting for democratic reforms, as it is perhaps ready to do in Russia. While in the latter country the working class must actively support bourgeois radicalism, in the former the situation is rather similar to the one we have described in connection with Britain and the United States. There is no longer a need for the working class to ease the road for bourgeois political and social success, and there is not even an opportunity for that, because it is no longer feudalism and bureaucratic absolutism which oppose social progress and the workers' movement, but the bourgeoisie itself. The enemy is the bourgeoisie along the whole front.

The working class must continue to use the weapons of the bourgeoisie to defend itself; but it will no longer be a fighter for alien, even enemy causes. The working class will begin to fight, beyond its own economic constituion and consolidation, for all the interests of the final struggle derived from its specific social situation: for the transformation of the entire society in its own image.

Social Democracy will have to face facts: will it remain on the trodden path, the path which was obviously that of bourgeois democracy, or is it capable of replacing its old programme and its traditional mode of action with new concepts and new means of struggle?

This will be the moment when the issue of party and trade union have to be resolved. If the transformation is successful, it will no doubt be painful, and the more painful and difficult the more developed the social democratic organization, the more elaborate its hierarchy, the greater the number of its representatives. In France it is obvious that a substantial portion of the party's members and its voters still belong to the bourgeoisie; the same can be statistically demonstrated for Italy and Germany. This adulterated organization cannot be dissolved without provoking enormous crises.

Where should the party find its new concepts? It will probably have to find them in the ideology and practice of that social formation which has best preserved its class character, because it could not be infiltrated by other classes: the revolutionary trade union movement, the creation most specific to the working class.

At the present stage of economic, social and political development we cannot know what shape this movement will eventually take. The future, and perhaps the immediate future, will show whether this movement is capable of producing more than just an action for the overthrow of bourgeois society: will it include constructive principles and a fervour for reconstruction? The French trade unions taught new methods and new ways for the political struggle of the working class: direct action and anti-militarism. But from the point of view of future society all this is but negative, the most recent manifestation of destructive forces. The economic backwardness of France – which we surmise mainly from the disintegrating divisions of its trade unions – does not allow the trade unions to reach a point of maturity where they could carry out truly constructive work. That is a correlate of the concentration of industry, vertical monopolies, cartels and trusts which demand great centralized industrial unions on a higher level than the old trade unions. We have no doubt, nevertheless, that the working class will be able to find its own way: the construction of the new society does not depend solely on its will, but is a necessity of social biology. The life and death of society depend upon it.

THE ROLE OF THE POLITICAL PARTY IN THE WORKERS' MOVEMENT
(Introduction to Marx's 'Critique of the Gotha Programme')

This compact article, the final re-statement of Szabó's rejection of Social Democratic political, that is parliamentary, parties was written for volume 2 of his Marx-Engels collection, but he found it so important that he published it as an article in 'Huszadik Század', pt II (1909, pp. 147-47) and also in French in 'Mouvement Socialiste', pt I (1910, pp. 5-20). Taking his cue from Marx's most explicit statements on Lasallean etatistic illusions, Szabó develops his critique from empirical data (on bourgeois votes for socialist parties and proletarian votes for non-socialist ones) and states clearly that through the German-type parties a 'new class' of professional politicians have taken over the leadership, in no way expressing the interests of the working class. These, he maintains, are represented only in the sphere of economic confrontation between workers and bourgeois, not in the political arena. This article marked the final break of Szabó with Social Democracy: a party that strengthened bourgeois democracy and the state - though it may have served progressive aims - was not the field with which a Marxist-proletarian theoretician and revolutionary had anything to do, not even as an oppositionary member.

The letter about the Gotha programme is one of Marx's least known writings. One would assume that the German socialists, according to whom Marxism and German Social Democracy are one and the same thing, would not miss an opportunity to acquaint the disciples and adepts with all the writings of the master, in order that they may learn from them. This is not so. Whole volumes of Marx have yet to be published in German: 'The Eastern Question', the 'Secret Diplomatic History of the Eighteenth Century', etc. Many shorter ones are buried in rare, old volumes of journals, if ever published at all. Such had also been the fate of the 'Critique of the Gotha Programme': for sixteen years (1875-91) only a few people were even aware of its existence, and it was only in 1891 that it finally saw print in the 'Neue Zeit'. Nor has it been re-edited since, except in a French translation as a separate pamphlet. Yet few Marxist documents are more interesting than this one. Besides some economic treatises which offer precise definitions of the economic theories of Marx, hardly any of his statements characterize Marxian socialism better. It states with utmost authenticity - not only in the opinion of Marx but, to my mind, objectively speaking as well – that Marxism and state socialism are not only not identical, but are mutually exclusive opposite formulations of both the future order of society, and of the forms and contents of the present-day working-class movement. This statement was very timely in 1875 – and that is why it remained secret; but it is topical even today. Perhaps more so than ever. If we want to differentiate clearly between the various tendencies within the contemporary working-class movement, we could hardly find a method more appropriate than to compare their respective attitudes towards the state. In our times of political working-class movements and of great parliamentary labour parties, and in an era of increasingly omnipotent states' all-round intervention, the attitude towards the state is of immediate relevance. It has become the most universal and most urgent practical problem which affects all other actions of the parties and labour organizations and reveals most clearly their true nature.

If we want to discover the nature of parties and political tendencies we should refrain from directing our attention to programmes, pamphlets, theories, that is to words. What Marx states in the Gotha letter: 'a single step by the actual movement is worth more than a dozen programmes' is a profound truth, which might well serve as a motto for every honest party programme. But it is likewise certain that this slogan would incur the fate of all other party principles: it would remain but pale theory, a dead letter, good enough to adorn the banner of the party and recruit new members, yet it would prevail only as far as it suits immediate party interest. Few facts have rendered public life more difficult to bear for many than the discrepancy between loudly proclaimed theories and practical reality – the most characteristic manifestation of contemporary politics. This manifestation is so general, so widespread in all political parties that it is impossible to see it as mere coincidence, or to ascribe it to human evilness or inadequacy. The causes of it seem to belong to the very nature of political parties and prevail on working-class parties not less. This fact becomes clearer day by day. Hence questions inevitably arise: what is a political party? What is the significance of controlling the state – the goal of every political party – for the working-class movement? Does this goal and the means to its achievement, the political party, embrace the entire workers' movement, or are there tasks and objectives of the working class which do not fit into the framework of a party? What, then, is the true, genuine, workers' movement? And what is the role of the political party within it?

There are a whole range of questions, related to the statement quoted from Marx, far more extensive in its connotations than could be solved within the limits of an introduction. After all, it includes all the practical problems of contemporary socialism, especially the issue of state socialism, around which, whether admittedly or not, most of the struggles of the various tendencies of socialism are taking place.

In every modern state where the proletariat is organized for mass action, the working-class movement is divided into basically two branches: the so-called economic or trade union movement and the so-called political movement. Each of these contains two clearly distinguishable tendencies: one advocates the principle of the autonomous organization of the working class, independently of other classes, furthermore, in contrast and in conflict with them; whereas the other tendency strives to find room for the workers' movement within the framework of the economic and political organizations of the upper classes. These tendencies and forms appear in the most diverse nuances and colours, and vary greatly in importance from country to country. The political traditions, the specific economic development, the demographic peculiarities, and many other factors interact to determine whether in a given country an autonomous trade union organization arose sooner and grew stronger, or, as in another, the autonomous political organization of the working class prevailed, or in a third, both of them together, or, in a fourth, the masses of workers may be still completely subordinated to the objectives of other classes. From this point of view I am perfectly justified in speaking of an English, a French, a German, or some other type of workers' movement.

At the early stage of the European workers' movement the socialists attempted to bring about a uniform organization of the movements in various countries. Of course, the International was one such attempt. So are the international socialist and trade union congresses of more recent years: their main purpose is to decide on general directives applicable to the working-class movement in every country. Nevertheless, the differences continue to be considerable both in theory and in practice.

Still, one cannot help noticing that one of the outstanding principles of German socialism has struck root in many countries and has contributed powerfully to the trend towards unification. This principle is that the two kinds of organization of the working class, the economic and the political, are of equal value, and are necessary and complementary forms of the same struggle. One is the weapon for obtaining immediate economic benefits and improvements in the working conditions, the other is intended to compel the state to exert power on behalf of the general social, cultural and political interests of the working class. The economic power of the working class is the base, but its advance is made smoother by political power, until the dictatorship of the proletariat will crown the process with the achievement of socialism.

The concept of an autonomous working-class movement evolved slowly. Some Marxists claim that its origins are to be found in 'The Communist Manifesto'. The phrase that 'every class struggle is a political struggle' would be the starting point and proof of this interpretation. But this is proof a posteriori. In fact, the formulation of the principle about the working class's need to organize itself as an independent party and to strive for control of parliament independently does not appear in the 'Manifesto', nor in the journals edited by Marx and Engels in 1848. It has long remained alien to the praxis of the workers' movement; in fact, the militant class movements had always placed emphasis on immediate economic struggle by which the direct violent revolution was to be prepared and provoked. The defeat of the revolutions of 1848 and the reaction that followed have indeed considerably cooled the fire of revolutionary zeal among the masses, but not in the minds of Marx and Engels. They continued to expect the revolution. Not they, but Lassalle decided in the early 1860s, that the aim of the workers' movement should be to influence legislation and eventually to control it. As a means to that end Lassalle posited universal suffrage and, wherever necessary, the struggle to obtain it; he had very little regard for the economic struggle.

The unquestionable success of the propaganda of Lassalle was convincing enough to the German Marxists, although the two factions of the socialist movement united only after many years of parallel development and of much, mainly personal, quarrelling. In his critical letter Marx, the most directly involved theoretical leader, indicates which of the tendencies prevailed in the process of unification. There can be no doubt that the praxis of the party today is, indeed, purely Lassallean.

Nevertheless, the theory of the new party contained some new elements. The emphasis on class struggle became more pronounced, the faith in the omnipotence of the state grew weaker. But the old formula for the working class and the class struggle got transformed in the process. No longer is it claimed that the workers form a class in the process of the struggle aimed at the protection of their wages against the bourgeoisie, and 'constantly form associations, in order to be equipped for the occasional uprisings'; but rather that the political party, fighting electoral battles and amassing votes, will be the means for coalescing the workers into a class and representing their class interests. The economic organizations and autonomous economic creations of the working class are not seen to constitute the nucleus of the future society which, according to Marx and others, has to evolve within the womb of the old society, but the party which, once it has attained political rule, will bring about the economic order through the power of the state. That is all the functions and the historical mission for the creation of socialism, which Marxism has assigned to the fighting organizations of the working class, have now been transferred to the state, or rather, to the political party organized for gaining control of it.

Of course, there was no lack of attempts to reconcile the new principle of the workers' political party with the theory of class struggle. The essence of the nature of the parties became an object of research. History has shown that political parties have always represented economic interests, that is classes; hence the struggle of parties was simply the transfer of the class struggle to the political arena; party and class were basically identical formations; and the party was an organ of the class struggle in the same right as, say, the trade unions. Perhaps even more so,

because its goals and means are more universal. Thus the economic movement performs only preparatory tasks; it guarantees
them through government and creates the whole structure of
future society. The party is the true agent of class struggle.

This theory of political parties, however, contains two basic
errors. As to the past, the error is a bold generalization and, to
the present, it simply does not accord with facts. Both errors
shake the theory to its very foundations.

When historical arguments are brought up to justify the theory
of parties, an essential factor is easily forgotten: that the system
of government in which political parties have assumed such significance in recent times, to wit the democratic representative
state, is barely more than two hundred years old, and barely
even a hundred on the continent. The role of the political party
in a representative system is quite different from its role where
representation is unknown; hence it has to be quite different from
what it had been, say, a century ago.

It is not necessary to repeat the debate regarding the theory of
representation at this juncture. It suffices to observe that the
period prior to parliamentarian rule did not know the principle of
representation, or knew it to a very limited extent. Hence every
action of the political parties in those times, even if initiated by
a brave minority, required the direct and active participation of
every single member of the party. Every party action entailed
responsibility and danger to every party member. In that age,
therefore, the political parties had a better chance of being the
political exponents of class struggle, indeed, they often were.

In a parliamentary regime the function of political parties is
quite different. The masses of those who, according to the class
theory of political parties, constitute the politically organized
class, encounter but seldom, sometimes not even during an entire
generation, a situation where they would have to take a direct
stand for their class interest, through action entailing responsibility and danger. The direct function of the masses is normally
limited to periodical elections, and some material contribution to
the party, but even this does not usually involve direct intervention. Since the vote is secret in most countries, it does not
entail risks even at such rare intervals; and the occasional material contributions do not affect government directly, but constitute the material base of the intermediaries between the masses
and the state.

Wherever there is a parliamentary system a new, hitherto unknown, class of participants in public affairs has evolved. The
existence of this class is quite obvious in the most highly developed democracies – the United States and Great Britain – but it
also exists, perhaps under a more patriarchal and sentimental
guise, in the states which assumed parliamentary forms only
recently. This is the new class of professional politicians. Those
who compose this class are usually no worse but rather more
intelligent than those whose interest they are supposed to represent. It includes members of parliament who come mainly from the

ranks of professionals, the great grey mass of agitators, political agents and party officials among whom but one or two individuals, members of some persecuted party, reach a level surpassing the moral and intellectual level of the general population. This class of professional politicians has become the actual, personal and direct fighter of political struggle in the modern democracies. They are to be found where the parties ultimately confront one another, in parliament and in government, or where the basis of the strength of political parties is determined, in electoral campaigns. They share in the government and make the state attractive or unattractive to the masses. They write the party programmes, they shape the slogans that render thinking superfluous, they provide patronage through public contracts, offices, privileges; they dictate the laws, and the administration obeys them. It is not the political parties, but their representatives who run the state and nothing moderates the rule of the professional politician except the executive organs, the power of bureaucracy.

This does not mean that political parties cannot be the expression of economic interests. Undoubtedly, most of the time they are. But what constitutes the clear and strict differentiation of class interests in the competition between parties, in the wrestling aimed at seducing each other's voters, in the efforts of the professional politicians to outbid each other with streams of words? Even contemporary parties could not exist without attempting to meet the needs of the masses; at the same time, the politicians could not exist if they were to represent but a single strictly differentiated economic class. Nowadays the battles of political parties take place inside parliament, and the basis of parliamentary power and influence resides in numbers, in the democratic principle of majority rule; who could struggle for parliamentary influence if he were to remain forever in a minority, however splendid his isolation?

Thus it is not possible to compare contemporary political parties with parties that existed before the representative system; or to infer from the clear-cut class character of former parties, that contemporary parties likewise bear a class character. The system of representation has dug a deep trench between the past and the present; in the parliamentary system the party cannot be class representation.

It is argued, on the other hand, that it is precisely the minority, that is the propertied classes, that make this claim and, consciously or unconsciously, use all their power to put it into practice. Otherwise they could never recruit enough voters from the propertyless classes to obtain a majority. On the other hand, the masses organized on the basis of the class struggle, that is contemporary Social Democratic parties, not only proclaim the principle of class party, but actually constitute a strict class representation and compel others, the bourgeois parties, to show their true colours. In other words, the entry of the Social Democratic party into parliament and its gain of strength therein allegedly brings about the same differentiation in the political arena as can be observed on the battlefield of economic struggles.

The examination of the composition of the major Social Democratic parties indicates that the foundation of this statement is no
more sound than the historical argument. From reliable statistics,
partly official, partly private, based on the votes in recent
elections in the German Empire, Austria, France and Italy, two
facts are brought into relief. One is that every significant bourgeois party receives a considerable portion of its votes from
industrial workers; the other, far more important, is that a major
segment of those who vote for the Social Democratic party do not
come from the working class, but from other social classes.

The first fact, namely that there are many workers among the
supporters of parties serving the propertied classes, hardly
requires numerical proof. If this were not the case, universal
suffrage would indeed be equivalent to the end of private property. Since in every country the propertyless far outnumber
those who own property, universal suffrage would theoretically
result in the rule of the propertyless over the propertied ones.
Yet this logical consequence of universal suffrage has never
occurred. What has happened, rather, is that while wealth is in
the hands of fewer and fewer individuals, the bourgeois parties,
even in the most industrialized countries, continue to have numerical superiority. The only explanation can be that large masses
of workers support them with their votes. In the most industrialized province of Italy, in Lombardy, there were 94,000 proletarian
electors during the latest elections, yet the socialist votes numbered only 65,000, and many of these came from the bourgeoisie.
In Puglia the Socialist Party received no more than 9,500 votes
from the 50,000 proletarian electors. And so on.

Much more important are the figures which show the participation of semi-proletarian and bourgeois elements in the Social
Democratic vote. The Social Democratic parties insist that they are
the parties of all the oppressed. It is clear, however, that not all
oppressed people are productive in capitalist society, that not
everyone is a member of the economic working class. The artisans
and small entrepreneurs, hard-pressed by big industry, the
lower echelons of the state and local bureaucracy, certain categories of those who do clerical work, all these people may well be
oppressed, but at a certain level of development of the means of
production they constitute an unproductive stratum. They are by
no means workers, hence they are not legitimate members of a
working-class party. Still, it was possible to determine that of
the 2,107,000 votes which the German Social Democratic Party
received in 1898, no less than 541,000 were bourgeois votes; and
that in 1903, when the party received three million votes, again
about 750,000 were accounted for by bourgeois elements. In both
elections this represents about a quarter of the total vote. At the
1904 elections in Italy the Socialist Party received 326,000 votes,
even though the proletarians eligible to vote numbered 256,000
and many of these, as we have seen, voted for bourgeois parties.
It is obvious that the ratio of semi-proletarian and bourgeois votes
is even higher than in Germany.

But the social composition of the voters in Germany is more significant than in Italy. The theory of class party originated in
Germany, and nowhere was it pushed as insistently as in that
country; nor is there another Social Democratic party in the
world with the following of the German party - hence it is clear
that even after forty years of unparalleled propaganda this party
is still not strictly a class party. It may be only a matter of time
before all organized workers, that is the persons who stand on
the basis of class struggle, vote for the party; but that semi-
proletarians, intellectuals and members of the propertied classes
also vote for it makes it impossible to maintain the fiction of a
class party.

If we discard the theory of the class party we must also dismiss
the theory it supports, namely that the political party is a means
and a part of the class struggle to the same extent as the economic organizations.

In the light of comparative history and of statistical evidence,
we can see that in a democratic republic most conspicuously, but
even in the more progressive representative monarchies, the political party is an occasional alliance to compel the government to
certain actions through the parliament. Hence parties can be the
agents or tools of class struggle only in so far as states and parliaments are. However, the role of the state and of parliament, no
matter how significant they may seem in the everyday struggle,
are much less relevant to social development than some may
presume.

Among the most valuable admonitions of Marx are those by which
the domination of ideologies is finished off. We must deal with
these elsewhere. All I want to say here is that a doctrine which
bases the progress of society on the economic forces of production
cannot coexist with the tenet of the omnipotence of an ideological
construct, the state. Thus it is impossible that the political struggle of the party for control of the state should play the same, let
alone a greater or more universal, role in the progress of society
than the economic struggle.

True class struggle takes place in the area of economic conflict.
That is where the representatives of the material forces of production, the active elements of opposite relations of production,
confront one another: economic classes are not occasional alliances,
not moods, nor slogans, nor heterogeneous groups brought together by professional hypnotists, but original, homogeneous
formations brought about by the compulsion of natural differentiation, the representatives of definite types of relations of production. In the state and in parliament the battle is fought around
the distribution of wealth; in the economic struggle the representatives of different forces of production confront one another.
Which of these forces are the springs of social progress: the
forces of the modes of production, or those of the distribution of
wealth? For Marxism, the philosophy of economic production, there
can be but one answer.

From the point of view of the mental prerequisites of socialism

the economic struggle also seems much more appropriate than the
political movement for educating the working class to socialist
thought and feeling. On the basis of the realist philosophy, to
which Feuerbach contributed the elaboration of historical materialism, we believe that it is mere fantasy and self-delusion to believe
in the possibility of acquiring knowledge from the outside, by
means of logic. It is direct experience, the continual, one might
even say, sensory contact with objective reality that constitutes
the philosopher's stone of our ideas, the only authentic measure
of its truth, the only basis for the unity and identity of being –
that is of objective truth and of thought or subjective reflection
('Denken und Sein'). If this be true for the individual, it is even
more true for the masses. An intellectually outstanding individual
may be capable of discovering the facts on the basis of pure speculation, but the masses are not. The truth of the masses is nothing but the subjective reflection of their immediate situation in the
objective environment, and every other belief or conviction, under
ordinary circumstances, lives only as long as it does not clash
with their sensory experience. If we believe that objective truth
is expressed in socialism, and if we claim that it is not arbitrary
speculation, but the necessary solution of the contradiction between the objective forces of production and the relations of
production, that it is not simply mood and suggestion, but the
only possible ideology of the future order of society – even though
for the time being it can only be expressed through logical
abstraction: then it is impossible to believe that the struggle of
the working class for its own reality, for its economic existence,
could be prepared by anything but the economic struggle. The
consciousness of the working class is raised day by day through
the most direct contact with the contradiction between forces and
relations of production, in which there is no mood nor speculation,
but solely the ineluctable logic of direct economic contradictions.
This economic struggle is everyday existence, everyday action,
everyday experience – the only thorough and reliable training
ground of the souls. Herein lies the overwhelming importance of
the economic movement for the class struggle of the workers and
for socialism.

I do not claim that the economic struggle of the working class,
once launched, would advance unhesitatingly towards class struggle. The economic organization of the workers keeps pace with the
evolution of the working class. 'The Communist Manifesto' describes vividly how class struggle develops from the struggle of
individual workers, of a factory, of the workers of an entire trade
against the individual bourgeois; it describes how the class struggle originates with the smashing of machinery and the burning
down of factories. This process of the class formation of the
workers coincides in time and space with the struggle of the bourgeoisie for political power; in this struggle the proletarians are
the auxiliary troops of the bourgeoisie, against their enemies, the
absolute monarchy and the land-owners.

It seems to me that the political role of the workers indicated by the 'Manifesto' some time ago does not reside, even today, in anything but the construction of political democracy. The economic organization of the proletariat is rendered considerably easier by certain legal and cultural circumstances such as political and civil rights, compulsory education, separation of church and state, etc. Bourgeois democracy, according to its inherent principles, can defeat its adversaries, absolutism and feudalism, only by numerical superiority, and it can attain such superiority only with the help of the proletariat. Hence the workers, as long as they yearn for democracy, are compelled to enter the arena of political action and support the democratic action of the bourgeoisie.

Such is the significance and function of the political party for the class struggle of the workers. Far from being the most direct, let alone the primary organ of class struggle, the workers' political party is formed precisely to support the bourgeoisie in their struggle for political democracy. Class struggle, after all, is fought between economic groups; it must be aimed primarily at the bourgeoisie. But the political struggle is not directed against the enemy of the working class, nor for the social and political organization of the working class - that is, socialism - but exactly for the social and political organization of its enemy, for bourgeois democracy.

Even the most radical phraseology of class struggle or the militant programmes of certain Social Democratic parties cannot alter this fact. To determine the true motives of actions from documents of the past, from the theories of the protagonists, from their programmes, their writings, their views regarding the goals and causes of their struggle is among the most difficult tasks of the historian. He will find that the interpretation given by the actors of history about the changes of their times rarely coincides with the actual events, that there is often an unbridgeable gap between their consciousness and reality. I think that the future historian of today's working-class movement will see the sanguine views about the function of Social Democratic parties as images which do not conform to reality. It is likely that he will find the source of the misapprehension in the above-expressed analysis of the nature of political parties and the essence of the class struggle.

A political workers' party capable of preparing and building bourgeois democracy in order to facilitate the organization of the working class and its class struggle can be a useful agent of social progress. The political party, however, which comes forth with the claim that it is the true class organization of the proletariat, the major and decisive agent of class struggle, which demands the role of leading the working class to socialism, is simply usurping the role that behoves only the economic organization and economic struggle, causes chaos and disorder in the workers' movement, and finally serves the cause of the enemy when the only task of the working class is no longer to strengthen or build bourgeois democracy, but rather to disorganize the already consolidated democratic state, to sweep away the rule of the victorious bourgeoisie with all its political appendages. Hence the role of the parliamentarian workers' party ends where the specific and direct action of the working class begins.

AMERICAN AND EUROPEAN
SOCIALISM

Szabó's article in the 1908 'Népakarat' (People's Will)
almanac, the annual of the Hungarian workers' paper edited
by Elek Bolgár in New York, was translated by Mark Stern
for the 'Daily People' (26 January 1908, p. 5), where it
appeared as the writing of 'Ervin Czabo, Budapest'.
Although, as we know from the correspondence, the article
was written on the request of Bolgár, whom Szabó had helped
to obtain the editorial post in New York, it was not only an
occasional favour. Disappointed in central European Social
Democracy, Szabó began to note the decline of French syndicalism as well and became increasingly interested in the
American working-class movement. As did many of his contemporaries, he expected that the American working class,
connected as it was to the most developed and centralized
capitalism, would proceed, without the detours of parliamentary struggles for liberties that were still on the agenda in
Europe, to the fight for socialism. Here he encourages his
countrymen working in America to participate in that struggle,
not to support petty-bourgeois moralizing complaints about
the trusts but to confront them with strong militant unions.

The 'Népszava', the official organ of the socialist party of Hungary, is read in America as well as in Hungary. Its opinions of
America and American socialism have probably had an influence
on the comrades living there. While the Hungarians living in
America add very little to the promotion of American socialism at
present, the 'Népszava', through them, influences it, however,
to a small extent, at least intermediately. What it says about
America should not be passed over in silence. Recently it discussed the 29 million dollar fine imposed upon the Oil Trust.
    On this occasion it called Rockefeller a scoundrel. Then it went
on to say that Harriman was also a genuine American scoundrel.
Other Trust magnates were not mentioned at the time, or they
would undoubtedly have been treated likewise. I am not quite
certain, I must confess, whether Rockefeller, Harriman and their
associates are really scoundrels, in the same way as I do not know
that they are heroes, industrial kings, phenomenal economic geniuses, etc. - things, I believe, that millionaires are usually called.
I hold that it is possible that geniuses as well as scoundrels may
be found among them, but all of this is of very little concern to
me, as a socialist.

Being a socialist, I am more careful in judging morals. I like to remember Marx's words: That we cannot censure individuals for the existing social conditions, but must trace evils and misery – the monopoly and extortions of the Trust among them – back to the economic system of production. Then again, I remember how our places, or rather our class attitudes, determine our entire moral being, our moral conceptions in the economic system of production.

There are scarcely any moral conceptions which are absolute, or which hold good for the whole of humanity at all times. On the contrary, it can be said that there are numerous actions which are held as good and proper by the proletariat while at the same time the bourgeoisie condemn them as bad and wicked, and vice versa. And why? Simply because, as a general principle, good or bad is determined by a man – and naturally so – from the view-point of his class. For instance, a strike-breaker is regarded as a criminal by the organization of workers, while in the eyes of the employers he is a good man. On the other hand, the employer, who on his own account and of his own free will, improves the conditions of his employees, will be condemned as a traitor by employers at war with labour organization while the labour press praises him. Is it not, therefore, ridiculous to establish moral classifications under such circumstances?

For this reason it would be much better if we set up moral standards for our own guidance only. I, for instance, would regard it as a most heinous crime if an officer of a labour organization should defraud his fellow workers of their funds, and the same would be said of the actions of him who would create dissension among his fellow workers engaged in a battle, thereby causing a break in the ranks; or of him who would violate any other basic principle of socialist morals. But the organizing capitalists, who lock their employees out, crush the small capitalist and build trusts, I shall not call scoundrels, except in such instances in which they violate generally adopted moral convictions – for instance, by commiting rape on children or destroying creations of science or art of historic value. All else is the result of the social – the class struggle; and as we want the class struggle we could not have it without the fighting of the enemy. We strike: they lock us out. 'C'est la guerre'.

'But', some may say, 'these men, by artifical means, increase the prices of the necessities of life. Misery and want follow their actions'. This is true, but I could regard this as a rascality only from such a social viewpoint, which bases all of its social demands on the equal distribution of income – to wit, on the interest of the consumers. Let it be well remembered, in the interests of the consumers, not of the working class exclusively – that is all men, including the millionaire banker and the lord of a manor, for they are also consumers. There was, and there still exists, such social-ism; but there is another, which bases its demands on the pro-duction of wealth, and the interests of the producer, of the wealth-producing classes. This is Marxian socialism, in short: Marxism, which many hear but still only a few understand.

Being a Marxist, I must say that in America the capitalist system of production has reached its highest stage of development.
Marx's much disputed prophecy has been fulfilled in most of the
branches of industry. The means of production are concentrated
in the hands of a few. Looking upon this condition, not from the
viewpoint of the frozen-out small capitalist, nor of the narrow-
minded trade unionist who sees nothing but his immediate material
interest, nor of the teacher of morals and the philanthropist, but
viewing them with the knowledge that the development of the system of producing wealth is the moving spring of social evolution,
I shall not curse nor abuse, but joyfully say: 'Lo, the time is
nearing when the working class shall step into the heritage of the
bourgeoisie'.

The bourgeoisie developed and raised the industrial production
to a stage where it made itself superfluous, for nobody believes
that, from the standpoint of production, there is any need for
Rockefeller or men of his kind. Now that the Trusts form has
been organized by them, and also put into operation in the most
important branches of national production, their social mission is
concluded; their further existence is parasitism, a barrier to progress. It is for the working class to organize within and also
beyond the several concentrated branches of industry, to imbue
its members with the knowledge of the necessity, usefulness and
possibilities, to inspire them with the ideals of the beauty and
grandness of the new order, and to train them for action: and
form the ranks of this enlightened, inspired and trained body
with the organs which shall, in their name, by their consent and
for them, organize and manage the new order of production.

With this we arrive at last at the heart of our theme. It is our
object to draw a comparison between American and European socialism. In order to do this, we needed the Trusts and millionaires,
for indeed, it is through them that the conditions of American
socialism differ from the European. They are the ones who gave
the working class its specific possibilities, determine its respective tactics, the peculiarities of its immediate ends and means.
What occupies the Socialist parties of Europe? First of all, the
struggle waged for the institution of political democracy – universal suffrage, government by parliament, the separation of church
and state, the restriction of the power of bureaucracy and militarism, the abolition of feudal privileges, etc. – almost without
exception things which are really the concern of the bourgeoisie
and which are destined to open the road for the development and
domination of industry and commerce. These problems, no doubt,
deeply affect the working class also but, at the same time, this
struggle brings into the ideology of the working class elements
which are to a great extent capable of blurring its purely socialist
conceptions, coming from its specific condition to such an extent
that they are pushed into the background and entirely ignored.

That the political and civil liberties – for it is these we speak
of: the taking part in the affairs of the government, the freedom
of thought, of conscience, of the press and other things – are

necessary rights and demands of the working class is self-evident, but it is proven that they are not even sufficient to secure immunity from interference on the part of the powers of government in the economic struggles of the working class. The liberties guaranteed by the laws are thrown aside even in the most democratic states whenever the economic struggles of the workers threaten the safety of the economic interests of the employing class as a whole, or its most powerful groups; and it is only the organized economic power of the workers which acts as a barrier against economic oppression. When the working class, in spite of all this, uses up the greatest part of its energy in a continuous struggle to gain these liberties, we, who do not believe that mass movements can be based on error or artificially created issues, must of necessity come to the conclusion that the industrial development of Europe is not sufficiently advanced for the workers to take up the real struggle for the socialist system of production as yet. The struggles adverted to are the necessary forerunners of the latter, and the question is, when and in what measure will the necessity arise for the onslaught against the last fortress of capitalism. This condition, it seems to us, has already arrived in the United States. Feudalism, militarism and bureaucracy being entirely absent, the bourgeoisie of America, in possession of all of the political rights and liberties, has freely developed its economic and political rule, which the Trust magnates are getting ready to crown with the final concentration of wealth production. Every Marxist must see in them the performers of an indispensable social function. In light of this there can be but one problem for the socialist of America. Seeing that political democracy alone will not secure the working class the bare freedom of movement even, that it cannot be a means and a road to the 'dictatorship of the proletariat', or for the transformation of the capitalist social system, they must use their entire agitational power for the strengthening of the economic organization of the working class and the spreading of a knowledge of social problems. The workers of America will be successful against the capitalist state and the Trusts, and march forward via their immediate economic and social demands only in such measure as the strength and clearness of their economic organization are developed. It would be an entirely erroneous position on the part of the socialists if they should demand, for instance, the regulation of the Trusts by the state. This would be a relapse to the narrow viewpoint of the trade unionists and this would also be doing the work of the middle class and small capitalists. This, too, is in opposition to the trend of social development, consequently a suicidal policy. No! let the Trusts develop; let the concentration of wealth production go on in all branches of industry. It will be so much the easier for the working class to be able to substitute the present-day management of production with its own organs. This does not mean that the working class shall stand idly by and watch the extortion and plunder of the Trusts, or even assist them.

The working class must stand and fight together to keep the

Trusts within such limits, where they may not threaten to under-
mine the proper living conditions and the organization of the
workers. The working class, crippled and disorganized, would
not be able to take up the struggle for the founding of the 'socialist system of production'. We believe that the holding of only what
they have will result, in the next few years perhaps, in bloody
battles, in real local struggles which will awaken the American
working class to their class position and social mission, and will
become the strongest leaven in its class organization and its class
struggle. In this conflict the millions of Hungarians living in
America must do their share honourably.

Part III
ON SOCIAL SCIENCE,
HISTORY AND LITERATURE

THE HUNGARIAN REVOLUTION

Among the specifically Hungarian topics of the Marx-Engels volumes, Szabó's attention was mainly drawn to the writings on the 1848 revolution. Ironically, this internationalist, who was most committed to the western patterns of socialism, completed only one book-length manuscript on 'Social and Party Struggles in the Hungarian Revolution of 1848-1849' (published posthumously by O. Jászi). This introductory essay on Engels's comments on 1848 and Marx's critique of Kossuth in exile was the first attempt at the book, Szabó's most significant and original contribution to historical scholarship. The assessment of Kossuth and the events of 1848-49 was, and in some way remains, a crucial issue of political and theoretical orientation in Hungary. The history of the revolution raised almost all the questions Szabó's contemporaries had to face: the form and leadership of the country's transformation from feudalism to capitalism, the problems of the emancipation of the serfs, the conflicts between Magyars and the other nationalities and the relationship between Budapest and Vienna. The majority of the 'left' declared itself uninterested in the Kossuth-cult of the ruling classes, and Szabó was no exception. The cleavage between 'progressive' versus 'national' beliefs was in a way an issue of mutual disinterest. Still, in this essay, Szabó attempted to come to grips with the complex issues of social, political and national conflicts of 1848. While he stood on firm ground when emphasizing - with Marx - the inconsistencies of Kossuth, this typically parochial gentry-made-revolutionary, he often oversimplified the social analysis of the revolution, denying its anti-feudal character. Considering the distortions and sheer forgeries of the official 'national' historians, the polemical overstatements are understandable. Szabó was not the only socialist or Marxist of his times who imagined that only such radical 'bourgeois revolutions' as the French could fulfil the task of opening the way to capitalist transformation. Only in the last few decades, partially following Gramsci's insights based on an Italian course of development not unlike the Hungarian one, did Marxists begin to discuss the different ways of 'incomplete' and 'truncated' transformations in which many elements of the obsolete 'feudal' system manage to survive. Hungarian Marxists - especially during the time of Communist attempts at a 'national front' - criticized his 'one-sidedness'. Present-day Hungarian historians accept much of Szabó's approach,

even though they judge the nobility of 1848 and its leader,
Kossuth, in a more positive sense.
   This article was first published in 'Huszadik Század', vol.
II (1904, pp. 404-14) and also, augmented by notes, in German translation in 'Neue Zeit', pt I (1904/5, pp. 782-7,
811-18). Kautsky found Szabó's comments so novel and
interesting that he suggested a separate publication together
with the Engels articles, but the plan did not materialize. We
have followed the German version.

I

Traditions are so deeply rooted in the minds that they can block
for quite a while the reception of new ideas even if these are of
the utmost importance and interest. The dead are ruling us - in
a good sense and in a bad. And dead truth can terribly hamper
the progress of live truth.
   The history of Hungary is a classic example of a vanity fair of
obsolete traditions. One is appalled by seeing what kind of stories
are stuffed into the heads of schoolchildren, what is being called
Hungarian history in the secondary schools and what kind of
ideas are disseminated among the public by journalists and so-
called historians. If one did not know that besides the inherent
force of tradition another major force is at work, namely the
influence of that class whose interest it is to colour the history of
the nation in a definite way, one could not understand how that
jumble of irrelevant anecdotes and false explanations, which is
being styled Hungarian national history, had been constructed.
   It would be a major service to the cultural development of the
country to clean from the minds those cobwebs which have been
spun by the historians and permit them to see the past of the
country clearly and truly: this would even offer a glance at the
conditions which underlie the future! But who shall bury the dead
haunting among us? Who shall expel the ghosts and spectres?
There is a mighty force in all of them.
   Take the Hungarian Revolution. The eyewitnesses of this great
event are still with us. One does not need to undertake careful
research for the vestiges and try to reconstruct the events with
the help of fantasy and mental experiments, as one has done for
the history of centuries long past. This history is here, at an
arm's length from us and still so far away, if we measure distance
with the standards of truth.
   The Hungarian Revolution of 1848 has been successfully depicted
as the eruption of the pure yearning of a whole nation for freedom,
as an event in which one social class crowned the unique merits
they had acquired in the struggles of many centuries by a deed of
unparalleled altruism. It is seen as a great upheaval in which the
poet's visionary words came true: 'Great times. The Scripture is
fulfilled: one flock, one house - one faith on earth: liberty!...
One soul, one heart, one arm... the fatherland is one!' (Petőfi's
poem, 1848).

But was it really so? History does not know miracles. There is no record of any event that would have wielded into one a people divided by divergent interests, nor of a class that would have resigned its privileges out of sheer magnanimity. Would Hungarian history have seen these miracles happening for the first time? We do not intend to denigrate the importance of the Hungarian Revolution by raising these questions. If there is an event in the history of the nation of which it can be proud then it is certainly 1848. And if the past ever permits conclusions for the future then the magnificent struggles of the revolution may nourish promising hopes. But that image of the revolution into which official history has cast it, those traditions of 1848 which are being hailed by the official propaganda neither grant the merits to whom they are due, nor offer such insights which can be utilized in mapping out the roads to a better future.

The Hungarian Revolution can only be understood if it is perceived of as a phase in the class struggle between the aristocracy and the lesser nobility.(1)

This class struggle was neither a uniquely Hungarian phenomenon, nor did it begin in the period preceding 1848. We find evidence for its beginnings in the thirteenth century, when the great feudal estates emerged, and we can detect its innumerable traces in Hungarian laws over the centuries. This struggle can be encountered in all countries where the slow development of industry and commerce forced the crown to look for other support than that of the bourgeoisie; in such countries it was always one part of the nobility which served as the ally of the monarchy against the other. In Hungary, the aristocratic great land-owners became the allies of the ruling House of Habsburg, hence the recurrent 'national' uprisings were the experiences of the class struggle of the minor nobility whose shoulders supported the 'national' anti-kings, such as Szapolyai, Báthory, Thököly and Rákóczi.(2) That these movements received - only in the nineteenth century, of course - the attribute, 'national', was warranted by one fact alone: that they happened to be fighting against a foreign ruling dynasty as the main ally of the Hungarian aristocracy. These struggles could never have been 'national' in the modern sense of the word.

This is, of course, no base for praise nor for blame. The national idea is a relatively young notion, a reflection of that economic revolution which began to spread its wings on the European continent at the beginning of the last century. Being, as it is, intrinsically connected with the establishment of the bourgeoisie as a class, the reproaches of chauvinist critics of the Hungarian nobility (such as Béla Grünwald (3) and others) are as unjust as the scorn of the critics of nationalism is misplaced, when addressed to the Hungarian nobility of the eighteenth century. The Hungarians could not have been national before the national idea was born. Obviously, then, references to the Hungarian nobility as a protagonist of historical progress, in the sense that they had preserved 'national' autonomy or the 'national' character of the

country, as so often emphasized by our patriotic authors, do not
make sense, at any rate not before the nineteenth century. That
the Hungarian aristocracy was national has not been maintained
even by its best friends and most devoted servants; that, however, the minor nobility was also lacking any national sentiment
is not difficult to demonstrate either.

The reign of Joseph II is often referred to as having given the
impetus to a national 'resurrection' when it forced the nobility to
defend its constitutional rights. Where was that nobility which is
supposed to have been moved by national instincts into this
battle? Was it perhaps the one which, 'during the reign of Maria
Theresa, in the counties where the language of the people was
not Magyar, began to use the language of the peasants and was
about to forget Hungarian'?(4) Or was it that of which 'the national feeling was suffocated by estate-consciousness'? Was it those
Hungarian nobles who felt greater solidarity with the Serbian,
Romanian, Croat or Slovak nobles whom they regarded - in the
spirit of a juridical fiction - as Hungarian gentlemen, than with
the Magyar peasants'? Or were they perhaps those 'Magyar landlords who dislike the Magyar serfs because they are more conscious, tolerate tyranny less and insist on their rights, and who,
therefore, frequently... expel and dislodge their Magyar serfs
and settle more servile and patient Slavs and Romanians' in their
places?

Did Joseph II really endanger that Hungarian language which
'was used nowhere in public life because it has been long ago
extirpated from Hungarian society', or did he hurt the national
feelings of those nobles who 'although they did not accept German
as the constitutionally legal language but neither did they Hungarian', or those of the counties which 'still twenty-seven years
later in 1811 had declared on the Diet that the Hungarian language
could not be made an official language because among their noble
members there is nobody who would speak it'? Or did the king
offend those who held Germanization 'rather an injustice than a
national insult and were worried that deserving patriots would
lose their positions just because they did not know German, but
were ready to transact business in German and of whom not a
single one has resigned his office for this reason'.

All these were quite obviously not driven to resistance against
the reforms of Joseph by the national idea. They defended not the
national idea but the interests of the noble estate which appeared
to be threatened by Joseph's certainly illegal, but essentially
modern reforms. If there was a class which in those times actually,
though unconsciously, acted as a defensive wall for the endangered nationality, then it was the peasantry, since the nobility
'virtually ceased to speak Hungarian everywhere where there
were no Hungarian peasants'.

If, however, the defence of the noble constitution against the
Habsburg dynasty was a merit, then this has to be divided equit-
ably amongst the Hungarians and the few 'long ago disintegrated
unconscious nationalities'. (Naturally only to the extent that they

were nobles themselves and thus in solidarity with the Hungarian
gentlemen.) Why, then, were the Magyars 'revolutionary' and the
Slavs 'counter-revolutionary'?
Because, says Engels, only the Hungarian nation was a factor
of progress which has become active in the course of history and
remained capable of survival ever since. Engels touches here on
the most difficult problem of Hungarian history and anticipates its
solution by saying that the Magyars, together with the Germans,
have defended the country from becoming Turkish; the Magyars
managed to develop a national bourgeoisie and they together with
the Magyar-feeling Germans took over the intellectual and commercial leadership in the country. In contrast, the Slavs did not
manage to develop a bourgeoisie and fell intellectually and materially under the overlordship of the Magyars.
In our minds, this dichotomy does not stand up to historical
criticism. What Engels has to say about the Magyars in the historical process is not correct and it is not true that the Magyars,
even less the Magyar bourgeoisie, represented historical progress.
What are the objective criteria of the historical progress of a
nation? The expansion of the sphere of transport, the development of economic techniques, the differentiation of economic
functions and increased differentiation of the population, a more
equal and wider dispersion of education, and so forth. In all
these areas, Hungary did not manage to make any mentionable
progress since the Turkish occupation of the country. Up to the
death of Matthias I (1490), the country kept pace more or less
with the more educated west. Urban burgher strata developed
which transmitted an active trade to the west; the technology of
agriculture, introduced by the first Christian missionaries, was
not seriously inferior to that of the western countries; the country had its own culture, high education and a lively intellectual
exchange with her neighbours. King Matthias's court was a meeting place of scholars, poets and artists of European fame, the
library he founded is world renowned.(5) With the Turkish conquest
all this came to an end.(6) The religious and defensive wars, the
class struggle between the aristocracy and the gentry which led
to recurrent civil wars have swept away the results of economic
development, and the cruel enserfment of the peasants after the
great uprising of 1514 eliminated the overwhelming majority of the
population from the number of those interested in independence
and cultural progress.(7) The cities regressed into poverty-
stricken market towns, got petrified in their narrow particularist
interests, and lost their earlier influence on legislation. There
was no splendid royal court, and since in those times arts and
sciences flourished only in cities and royal residences, they found
no shelter in Hungary. The last connection which could have
helped the intellectual invigoration of Hungary from abroad had
been severed. This absolute stagnation lasted for three centuries.
   At the Diet of Pozsony (1687), the dynasty and the aristocracy
finally achieved complete victory.(8) When the financial and power
interests of the absolute monarchy and the economic development

of its other countries (above all, Austria) was given preference,
then Hungary was obliged to accept this secondary position since
there were no social strata in the exhausted and impotent nation
which could have made the necessary sacrifices for progress. Not
the nobility, nor the bourgeoisie, but the monarchy took the historical initiative.

The reigns of Maria Theresa and Joseph II mobilized all forces
in order to liberate Hungary from the oppressive fetters of feudalism and to force her on the road to industrial development; but
all attempts failed because of the feebleness and narrow-minded-
ness of the bourgeoisie and the resistance of the nobility defend-
ing its privileges to the last.(9) The most important obstacle in
the development of agriculture was the oppression and the ignorance of the serfs. The serf could not and the landlord would not
invest in their estates. Boon work ('robot') used up, mainly because of the bad conditions of the roads, the most valuable time
of the serfs. The tyranny of the manorial courts held them in
continuous insecurity. They were uninterested in their work, and
the yield of Hungarian soil remained far behind that of the neigh-
bouring countries. The burghers held fast to their guild privileges. The cities were so scarce that they could gain no significant
influence on the local administration of the counties, hence the
roads and bridges, more or less kept up from the taxes of the
serfs, were in a disastrous condition. How would crafts and commerce have developed under such conditions?

Maria Theresa attempted to loosen the chains of the serfs, but
the nobles resisted. She tried to reduce the burdens of the peasants by having the nobles share the taxes, but they did not yield
from their privilege of freedom of taxation. She ordered the foundation of elementary schools but the nobles preferred to leave the
peasants uneducated. She tried to disseminate knowledge about
rational economy but the local administrators were uninterested.
Almost annually statutes were issued about the repair of roads,
but the counties consciously neglected these means of transport-
ation in order to hamper other landlords in competing with them on
the grain market.

The reign of Joseph II was, indeed, a veritable tragic drama.
Ruthlessly did he try to cross the parochialism of the counties and
cities, to modernize the administration of justice, to abolish the
guilds, to liberate the serfs, to introduce a free press and religious tolerance. After his death, the noble reaction demolished the
entire work of his life. The old privileges, the autonomy of the
noble counties were guaranteed, the guilds and the seigneurial
courts restored and all reforms cancelled.(10)

Is it a wonder that, under such conditions, the ruling dynasty
became fully alienated from the country and placed the emphasis
of development on Austria? That they concentrated at any cost on
the economic growth of that part of the realm? What the Hungarian
nobility refused and what the bourgeoisie of Hungary was unable
to offer, the expenses of a state administration, were collected
from the developed manufacture and commerce of Austria, for which

she received Hungary as her colony. This is the origin of the
famous customs politics of the Habsburg dynasty.(11)
     As Engels's view, that the Hungarians, while protecting their
nationality and grasping the historical initiative, became a 'revolutionary' nation, is incorrect, so it is unjust to apostrophize the
Slavic nations as 'anti-revolutionary'. While, for example, the
tone of the Serb national congress of 1744 was not essentially
different from the contemporary politics of 'gravamina' at the
Hungarian Diet, in some points it was more national and in a few
even surprisingly democratic.(12) It contained a request for
further undisturbed enjoyment of privileges, protested against
the 'really inhuman oppression and torture' of Serbs by Hungarian landords and wrote that the Serbian nation was, as is well
known, not a servile, but a free people with the right to settle
and move about freely. They protested against the tithe to the
Roman Catholic Church and demanded rather that it should be,
together with the general tax of the Serbs, collected in a national
treasury which should be administered by elected and trusted
persons and would serve to pay the bishops, finance schools and
churches, and cover other community expenses. Here we see the
same defence of traditional rights as by the Hungarians but with
a more national and democratic tendency. The Hungarian Diet's
policy of protecting the nobility's interests did not include any of
these elements and was much less in harmony with the demands
of historical progress. Engaged in this struggle alone, the Hungarian nobility refused to grasp the historical initiative.
     How, then, can we explain the reform period during which there
was more political life in Hungary than in the whole of the German
Empire, and the feudal mould of the old Hungarian constitution
was much better exploited in the interests of democracy than the
modern frame of some of the German constitutions? Where did the
pacified Hungarian people, unused to any struggle, get the
energy to fight through their courageous revolution? What were
the forces, which were the new factors that appeared on the field
of battle?
     It is not our task at this point to inquire into the moving forces
of the Hungarian Revolution. We have to limit ourselves to a few
items which shed light on Engels's commentaries.
     Hungarian historiography is unequivocal in dating the period of
'national reform' from the year 1825, the foundation of the Hungarian Academy of Sciences.(13) It is easy enough to reduce ad
absurdum the explanation implied herein, that the whole issue of
social reform and national independence was caused by the unfolding of national literature. It is typical of the haughtiness of poets
and the stubbornness of literary historians to regard the foundation of an academy of writers as the pivot of great social transformations. Academies by their very nature serve conservative
interests, even if not always consciously, through the sheer fact
that they defend the old obsolete science and its representatives
against the new and emerging science and the young generation
of authors. Would the Hungarian Academy have been an exception

that was unjustly attacked by the revolutionary writers and
scorned and despised by the radical poets such as Petöfi?
In fact Hungarian literature was, until the 1840s, by no means
national and even less revolutionary, even if we understand reformist as revolutionary. The famous bodyguards of Maria Theresa,
the protagonist of Hungarian literary renaissance, and all Hungarian authors of the eighteenth century, Rádai, Baron Amadé,
Baron Orczy, Barcsay, Count Teleki, Bessenyei, Ányos, Faludi,
Révay, Virág and all the rest, nobles and churchmen, sang with
their feeble voices the praise of the nobility and of the dynasty.(14)
There was no trace of national spirit anywhere. The great struggles of ideas abroad did not reach their ears. One or other may
have spoken about the humanitarian ideals of idealist philosophy,
but in the same breath they praised the satisfied and happy poverty of the Hungarian peasant. Even Kazinczy, the most famous
author of this time and the great innovator of the language, could
not tolerate patriotism in poetry and actually denounced it quite
decisively; the translation of the Germanizing statutes of Joseph
II was 'an enjoyment' for him, as he admitted.(15) After the Diet
of 1811, patriotic poetry became totally silent, although in the
first years of the reign of Francis I it did briefly appear in form
of praise of noble gloire. Patriotic poetry received a new impetus
by the great epic poem of Vörösmarty's 'Zalán futása' (The Flight
of Zalán) (1823), but even he only brought 'the old glory from
the nightly shadows to the light'.(16) Democratic ideas do not
appear anywhere in the literature and the few who believed in the
future of the nation did not expect the dawn from the reforms.
Even if the idea of nationality in the form of equality and independence of the whole Magyar-speaking people or the political
trends of the west had been propagated in the poetry of those
times: what kind of impact would they have had? Hungarian
authors had barely any readers. The first drama by József Katona,
'Bánk Bán' (Banus Bank), in which national bitterness and the
sufferings of the serfs were brought to the scene with dramatic
force, was not staged anywhere. Only a few copies were sold from
the first edition of 'Zalán futása'. With the exception of the last
two or three years before the revolution hardly any Hungarian
book had been published without the support of an aristocratic
sponsor or on the basis of subscription. How revolutionary or
national could that tone have been which found the approval of a
Hungarian magnate, and how wide the circle in which a book could
be distributed by the friends of the author soliciting signatures?
In a word, neither in the preparation of national nor in that of
political reform, did Magyar belles lettres play a significant role.
After Bacsányi, the only one who empathized with the ideals of
the French Revolution, Petöfi was the first national and revolutionary Hungarian author in a European sense, but his influence
was not felt before the mid-1840s.(17)
    If one would still like to assign the merit for the reform to a
person and to a literary work, the name of Count Stephen Széchenyi comes to mind,(18) whose essay on 'Hitel' (Credit) (1830)

opened the agitation for bourgeois reforms. For him the idea of
nationality meant not lamentations over long past military glories
but, similarly to western Europe, an ideal that articulates the
economic and social regeneration of the country and a moral
demand which mobilizes the necessary self-sacrificing spirit
against the restricting and hampering forces of inertia. However,
even Széchenyi, who subscribed to the ideas of the classical economist of bourgeois society, Adam Smith, and of its classical philosopher, Bentham, synthesized the necessities of a bourgeois
society in a peculiar way with the interests of his own class.
While he sincerely demanded the abolition of serfdom and of
'aviticitas',(19) the development of manufacturing and commerce,
he wished that this enormous economic revolution, which would
liberate a class from civic slavery and make another new class
emerge in its stead, should not overthrow the existing political
power structure. The new Hungary was supposed to emerge in
concert with the dynasty and the preservation of the constitutional
and social overlordship of the aristocracy. This incompatibility of
his realistic economic and his utopian political programmes, is the
key to the tragedy of Count Széchenyi.
   Széchenyi did not see that even if he could gain the support of
the aristocracy for his reform programme and convince them to
work for it, this could not be achieved without dissolving those
ties which had bound the core of the Hungarian high nobility to
the monarchy in the course of many centuries of joint struggle.
The dynasty had, by this time, an entirely different attitude towards the progress of Hungary than it had a few decades earlier.
The times of Maria Theresa and Joseph II were long past. The
tempest of the French Revolution and the Napoleonic Wars aroused
the reaction: its centre was Austria, its torch-bearer Metternich,
the true ruler of the empire. Had the aristocracy decided to follow
the course of reforms, it would have had to choose between the
court which secured their domination and Széchenyi whose economic projects would have endangered this supremacy. Széchenyi
did not see that besides the aristocracy there was only one class
in Hungary which he could address: the lesser nobility. Széchenyi,
the aristocrat, hated the Hungarian gentry passionately and despised them. The centuries-old class struggle of these forces
clashed in his person. This, however, did not change the fact that
his ideas could get roots only in so far as they spread in the
circles of the common nobility. As the popularity of his reforming
ideas grew so, inevitably, did the traditional hatred against the
dynasty and the aristocracy which stood in the way of the very
same reforms. This is the core of his tragic fate: Széchenyi could
not build on the one side without on the other side demolishing his
own faulty construction.
   There was another conflict beyond this. While through his personal failure Széchenyi became politically more and more conservative and a spokesman of dynastic interests, the power of the
contradiction and the heat of the battle pushed Kossuth, this typical representative of the lesser nobility, steadily to the left in the

direction of democracy and anti-Austrian sentiments. Here lies
the origin of the close connection between the ideas of social
reform and of national independence which reached its completion
and sanction in 1848 through the final political victory of the
lesser nobility and the war of independence.

It would be a complete error to believe that the revolution could
have changed the pre-1848 political balance of power in any way
other than by replacing the domination of the aristocracy with
that of the lesser nobility. When the last feudal Diet of 1847 tore
down the legal barriers on the road to the development of a bourgeois society, it could not hand over political power to the
bourgeoisie or the peasantry, nor even to a new parliamentary
coalition that the representatives of these classes and the lesser
nobility would have formed in opposition to the aristocracy and
the dynasty. This could not happen because a bourgeoisie barely
existed and the peasantry, after many centuries of oppression,
was politically entirely immature; therefore the struggle for power
could end only with the victory of one of the two old opponents.
The lesser nobility carried the day, at least until the end of the
war of independence. The origins of the 1848 legislation and even
more the implementation of the laws proves this beyond any doubt.

Formally, the laws of 1848 are very similar in character to western bourgeois reforms: equality before the law, popular representation, parliamentary government, freedom of the press, etc.;
exactly the same as in France, Belgium or in the Frankfurt parliament. But we ought not to forget that the overwhelming part of
the political reforms was not the fruit of the spontaneous will of
the Estates. When the revolution broke out the masses of the
lesser nobility were no closer to the idea of democracy than the
aristocracy. Only a few young people were enthusiastic for the
radical ideas of the west, while even the leaders of the opposition
differed from the conservatives mainly in regard to the speed of
progress. The issue of the agrarian reform was an exception: it
had become a concern of all, high and lesser nobles alike. At the
elections to the Diet of 1841, the demand of general taxation was
defeated in almost all counties; the nobility resisted it. However,
at the Diet of 1843-44, the magnates and the common nobles
agreed unanimously to codify the right of non-nobles to property,
though their eligibility to offices was accepted by the Lower House
only after the magnates had done so, 'as if they were ashamed'.
In the Diet of 1847, both houses passed the laws on general taxation and the voluntary commutation of seigneurial dues; the
abolition of 'aviticitas' was actually proposed by Pál Somsich, the
leader of the conservative government party.

Clearly, the general economic misery, the inferior value of servile labour, the low prices and slack trade of agrarian products -
imposed by Austrian customs policy - and the necessity for credit
knocked the economic reform into the majority of the nobles, high
and low. The same general consensus was, in turn, in full support
of the political privileges of the nobility, barely assailed even by
the opposition. Only a small number of young intellectuals such as

Petőfi, Táncsics, Pál Vasvári, followers of the French socialists
(Fourier, Lamennais, Cabet, Blanc) demanded a democratic transformation of the constitution. Kossuth himself went out of his way
to assure the nobility of the moderate plans of the opposition when
in 1847, Bertalan Szemere proposed the bill on general taxation.
'The Hungarian nobility', so Kossuth said, 'has been ordained
to be the foundation of the nation by a thousand years of history.
That Hungary became what Hungary is, is its work. The Hungarian nobility has never learned to bear a yoke, never let the golden
thread of freedom fall out of its hands and never granted full
rights to absolutism. All this is the work of the Hungarian nobility.' After these somewhat peculiar words from the mouth of a
democratic leader Kossuth continued:

> I ask you, who could be so foolish as to want to destroy the
> political status of this nobility? We, certainly not.... No, we
> wish that the nobility retains in the public life of this nation
> that political weight to which it is called through its history,
> its property, its experiences in constitutional life and through
> the thousands of conditions which are enmeshed in the cen-
> turies... I do not wish that the nobility be destroyed, but
> rather that it be among the rest of the citizenry as the faith-
> ful first-born among the brothers whose lead conveys self-
> assurance to the siblings. A commander of the nation it shall
> not be, a leader of it, it can be: a splendid vocation which it
> ought to retain.

This radical speech was delivered on 29 November 1847, three and
a half months before the democratic revolution. No less characteristic is the way in which the representation of the cities was
debated in the Lower House shortly before the revolution in January and February 1848.(20)
    All this proves that even if some men of the opposition in the
Diet were more radical than their party, the attitude to democratic
reform was far from being so favourable as to have led to the laws
of March. External events had to force legal and political transformations in the wake of the economic reform: they were the
February Revolution in Paris and the March Days in Pest.
    The news of the Paris Revolution of 23 February reached Pozsony
just when the opposition, disheartened by a defeat in the question
of the administrators, was about to embark on the old politics of
'gravamina' and let the fruits of many years' struggle be buried
in the mud of constitutional debates. The upset of the government
caused by news of the Paris events was first utilized by Kossuth.
On 3 March, he submitted a draft resolution containing the well-
known demands of the opposition. The Lower House passed it
unanimously, which was the less difficult as the draft went only in
a few points beyond oft-debated demands. However, the issue of
a parliamentary government was raised for the first time. Otherwise, the tone of the address was by no means resolute, and the
speech of Kossuth was full of dynastic phrases: 'We wish that the

splendour of the ruling dynasty be eternal.... My proposals are based on a dynastic point of view and I thank God that this point of view is closely connected with the interest of our fatherland.... My proposal is dictated by my devotion to the dynasty', and so on. Kossuth and the parliamentary opposition abided by the road of 'wise' moderation even when the House of Magnates refused to pass the bill. Not even the news of the Vienna Revolution of 13 March moved Kossuth. 'We have been', so spoke he to the Estates, 'granted the sublime task, to lead the movements wisely, and we have to be concerned that their reins remain in our hands; because only then can we proceed on the constitutional path. Once they are torn from our hands, then only God knows the consequences. Therefore it is salutary that our representations reach the throne before news of the events has spread in the country.... No one should dare beyond these bounds, but to these bounds - all ahead!'

These bounds, of course, were there, where the parliamentary rule of the nobility ends and the dictatorship of the streets and fields begins. Kossuth, the 'Hungarian Danton' demanded on 14 March not even as much as the 'cowardly' Viennese had already achieved with arms in their hands.

Thus it is one of the greatest historical errors to assign the nobility and Kossuth the merit of the democratic legislation of March 1848. Even if the Pozsony Diet would have gone as far as accepting the most radical proposal of Kossuth by submitting the draft bill to the king without the approval of the Upper House, their representations would have amounted only to four of the twelve demands of the Pest Revolution of 15 March.(21) It was the 'Youth of March' who gave the decisive impetus to the democratic reform. There can be no doubt that Petőfi spoke the truth when he wrote in his diary that the Pozsony Diet was frightened by rumours of a peasant uprising. Anton Springer, the liberal Austrian historian, maintains that the first news of the Pest uprising that reached Pozsony spoke of a peasant revolt; Kossuth confirms this when, in a speech on 18 March he 'opposed the view that the Diet would have received its impetus for its by then successful acts from the movements in Pest'.(22) This view was, as we have seen, very well founded indeed.

All these facts confirm that, throughout the whole revolution, the nobility did not go beyond the lines set by its well-conceived class interests. This fact is underlined by the evidence of the laws of 1848. Barely were the first days of fear past, barely did the general enthusiasm, which every fighting class has to ignite in all the other classes, cool off and barely was the circumspect codification begun, when the truly revolutionary and even the sincerely liberal elements were presented with an unexpected surprise. Those reform demands which coincided with the interests of the nobility were fulfilled by the legislation. Only two among them could have endangered the absolute dominion of the noble class: popular representation and (by implication) the freedom of the press. Both were appropriately destroyed. The election laws tied the vote to such a high census that the people were right away left out from the 'representation of the people', and the press law... well, it hardly needs a more devastating comment than that of the people of Pest who burnt it on the streets. Even 'Pesti Hirlap', by no means a revolutionary paper, wrote: 'Did we writers fight for many years and put our personal freedom on the line only to be transferred from the servitude of the government to that of the capitalists? We rather break our quills than live with the freedom of this press law.'

If one would have doubts whether the revolution placed the lesser nobility in the saddle, the procedures in the implementation of the laws would silence him altogether. Who was it who suppressed the movements of the consistent democrats at all costs - including the loss of liberty and equality? The government. Who destroyed the journal of Táncsics because 'it poisons the air', because 'it brings up the peasants against the nobles' - actually, of course, because it wrote 'in the interest of the great masses with a loud voice of conviction and justice'? Gábriel Kazinczy and his noble comrades. Who threatened a man with arrest and jail 'because of the distribution of the poems of Petőfi'? A noble judge in the county of Pest. Who gave the instruction that 'those... great land-owners who do not reside continuously in the village, do not... need to pay the community taxes'? Another noble judge in the county of Szabolcs. Who was it who, as late as November 1848, demanded boon work and refused to pay taxes? The landowners in Garam-Vezekény, Zseliz, Tápió-Szele and others. Who was it who defeated the proposal of Móric Perczel to lift all peasant servitudes in order to win the country folk for the national insurrection by a counter-proposal that rather the land-owners should be granted an extraordinary subsidy for the sudden loss of their income from 'robot'? And as Táncsics complained that the privileges were still protected - who replied on 14 December 1848 that 'the task now is to rescue the fatherland and the popular papers would do better not to babble about land'? It was Louis Kossuth who distinguished himself by these two answers. He demonstrated thus what he has always been, an absolute representative of the Hungarian lesser nobility. Only if we see him as such, can we understand fully his personality.

II LOUIS KOSSUTH (23)

Few heroes of the 1840s were able to avoid an embarrassing dilemma in later years. The émigrés of the 1848 Revolution, those who raised the flag of liberty and equality, who dreamt of the fraternity of all classes and all nations, who fought for the republic on the barricades and founded democratic institutions in the constitutional assemblies, experienced a bitter disappointment when, after the passing of the first attacks of counter-revolution the constitutional conditions were restored and the bourgeois reforms of the revolution implemented. The guiding ideals of their

youth and the slogans of their struggles withered away. The
class for which they actually entered the field, the bourgeoisie,
in fact achieved power, but its political rule was sustained at
the price of the disenfranchisement of the wide masses; the concept of equality falsified by increasing economic inequality, and
the humanitarian and democratic ideals replaced by a new slogan:
'enrichissez-vous, messieurs!' These poignant words of Guizot
had clearly replaced the former 'liberté-egalité-fraternité'.

Some of them managed to remain true to the memories of their
past and, if they were again active, to continue proclaiming
democracy in the new bourgeois society, even if against and in
opposition to the governments of the bourgeoisie and their former
comrades-in-arms. The majority of the bourgeois revolutionaries,
however, jumped happily on the bandwagon of liberated economic
speculations and wallowed in the liberal parliamentary corruption.

Louis Kossuth had been saved of these not only by his voluntary exile. The honourable poverty of his old years proves that
material interests never did influence his deeds. But his inconsistent character could not save the admirers of the revolutionary
Kossuth from other kinds of disappointments. It is not a pleasant
task to address this issue. As long as a historical personality,
such as Kossuth, can be appropriated by a political party and the
occasionally surfacing discussions about his person and historical
role are silenced by clubs and whips, it is difficult for those
workers of Hungarian literature who are not as skilled in handling
these instruments of debate as the patented patriots, to comment
on the Kossuth-question. Not fear, but rather disgust halts their
pens. This disgust for the highwayman of our scientific life is
overcome only by the feeling that it is our duty to document at
least one of the harsh criticisms of Kossuth by Marx, which may
appear overstated to the otherwise benevolent reader prejudiced
by the legends fabricated by the holders of the 'Kossuth-
franchise'. We shall do this by the force of unquestionable facts,
and where we have to pass judgment, we shall do it by quoting
the words of such authors whose patriotism has been at least as
well tested as that of the club-swinging national gentlemen.

Most contemporaries of Kossuth agreed that he lacked nothing
more than personal initiative and courage for original views. Such
a man, if driven, as he was, by ambition and vanity, can succeed
only if he keeps espousing the momentarily popular ideas and
ideals. Kossuth had all the faculties to do so. He was a past
master of the secret of mass appeal: to call only on such sentiments that are already shared by his public and to propagate only
such ideas that are already popular. He could adapt to the mood
of his audience in a way that they believed that their leader was
speaking to them, although in fact they heard only their own
mouthpiece talking. 'He was always wont to mount the pedestal of
ideas already discussed and of proposals that had been elaborated
before him. And the public perceives of him as holding the guiding torch of progress and reform, while he had actually not been
an original mind.' As a diplomat, as a statesman, or as a

commander-in-chief he topped failure with failure; there was barely a governmental measure which would not have been frustrated by his subjectivity, contradictory views or its incompleteness – but every single speech or article added a stone to the column of his popularity and individual success.(24)

No doubt, Kossuth was deeply motivated by the love for his country. But he was so convinced that the fate of Hungary was intrinsically connected to his personal standing that he reckoned every proof of his own popularity as a triumph of the country's cause. It is easy to see that he therefore looked so hard for occasions of personal success that he often exchanged them for interests of Hungary – while he meant to act exactly for them.

It is also true that Kossuth was frequently ready to sacrifice what he had called his conviction for a rhetorical coup. There are hardly any details in his social and political views which he would have held consistently and under all circumstances. His relation to his audience was the exact opposite of that of great orators: while those attempt to win the listeners for their ideas, Kossuth was won well in advance for the feelings of his audience.

This is what Marx accused Kossuth of when he refused to accept him as a character witness for the political integrity of Karl Vogt. Kossuth's own words will be adduced as proof for the correctness of Marx's accusations; these have been taken from two books, both of which were written by true admirers of Kossuth: Ludwig von Alvensleben and P. C. Headley.(25) They permit us to follow Kossuth from his Turkish exile in Kiutahia to England and America.

Before his departure for the United States, on 27 March 1850, Kossuth addressed a manifesto to his hosts. We cannot comment on all parts of this writing, although it presents many of the light and the dark sides of his character. We can quote only briefly the boastings and flatteries that went far beyond the usual rhetorical licence: 'Two years ago, by God's providence, I, who would only be a humble citizen held in my hands the destiny of the reigning house of Austria...', or: '... we were supported, first, above everything, by our unshaken confidence in God... secondly by a love of country and the holy desire of liberty, and thirdly, by your example, noble Americans, you the chosen nation of the God of Liberty!' We shall refrain from commenting on the obvious deviations from the truth in such sentences as: 'How often have I and other leaders with me said to my countrymen, that they must be strictly just, and seek their future greatness not in the predominance of one race, but in the perfect equality of all? My counsel was adopted and made the basis of government.' We are mainly concerned here with his anxiousness to assure the religious American bourgeois that the Hungarians 'were not influenced by the theories of Communists or Socialists, nor were they what the Conservatives call anarchists'.(26)

A year and a half later, on 28 September 1851, when Napoleon III refused to grant him permission to travel through France to England, he issued in Marseille a manifesto to the French people. He wrote:

I have heard my name mentioned together with the Marseillaise and with calls: Long live the Republic! - with the only legitimate slogan in France, the only one the legality of which had been paid for by the blood of the martyrs of liberty. It is more than natural to love liberty, it is a small matter to suffer for it, almost less than a simple duty - but it is a great honour to be regarded by the French people as one with the ideal of Liberty.... Last night one of your brethren, one of our brethren, a worker from Marseille...

and so on.(27)

The party which in those days issued the call for the republic was the French Social Democratic Party, to wit. No wonder, hence, that barely had Kossuth set his foot on English soil, on 6 November, than a delegation of French socialists presented him with a salutation:

Citoyen! As republicans, revolutionaries and socialists we feel akin to you.... We congratulate you to your manifesto to the city of Marseille. When you joined our great slogan, 'Vive la république!' you have by this one deed proclaimed the solidarity of all people. You have chosen the side of those who suffer all around the world, the side of the oppressed, of those whom the cosmopolitan genius of the revolution can alone liberate. You will encounter many attempts and you will receive many emulations in order to be moved away from the cause of democracy. Permit us to hope that these attempts will be in vain...

The subscribers included: Babut, tailor, Bidet, watchmaker, Louis Blanc, Member of the Provisional Government, exilé, etc.(28)

The French socialists could not have known that a day before their delegation arrived in London, Kossuth would speak about socialism thus:

I regard it as an additional proof of the harmony of the two people that neither in Italy nor in Hungary did those ideas find resonance which are regarded as incompatible with the security of property. We Hungarians have nothing to do with this theory, as we have no need for it. Hungary is an essentially agrarian country.... Hence we have no use for socialism or communism, two things, of which I was unable to acquire a clear picture in spite of extensive studies...(29)

What kind of reply could Kossuth give to the French socialists, that Kossuth, who two days after his landing in Southampton, on 25 October had already replaced America 'that has been our leading star in the revolution' with 'free England'?(30) He answered:

I am pleased by the sentiments expressed in this address of the French democrats.... Louis Bonaparte brought it to the

point that the Republic of France... is no more a refuge,
not even a way station for republicans from other countries..
.. I have confirmed in my manifesto that I wish a republican
government for my country. I am convinced that no other
political form is possible in Europe, but the republic based
on general suffrage and the ideal of the solidarity of people
and independence of all nations.... If I have not repeated
in England what I said in Marseille, I did so because I do
not wish to interfere with the internal matters of a country
that has offered me hospitality and of which I hope to
receive help for Hungary – my country, that I wish to see,
I repeat, to become a republic.(31)

Thus Kossuth was a republican on 6 November in London for the
French socialists and was so in respect to all countries. On 11
November he addressed an English audience in Manchester thus.

Here I take the opportunity to declare that it is true, I for
my own country and for myself, have convictions; I consider that after what has happened in Hungary, if it were
the most monarchical country in Europe, still the mere
establishment of it is impossible, because the treachery of
the House of Habsburg has blotted out every hope of it. But
it never came to my mind to have the pretension to go round
the world to preach government principles. Wherever I go, I
acknowledge the right of every nation to govern itself as it
pleases, and I will say that I believe freedom can dwell under
different forms of government. This I say, because gentlemen
whom I have had the honour to answer, upon an address
presented to me – of course, not having quite understood my
words – have given such a report that I should have said, I
considered in Europe there was no other... really constitutional form of government possible... than a republic. That
was a misunderstanding. I never said so. I consider that a
form of government may be different, according to the peculiar circumstances of a nation. Freedom exists in England
under monarchical as under republican government. There
social order is established. Combine my republican convictions with the principles of respect for the security of persons
and property.(32)

We do not wish to debate with Kossuth or to recall how often did
he offer the crown of the Hungarian republic (!) – once to General
Görgey, once to a Coburg prince, a Russian prince, or Louis
Napoleon, etc. We do not ask, why did the editor of the German
panegyrics of Kossuth accept the report of the 'Daily News',
'enthusiastic admirers of Kossuth',(33) if Kossuth spoke differ-
ently. Let us only quote, finally, what Kossuth said a short while
later to the republican citizens of the United States in Washington:
'Now, matters stand thus: That either the Continent of Europe
has no future at all, or this future is American Republicanism.'(34)

174   *On social science, history and literature*

The continent of Europe - means the whole of Europe!
Having read Kossuth's tergiversations in this one issue, the
reader may perhaps agree that there is no need to prove the
other accusations of Marx. The judgment on Kossuth's political
character has been passed - by the orator Kossuth himself.

NOTES

1   While Szabó used the term 'middle' (or 'moyenne') nobility
    in contrast to the higher nobility (aristocracy) and the poor
    nobles, we decided for the better-sounding 'lesser' nobility.
    According to Hungarian legal theory all nobles were equal,
    but in reality the major nobles (barons) had already emerged
    as a separate group in the Middle Ages. Among the lesser
    nobles the leading men were the relatively few 'bene posses-
    sionati' - land-owners with a few thousand acres - followed
    by some three thousand families of what can be termed
    'gentry'; a great number of legally 'nobles' actually lived
    the life of peasants. For literature and statistics see Béla K.
    Király, 'Hungary in the Late Eighteenth Century' (New York,
    1969), pp. 14-42. [Editors' note]
2   János Szapolyai reigned as King John I (1526-40); István
    Báthory was Prince of Transylvania (1571-86) and King of
    Poland (1576-86); Imre Thököly was Reigning Prince of Upper
    Hungary (1682-85) and briefly (in 1690) of Transylvania.
    [Editors' note]
3   Béla von Grünwald, scion of an old Hungaricized German
    noble family was a deputy high sheriff (highest elected officer
    in a county) and later a member of parliament. As most of the
    'Magyaronen' (renegades), he was an ardent chauvinist, but
    still one of the best educated and civilized statesmen of Hung-
    ary. He had a good eye for economic and social forces in
    history and has so far been the only author who perceived of
    the country's history as that of antagonistic classes. The
    publication of his 'Régi Magyarország' (Old Hungary) (Buda-
    pest, 1884) was received with outrage by all reactionary
    forces and would still deserve to be translated. [Author's
    note]
4   The quotations in the following paragraphs are from Grünwald,
    op. cit., pp. 119, 127, 466-7. [Editors' note]
5   See Csaba Csapodi, 'The Corvinian Library: History and
    Stock', translated by I. Gombos (Budapest, 1973). [Editors'
    note]
6   At the beginning of the sixteenth century [actually only in
    1541 - Editors' note] the country was split into a national
    (Transylvanian), a Turkish and a Habsburg territory.
    [Author's note]
7   On the so-called Dózsa-uprising, see Gusztáv Heckenast (ed.)
    'Aus der Geschichte der ostmitteleuropäischen Bauernbeweg-
    ungen im 16.-17. Jahrhundert' (Budapest, 1977) and Janos

M. Bak, Quincentennial of the Birth of György Székely-Dózsa, 'East Central Europe/Europe Centre-Est', vol. 1 (1974), pp. 153-7. [Editors' note]

8 At the diet of Pozsony (Pressburg) in 1687 the elective monarchy was abolished and the hereditary rights of Habsburg acknowledged. At the same time the nobility resigned its right of resistance ('ius resistendi'), the division of the Diet into an Upper House of 'magnates' and Lower House of common nobles was codified and the right of personal attendance of every nobleman formally replaced by representation. [Author's note]

9 From the more recent literature see, for example, Ernst Wangermann, 'From Joseph II to the Jacobin Trials', 2nd edn. (London, 1969). [Editors' note]

10 One should, however, beware of overestimating the self-government of the noble counties. While they indeed had far-reaching rights to self-administration they actually administered as little as possible and used their autonomy mainly for taking care of impoverished nobles and securing additional income to the rich ones. Most of the county offices were, though not de jure, but de facto hereditary, and yielded - as Grünwald, op. cit., has demostrated - far too high incomes, out of proportion not only to their duties but also to modern civil service salaries; of course, all this was at the expense of the tax-paying serfs. [Author's note]

11 In order to secure a safe market for Austrian industrial goods and cheap raw material for Austrian manufacturing industry, Hungary's import and export trade with foreign countries was restricted by protective tariffs, while Austrian commerce received considerable privileges. This explains that, around 1780, out of 15 million Fl. worth of Hungarian export 14 million went to Austria and 90 per cent of the country's import came from Vienna. [Author's note]

12 On the Serb National Congress see J. Jireček, 'Die Serbische Privilegien Verhandlungs-Congresse und Synoden' (Vienna, 1857); D. Ruvaroc, 'Narodni sabor od 1744' (Belgrade, 1903). [Editors' note] 'Gravamina' were those complaints regarding the constitutional relations between crown and nation and the rights of the Diet which the opposition raised and debated for years on end instead of presenting any constructive programme for legislation. Radical and stubborn though this kind of filibuster may have seemed to be, in fact it left the door wide open for royal absolutism. Also, it served as the best method for waylaying any reform plans of the government which were always seen as infringements on the nation's rights as they did not fulfil certain legal demands. [Author's note]

13 In 1825 Count Stephen Széchenyi offered his one year's income, 60,000 Fl., for the foundation of a Hungarian Academy. [Author's note]

14 On these authors see Albert Tezla, 'Hungarian Authors. A Bibliographical Handbook' (Cambridge, Mass., 1970). [Editors' note]

15 On Ferenc Kazinczy (1759–1831) see Tezla, op. cit., pp.
    301–10. The quotation is from Grünwald, op. cit., p. 469.
    [Editors' note]
16 On the literature of the 'Vormärz', see Tezla, op. cit.,
    passim (cf. p. 757); also: George Bárány, Hoping against
    Hope: The Enlightened Age in Hungary, 'American Historical
    Review', vol. 76 (1971), pp. 319–57; G. F. Cushing, The
    Birth of National Literature in Hungary, 'Slavonic and East
    European Review', vol. 38 (1960), pp. 459–75. [Editors' note]
17 Tezla, op. cit., pp. 463–89. [Editors' note]
18 See George Bárány, 'Stephen Széchenyi and the Awakening
    of Hungarian Nationalism 1791–1841' (Princeton, 1968) and
    György Spira, 'A Hungarian Count in the Revolution of 1848',
    translated by T. Land and R. E. Allen (Budapest, 1974).
    [Editors' note]
19 The dissolution of archaic society ('Gentilverfassung') brought
    disastrous consequences for the nobility. In order to prevent
    their impoverishment, in 1351 King Louis I (the Great) issued
    the so-called decree of 'aviticitas' [now in 'Decreta Regni
    Hungariae 1301–1457' (Budapest, 1976), pp. 124–40 with com-
    mentary – Editors' note] by which landed property became
    inalienable: it was not to be sold, mortgaged or given away,
    but to descend in the male line of the family and, only lacking
    an heir, escheat to the crown. [Author's note]
20 Until 1848 only the free royal cities had the right to send
    deputies to the Diet. However, the cities altogether had only
    one vote, the same as every single noble deputy. [Author's
    note]
21 The 'Twelve Points' of the Pest Revolution on 15 March were:
    1. Freedom of the press, abolition of censorship; 2. Account-
    able (i.e. parliamentary) government; 3. Annual session of
    the Diet in Pest; 4. Equality before the law, freedom of rel-
    igion; 5. National Guard; 6. Equal taxation; 7. Abolition of
    'robot' (boon work); 8. Trial by jury; 9. National bank;
    10. Oath of the army on the Hungarian constitution; 11. Rel-
    ease of political prisoners; 12. Union with Transylvania. The
    Diet's representations contained only points 2, 3, 6 and 7.
    [Author's note]
22 Michael Horváth, 'Fünfundzwanzig Jahre aus der Geschichte
    Ungarns von 1823 bis 1848', vol. 2 (Leipzig, 1867), pp. 611.
    [Author's note]
23 In the German text, prepared by Szabó for 'Neue Zeit', which
    we have mostly followed so far, this second section was sum-
    marized in a postscript:
        In the Hungarian original of this Introduction, a second
        chapter treats Kossuth and presents documentary proof
        that every accusation which Marx raised against him in
        'Herr Vogt' (pp. 121–30) rests on unquestionable facts.
        We admit that initially we did not expect to be able to
        adduce this proof for all points. We were afraid that
        Marx could have accepted in the heat of the polemic one

or other accusation from Kossuth's opponents without
checking their authenticity. Our fears were unfounded
as our inquiries have shown many weaknesses in
Kossuth's character which make Marx's treatment of him
appear as a rather mild one. Hence, we refer anyone who
wants to learn about Kossuth's historical personality from
all sides to these passages. Although the facts mentioned
there are of no great import, they may serve to support
and complement our characterization of the role of Kossuth
in the Hungarian revolution.
We chose to translate the full text from the Hungarian version.
[Editors' note]

24 Cf. Antal Csengery, 'Jellemrajzok' (Character sketches)
(Budapest, 1898), pp. 111–15; Horváth (see n. 22) vol. 2,
pp. 552, 572; Bertalan Szemere, 'Ludwig Kossuth' (Hamburg,
1853), pp. 85, 94 and passim – not mentioning any of Kossuth's political opponents or personal enemies. [Author's note]
25 L. von Alvensleben was the unnamed author of 'Kossuth nach
der Kapitulation von Világos', vol. 1 (Weimar, 1852) (henceforth: Kossuth); the other work is P. C. Headley, 'Life of
Louis Kossuth', with an introduction by Horace Greeley
(Auburn, 1852) (henceforth: Headley). [Author's note]
26 Headley, pp. 315, 318, 327, 320. [The following are all notes
made by the author]
27 Kossuth, pp. 65–6.
28 Ibid., pp. 100–2.
29 Ibid., pp. 99–100.
30 Headley, pp. 237, 238.
31 Kossuth, pp. 102–3.
32 Headley, p. 373.
33 Kossuth, pp. 89, 96.
34 Headley, p. 460.

THE AGRARIAN QUESTION IN HUNGARY

This is the only significant writing of Szabó on the questions
of rural Hungary, although he was very much interested in
the peasantry (for example, in the context of the 1848 Revolution) and participated in the presentation of a draft programme on the agrarian question to the Social Democratic
Party. The draft was not discussed at the 1908 Congress,
and Hungarian socialists did not work out a peasant policy
until very much later. Szabó's approach to the agrarian
question was influenced by both Kautsky's writings and his
Russian revolutionary friends; it is a consistently class-
conscious analysis, emphasizing the significance of the rural
poor in a country that has often been called that of 'three
million beggars'. While Szabó may have overstated the 'feudal'
character of the Hungarian countryside, which in his time
was increasingly permeated by capitalist market relations, the
overwhelming power of the latifundia justified this polemical
term. While the Social Democratic Party still regarded the
countryside as a 'reactionary mass', Szabó, who – according
to Jászi – felt deep sympathies for rural people, touched
upon one of the crucial issues in socialist politics. The dogmatic perception of agrarian transformation caused some of
the gravest difficulties for socialists and communists in 1919
as well as after 1948. The article was originally planned for
a Russian journal, 'Nauchnaiia Mysl', but Szabó then offered
it to Kautsky who published it in 'Neue Zeit', pt 2 (1908),
pp. 58-63; the translation is reprinted, with the permission
of UCIS University of Pittsburgh, from 'Peasant Studies'
vol. 7 (1978), pp. 28-37.

Even a cursory view of Hungary's economic structure and social
organization would suffice to detect a feudal organism with minor
beginnings of industrial capitalism hidden behind the façade of a
parliamentary régime and Western liberal institutions. Not less
than 36.8% of arable land belongs to latifundia, i.e. to estates
over 500 cadastral acres (=287.5 ha). In 1870 some 20% of the
arable was in entail, and during the following 25 years of the so-
called Liberal era, this percentage grew to 34.8%; it is certainly
even higher now. In 1900 only 1.5 million people, i.e. 17.5% of the
earning population, were employed in mining, manufacturing,
trades and commerce, while agriculture supplied the livelihood of
6.3 millions, i.e. 71.9%. Direct taxation is so apportioned to the

agrarian and non-agrarian population that the former is assessed
for a calculated net income of 143.8 million florins, while the latter
is taxed for 480.7 millions; this would mean that almost three
quarters of the active population are producing barely a quarter
of the net output of 17.5% of the producers. The distribution of
the tax burden within the agricultural sector has been described
by an obviously trustworthy author, the director of the industrialists' association, as follows: 10 *Kronen* net assessed income is
charged up to 60% income tax, 20 *Kronen* to 30%, 100 *Kronen* to
6%, 1000 *Kronen* to 1.2%, 10000 *Kronen* to 0.12% and 100000 *Kronen*
to a mere 0.01%. The ratio for the land tax is about the same, so
one may be bold enough to summarize the result of the abolition of
serfdom and the introduction of general taxation in 1848 by stat-
ing that now only 2000 great land-owners are virtually tax exempt,
while before all noblemen enjoyed this freedom. Even if the
owners of the great estates pay some taxes, these are more than
refunded to them in form of immediate economic or economically
useful political privileges. This over-all ratio of social forces is
neatly reflected in the most influential sectors of legislative and
executive power. The Hungarian parliament consists of an upper
house of magnates, where only great land-owners sit by hereditary right, and a house of representatives, which is elected by
a mere 6.1% of the population (ca. 1.1 million voters). The higher
echelons of the civil service are almost exclusively recruited from
the ranks of the gentry and the moyenne nobility.

One only needs to place oneself mentally in this milieu in order
to find a key to all those processes and struggles in Hungary
which so often baffle outside observers. The Hungarian revolution of 1848 was not a bourgeois but an agrarian revolution. The
liberation of serfs resulted mainly in making wage labor easily
available for the latifundia and in 50 years led to the emergence
of 2 million landless agrarian proletarians. The workers of the
slowly developing manufacturing industry - about 600,000 in 1900 -
are confronted not only by bourgeois entrepreneurs but also by
a privileged phalanx of agrarians standing behind them and controlling the entire economic and political legislation. In the last
resort, all problems of contemporary Hungary are contained in the
problem of latifundia.

Therefore, it was and remains the most urgent question for the
Hungarian working-class movement to find the best way to tackle
this problem in practical terms. However, those most responsible
for doing so have shown very little interest in it.

Karl Kautsky has recently shown us that for Hungary - as for
Russia - the agrarian question has an entirely different significance than for Western Europe. The Hungarian peasant is still a
revolutionary factor. 'His desperate lot can be changed only by
overthrowing the presently prevailing mode of production which
ruthlessly utilizes the remnants of feudalism for capitalist exploitation and by overpowering the presently ruling aristocracy.' That
is the reason why the agrarian question is the most particularly
important question for the proletariat of this country.

Economic events of recent years have brought the practical
aspect of the agrarian question even more to the fore than the
theoretical considerations. Hungary's agriculture is almost exclusively extensive. The net assessed income of some 90% of the
farms (over two million production units) is less than 100 *Kronen*.
(Actually it is up to 200-240 *Kr.* considering that the actual income is underassessed by 2-2.5 times.) The tax burden under the
present regressive system amounts to anything from 97.5% for the
smallest to 39.3% for the medium sized farms. This means that 90%
of landowners would have to end up on poor relief in a year if
they were not supported by artifical means. It is, however, in
the immediate interest of the great landowners, who also farm
extensively, to keep the dwarf- and small-holders artificially alive,
since these are the best wage-laborers for the latifundia. While
the great landowners may be able to depress the wages of the proletarian laborers to the minimum of living costs, the small-holders
who are regularly forced to work on the latifundia can be paid
even less - utilizing the 'iron law of wages' - because they are
able to augment the earned income from the products of their
dwarf holdings.

However, the peasants on the dwarf- and small-plot farms, need
more than the wages earned on the great estates in order to survive. In 1895 1,044,733 plots changed hands, in 1904 this number
rose to 1,365,077, and in 1902 the tax arrears had reached 100% in
one third of the villages. (The world record must be held by that
community which built up tax arrears of not less than 4252%. Some
competition may come from Russia, where the tax arrears in 1898
in some of the most fertile gubernia reached...232% and conditions
are much worse elsewhere.) Thus it is not surprising that in the
decade between 1890 and 1900 the number of independent farmers
decreased by 100,000 while that of landless agrarian laborers
increased by 200,000, i.e. 11%. Clearly, the winners were the
owners of latifundia.

How could the rest of the small-holders manage to survive under
these conditions? The answer is unequivocal: due to emigration.
Since the late '90s an increasing stream of emigrants has left all
parts of the country. From 1896 to 1900 there were only 32,000
emigrants annually; this figure grew between 1900 and 1905 to
110,000, in 1905 to 170,000, in 1906 to 186,000 and in the first
half of 1907 alone to 124,000. This enormous loss of population
was, unfortunately, not only a colossal safety valve which let off
the steam of discontent and of a threatening bloody rebellion, but
also served as a great source of money and credit to the small
landowners. The amounts sent back to these peasants from abroad
has been calculated for the last two years as 150 to 200 million
Kronen annually. This explains the survival of many a small
holding.

The happiness of the great landowners was not long undisturbed.
As long as it remained within the limits of the interests of the latifundia, emigration was well tolerated and even supported - so
much so that the emigration business was organized by the govern-

ment and a minimum of 30,000 passengers per year were guaranteed to a shipping company that had been granted a state monopoly. When, however, the ten thousands grew into hundreds of thousands, less welcome consequences for the latifundia became obvious. The great estates depend on the reliable supply of labor from the neighboring small farms, as they cannot successfully compete on the commodity market unless the costs of production are kept down by paying starvation wages to utterly exploited workers. This worked well as long as dispossessed small-holders were available in ever increasing numbers. Soon, however, not only more and more laborers emigrated but less and less of them returned. Those who did return, aware of the financial and cultural conditions of American workers, raised claims, and the good times were over. There was not only a shortage of agricultural labor but also an agrarian workers' movement, more stable, more conscious and more successful than all earlier sporadic attempts at organizing the agrarian proletariat. The Social-Democratic *National Union of Laborers of Hungary* registered 24,000 members by the end of 1906; other smaller associations of laborers and small-holders counted perhaps another 10,000. Very small though these numbers may be in comparison to two million agrarian proletarians, they are not to be underestimated in contrast to preceding attempts and their meager results. In spite of the most ferocious persecution and the officially organized strike-breaker services ('governmental work reserves' and 'state harvest machines'), agrarian wages and working conditions improved considerably during the past couple of years. In some areas the wage increase was as much as 100%, and landowners were happy to get enough hands to bring in the harvest at all.

These are conditions which the feudal latifundium cannot tolerate for long. The besieged agrarians demand from the state near incredible financial and reactionary political measures. They ask for almost complete tax reductions for the latifundia, subsidies, and all kinds of positive and negative preferential treatments as well as the abolition of the last remnants of political rights for agricultural laborers and their leaders, the industrial working class. No government was as harsh against the workers' organizations as the present 'national-democratic' coalition: not only were several hundred locals of the laborers' union dissolved, but quite a few national organizations of industrial workers were treated in the same way. The entire machine of the legislation and administration is busy oppressing and destroying those few liberal economic, political, and intellectual achievements and institutions which have emerged in Hungary since 1848.

A new tax reform is in the works, which will increase beyond measure the obstacles in the way of raising workers' standard of living and of industrial development; the recent law on general education makes Magyarization, not education, the first task of elementary schools (one may imagine what this means in a poor country with 40% illiteracy); so-called workers' protection laws are passed which make 500,000 agricultural household-servants into

virtual serfs; Magyar chauvinism is fostered by increased persecution of the Slav minorities in order to divert attention from the
sufferings of the Magyar poor. In brief: we witness a paroxysm
of all feudal and reactionary forces unparalleled in our history,
which we cannot interpret in any other way but as symptoms of
the beginning final disintegration of an outdated social system, of
feudalism.

But signs are increasing which in turn suggest that the agrarians themselves are scared by their luck. The value and hidden
meaning of 'peasant-friendly' policies of agrarians, here and
abroad, are only too well known to all of us. We can easily recognize the interests of the highly indebted landowners and the
real-estate bankers in the parcelling out of some parts of certain
latifundia. This has been done in the last few years with government support, certainly not out of love to the peasants. The
'beneficiaries' not only lose their last pennies in these usurious
transactions, but - as even an agrarian source admitted - they
are likely to lose their newly acquired goods and chattels in a few
years' time, due to the high prices of credit. Still, we should not
underestimate the symptomatic value of some of these policies 'in
favour of' the peasantry, especially if they are to become widespread.

In agrarian and governmental circles there is talk about a bill
enabling mass parcelling of land, with a budget of 100 million
Kronen of public funds. A private bill introduced a few days ago
by one of the great landowners goes even further, practically
demanding that the state take over the entails either by purchase
or through long-term leases. Even though this radical proposal
would hardly be accepted right now, it suggests the direction that
will have to be taken sooner or later.

It is the task of the organized socialist working class to direct
this development towards a socialist solution. The important thing
here is not the technical superiority of the small farm, but the
obsolescence of the feudal form of latifundia, of the extensively
cultivated great estates. Cheap credit is needed if they are to be
transformed into intensive agricultural enterprises. That is not
available in Hungary, however, because the country is not a commercial center, and, due to the prohibitive agrarian and customs
policies, industry could not develop even to the degree that would
have lured relevant amounts of surplus capital into the country.
Thus the feudal great landowners have no other choice but partial
liquidation: a portion is sacrificed in order to keep the rest.

This trend to dissolution has to be countered by socialist reorgan-
ization proposals and experiments. The Socialist Party must win
the agrarian proletariat's support for this demand: that the land
which becomes available due to economic pressures should not
simply change one private owner for another but should be returned to the possession of the community (actually perhaps to
the villages or the districts) and utilized for the benefit of the
entire nation. Whether this common property should then be cultivated in individual or collective leases, short or long term ones,

is another question. This will have to be decided in consideration of the local situation, the state of technology, world market conditions, and the intellectual progress of the rural population. The next congress of the Party will have to consider this problem. The *National Organization Committee of Agrarian Laborers* will submit a program to the congress. Although we are convinced that one step of actual movement is worth a hundred programs, in this case we still believe that the position taken by the Party in the agrarian question will influence the development of Hungarian socialism for many decades.

CAN POLITICS EVER BE SCIENTIFIC?

This short piece was written for the anniversary issue of
'Huszadik Század' (1910, pt I, pp. 133-6), for which all
editors, authors and friends of the journal were asked to
submit a piece on a problem they were most interested in.
Szabó's choice was characteristic for his lifelong quandary:
the relationship of theory and practice, of (individual and
group) consciousness and social progress, of intellectual
efforts and development of society. Polemizing with Gyula
Pikler, who in the same issue wrote about his dissatisfaction
with historical materialism (ibid., pp. 123-5), that he found
himself unable to explain ideological changes, mental transformations and meaning of such terms as the means of
production 'opposing' development, Szabó in a way replies
to him by developing his view of the interrelations between
ideas, consciousness and development. He offers a succinct
statement on 'ideology' and 'false consciousness' and
expresses his conviction that 'rationality' will increase with
the development of technology and world economy - towards
socialism and greater freedom.

Politics would be scientific if its calculations were based on the
workings of a force which sociology recognizes as the most powerful among the moving factors of society. Such politics would then
become rational from two aspects: from the psychological aspect,
because it would entail action that is conscious, guided by the
intellect; and from the economic aspect, because the principle of
economy - the least sacrifice for the sake of the greatest good -
would then prevail. Hence the scientific politician would be one
whose social action takes place in the direction of least resistance,
and whose consciousness coincides, and becomes identical with his
action.
    Some sociological systems claim that social evolution has always
been guided by a rational intellect conscious of its objectives. If
these systems are valid, it would seem that humanity has always
pursued scientific politics. Perhaps the most ambitious among
these theories is the theory of insight expostulated by Gyula
Pikler.(1) He argues that people create the family, the tribe, the
nation, just as consciously as they might establish a club or a
corporation. He likewise argues that people have always created
institutions which have ensured the greatest satisfaction of their
needs in accordance with the knowledge available to them at the

time. Hence social evolution was conscious, and it has been tele-
ologically oriented by human intellect from the very beginning.
All that is required for the future is to determine what would
guarantee most fully the satisfaction of human needs and then to
convince others of the validity of our findings.
I could not help thinking of this truly representative theory of
rational sociology while reading two recent works by German
sociologists; two works that often confirm, and sometimes are
supported with new arguments, the views of which I had reiter-
ated myself while arguing against a rationalist interpretation of
social development.
It is Müller-Lyer who expresses the contradiction between conscious and unconscious social progress most clearly.

This grandiose process of transformation of human affairs
which we term culture has travelled along the major part of
its way without people having the least inkling of where the
way would lead them; their awareness could no more perceive
the slow evolution of culture than they could perceive, from
their terrestrial abode, their voyage around the sun. (2)

As for Vierkandt, he explains why this is so: because the historical structure of human consciousness is characterized by a certain
permanence ('Stetigkeit') which consists in the fact that every
aspect of consciousness is determined not simply by an outside
stimulus - the immediate experience - but by the whole gamut of
previous experiences and impressions; tradition, imitation, the
pressure of habit dominate human consciousness both in theory
and in practice much more than spontaneous initiative or rational
insight. (3)
The entire study by Vierkandt strives to explain why it cannot
be argued that social action is conscious; namely, because our
actions are guided not by reason, but by emotion. Actually he
demonstrates what Spencer had already postulated and others
after him. His thesis, however, is enhanced by the fact that it is
based on a plethora of data taken from ethnology, prehistory and
contemporary life. Nevertheless, I would like to contribute one or
two thoughts to his arguments.
Thus, for instance, sociologists have paid scant attention to a
phenomenon long ago conceded by realistic philosophy with regard
to individual consciousness, but which has almost never been
applied to mass consciousness, even though it seems more applicable to it: the observation that the sole source of our consciousness and cognition is sensual experience, that man arrives at a
knowledge of objective reality only through his senses, through
direct feeling and sensory experience. Some persons with an
exceptional mind may arrive at other kinds of cognition, developing data acquired through the senses with the help of logic - still,
the only test of the validity of these thoughts remains practive,
contact with reality. What follows from all this? The fact that they
cannot realize - at least the masses cannot realize, for their

186 On social science, history and literature

intellectuality functions less well than that of the individual - the need of something, as long as that thing has no existence in the real world, as long as it cannot be experienced through the senses. That is practice precedes theory in the life of the masses, action precedes consciousness rather than the other way around; for one cannot have something in consciousness before feeling it through the senses. Hence something may be happening for a long time, a social institution may exist for a long period, before it reaches the consciousness of mankind and the need for it is realized.

Data taken from prehistory provide factual evidence for this theory. The use of fire (see the work of Karl von den Steinen),(4) the invention of the plough, of the cart and of roads (see E. Hahn) (5) suggest this; so does the institution of exogamy, which must have existed for thousands and tens of thousands of years before people were even capable of understanding its utility. And many other examples.

On the other hand, it is unquestionable that at a higher stage of development people have been more and more anxious - before and after the event - to give an account of their action to themselves. Such accounting, however, is filled with illusions often at direct variance with reality.

Even the individual does not know himself. His self-image is the offspring of his desires, the justification of his actions, short-comings transformed into virtues. How could the masses know themselves any better?

Society's consciousness of itself is expressed in theories, principles and ideologies. Historical materialism has compelled sociology to seek the reality of economy behind the theories and ideologies, because ideologies provide but a distorted image of society. The method of historical materialism is resorted to increasingly; and does this not indicate that science regards ideologies more and more as illusions, even though they have been humanity's conscious accounts of its own existence?

What tremendous forces have always acted and act even today to prevent humanity from knowing itself, from realizing what its true needs are, only to make sure that its consciousness becomes and remains a false one! Action, change and progress succeed against this consciousness or, colloquially speaking, against men's 'better judgment'.

We would be denying the great cultural role of need, of violence and of compulsion to work if we were to argue that all cultural progress has been the result of insight. War, slavery and serf-dom have been maintained by force, as is wage-labour today. Illusion, often self-deluding rather than completely artificial, has been supporting the use of force and the rule of class for a long time; it pretends that these institutions are necessary. We find ample evidence among contemporary labour movements that this pretension has been persuasive enough.

All this goes to prove that humanity could hardly have known what it was doing when it was raising its social forms and

institutions to higher and higher degrees of perfection. Nor has
humanity proceeded rationally in this work, that is it did not
operate according to the principle of the smallest sacrifice for the
greatest good; and that is proven sufficiently by the domination
of irrational traditions and habits, discoveries rejected hundreds
and hundreds of times, initiators and innovators mocked, tortured,
assassinated a thousand times, suffering martyrdom of all kinds.

Should we therefore give up the hope of ever developing scientific politics by which social progress would become rational, that
is conscious and economical? I do not believe that civilized humanity will change in the foreseeable future to such an extent that
irrational feelings will play no part among the motives of its
actions; but I do see indications that rational considerations play
an ever increasing role.

The fact that the only test of the validity of our thoughts is
life, reality and practice means, for the evolution of consciousness, that the smaller the circle affected by the actions of an
individual, the less frequently will he face the test of the reality
for his thinking. The wider the circle, the more frequent the test
of the validity of his thinking. At the same time the responsibility
and the risks involved in the actions are increasing and demanding foresight and rational planning. That is the smaller the circle
in which the life of the individual moves, the larger the possibility of a false consciousness; the greater the radius of his actions,
the more realistic his consciousness.

Since the most basic function of life is economy and the spread
of the sphere of economy manifests itself primarily in the division
of labour, it can be argued that the increase in the division of
labour signifies an increase in rationality – on the level of our
consciousness as well as of our actions.

Another process of evolution also brings us towards the rationalization of our consicousness. If illusion is one of the principal
results of compulsion and violence, then less compulsion and less
force must cause less illusion. It is clear that the whole history of
mankind indicates progress from a state of greater compulsion to
one of lesser. Need for food entails war, forced labour; increasing economy leads towards liberty. One cannot deny that the
wealth of mankind is on the increase; hence the need for compulsion and violence is diminishing. The decrease in illusion accom-
panies increasing freedom.

Thus both basic tendencies of evolution in society act towards
the rationalization of our social consciousness. But the rationalization of our consciousness means more than simple intellectual
betterment. It also means the acceleration of social progress; to
the extent that among the motives of our actions the conscious
ones are on the increase, and irrational emotions, such as traditions, habits, the primitive hatred of everything new or different,
are losing ground. Hence fewer obstacles to innovation and to
initiative; more chances for innovators, initiators, for great men,
etc. Thus intellectual force will become a direct agent of social
progress with an ever more rapid impact.

The spread of mankind's economy means world economy; the increase of freedom means socialism; the development of human understanding means intellectualism – these are the requirements for the rationalization of social action.

NOTES

1   Gyula (Julius) Pikler (1864–1937), professor of law at the University of Budapest, a sociologist, adherent of the psychological school of sociology, was one of the first men to gather social scientists on his chair and, although opposed to Marxism, remained a loyal supporter of the younger sociologists as president of the Sociological Society. His place in Hungarian social science at the time of Szabó's writing is well characterized by E. Bolgár, Entwicklung und Literatur der Soziologie in Ungarn, 'Monatsschrift für Soziologie', vol. 10 (1909), pp. 324–34. [Editors' note]
2   Franz Karl Müller-Lyer, 'Phasen der Kultur und Richtlinien des Fortschritts' (Munich, 1908 [correctly: 1906 – Editors' note]). [Author's note]
3   Alfred Vierkandt, 'Die Stetigkeit im Kulturwandel' (Leipzig, 1908 [correctly: 1906]). [Author's note]
4   Karl von den Steinen (1855–1929), ethnographer and traveller, explored Central Brazil in 1887–88 and the Marquesas Islands in 1897–98. He wrote about the use of fire among the Bururu. [Editors' note]
5   Eduard Hahn (1856–1928), geographer and pupil of Ernst Haeckel, wrote several articles on the early development of agriculture. [Editors' note]

THE TASKS OF THE SOCIOLOGICAL SOCIETY
(Presidential address)

Szabó gave the presidential address on the anniversary convention of the Society on 23 November 1912, although formally he had been (since 1907) only its vice-president, but Gyula Pikler, the president, lived abroad and the actual leadership was indeed in Szabó's and the energetic Jászi's hands. The foundation of the Society in 1901 - a year after the start of 'Huszadik Század' - and, even more, the decisive shift to the 'left' after its crisis in 1906, when the supporters of the nationalist-conservative government left and founded a counter-society, were indeed historical events in Hungarian intellectual life. The Society served, under the given conditions, simultaneously as a scholarly body and as a forum of scientific propaganda, and did both tasks with great success. Szabó was often attacked and mocked by socialists for engaging in this mixed, bourgeois enterprise, and has been faulted for it in retrospect by Communist critics. How he himself judged the compatibility of revolutionary politics and detached, but seriously critical, hence progressive social science, is best expressed in this speech. It was printed, together with other matters of the convention inter alia the greetings from the Fabian Society, in 'Huszadik Század', pt II, 1912, pp. 459-70.

Many of those present here today may have learnt about this celebration with surprise. A decade is not such a long span of time that one needs to toast the anniversary. Under normal conditions we would not have thought of it either. Yet we must not forget that the very existence of this Society, its development, and the place it now occupies in Hungary's intellectual life, are extraordinary occurrences. This Society did not grow up in the comfortable hotbed of conventions, traditions and custom - but has been earning its right to survival by dynamic daily activity. Who could blame us for gathering today if only to commemorate ten years of work and to once again profess our faith in what is right and good? Who could argue that, after years of serious work and struggle, we do not have the right to reiterate proudly and solemnly what our enemies keep saying with animosity: that the work and struggle of this Society have already left a visible mark on the development of our nation? Who would blame us if, sincerely convinced of the usefulness of our work for the cultural, scientific, economic and social progress of Hungary, we should proclaim it for once, loud and clear?

189

However, I would rather that this ceremonial occasion did not limit itself to that. The person who treads along the wide and smooth highway of conventions need not mind his or her step. But if we claim that our activities have cut a new path in Hungary's public life, we must not be satisfied, even on such ceremonial occasions, with the customary eulogies. We must seize the occasion to recapitulate not merely the positive things about ourselves and our tenets. Excessive zeal has led us too often to self-praise and to a profession of our faith; even more often, we have been compelled to do so by the attacks of our opponents. But if we want to endow this celebration with the legitimacy it deserves, we can only achieve that by making it a day for self-criticism.

In what resides the exceptional situation of the Sociological Society? The scientific work of mankind is carried out under the aegis of the same great natural law which motivates and guides the actions of each and every individual: the will to survive. In this sense there can be no science without self-interest, just as there can be no economy, no legislation and no government without interest, nor any function of the instinct of survival that manifests itself socially.

Does this mean that the search for truth - which is the abstract or common goal and object of all scholarly endeavours - can also be in the direct service of particular interests? All social will and activity manifests itself or happens through the individual. In earlier times, when the lack of differentiation of social activities and the small size and homogeneity of human communities presupposed the complete identity of individual and social interests, the search for the truth could have been in the interest of both the individual and the society. This was that ideal state so difficult to even imagine on the basis of our ethnological data and our knowledge of prehistory. From that time on, the development of the social division of labour has increasingly assigned the performance of different social functions to different groups of individuals. In this manner science has also become separated from other functions; the search for truth became the profession of a special group of individuals, namely the scholars - just as material production, warfare, art, etc. became the task of other groups. And all these separate social functions strive equally to become autonomous vis-à-vis the others, that is vis-à-vis society.

But it is precisely in this very natural and powerful striving for autonomy that we recognize the supreme interest of society's unified goal. For what does autonomy signify? Nothing more than that the differentiated social organs which act through individuals or their agglomerations, usually designated as social class, stratum or group, consider themselves autonomous and wish to live an independent existence. Their own. Not that of anybody else. And for the sake of their own goals.

It is in this process that we detect the great and decisive universal justification of the principle of 'l'art pour l'art' valid for all areas of human creativity. While social need brought about the differentiated social functions for the satisfaction of a basic common interest, this same need can be satisfied only as long as the social functions follow the direction of their respective causes; that is if the cause of their being is at the same time their end. Society has created different organs for different goals. Thus the search for truth becomes the only aim of the scientific function, independent from any other end or interest; and the scientist becomes a faithful and effective agent of the general social interest only if he is not influenced by any motive or goal other than the discovery of truth – only if science is pursued for the sake of science. A perfect society would be one in which every differentiated social function became autonomous in this same manner, and in which the social functions were carried out by functionaries who individually have no vested interest in the immediate social utility of their work, who work solely in the service of the causa causans, of the common social needs. The greatest social good can best be satisfied by the greatest individual disinterest.

To what point have we approached this ideal state? How far have we progressed in the social division of labour, in the differentiation of functions? To what extent has the scientific function differentiated itself from, let us say, the political, the religious, or the educational ones in our country? To what extent is it recognized as self-directed, and how is its independent, interest-free pursuit ensured?

Nobody can rightly claim that the ideal state has been attained in any part of the world. Even in the most prosperous and civilized states it happens but rarely that those who have enriched the scientific treasury of mankind with its most precious possessions live exclusively for this function; and there is not a single country where the temptation of alien interests has not endeavoured to capture the new scientific truths. Poverty-stricken inventors, researchers compelled to serve in diploma factories, thinkers chased away from their university chairs or cowed into submission are to be found everywhere in the world. Nobody will deny, nevertheless, that our country is still further from that state of social differentiation which would guarantee the absolute freedom and disinterest of scientific research. It is as if we were still standing with both our feet in that era when the political function constituted the most distinguished social activity. This era is also characterized by the fact that the ruling social group allows autonomy to the newer social functions only to the extent that these can be used for the enhancement of its domination. In contrast to the greater differentiation, hence greater freedom, found in industrial societies, we are still living in a period of almost uncontrolled state omnipotence in which all initiative, whether political, economic, moral, cultural, or whatever, originates with the state and serves the ends of the state's ruling class. Hence there is hardly a country to the west of us in which the academic character of science and scholarship prevails so conspicuously, often even in the most abstract sciences, as in our own country.

How much more so is this the case in an area concerned precisely with the scientific problems of the nature and essence of the state itself! Whereas in certain branches of scholarship, say the natural sciences, a civilized law exists even in this country which facilitates and promotes the search for scientific truth – not a law of war but a law of commerce that guarantees the free exchange of values – in the area of the social sciences, club law is still pretty much supreme. The kind of respect for science which accepts the truth eagerly and lovingly, wherever it may come from, even if it be from the adversary – this kind of respect is almost unknown in the social sciences. In this sphere only that which can be useful to others is considered true; and the person who serves truth for its own sake is often ostracized not only from the community of interests that calls itself scholarly, but often even from the national community.

This was the social environment in which the Sociological Society got launched some eleven years ago. Is it a wonder under these conditions that the atmosphere of pleasant feelings which surrounded the Society at its birth dissipated rapidly the more consistently the spirit of unfettered scientific investigation triumphed? Could it be the fault of the youth who dominated the Society that, little by little, not only the ignorant and the malevolent, but even many of those among the Society's founders or friends who had a sincere respect for science, did not dare to face the club law of this field? Can we be astonished that the open enmity of the ruling circles, together with the withdrawal of the passive or timid souls, gradually changed the original character of the Society?

Let us confess that the Society did not adhere closely to the programme it had set for itself at its foundation. This is a latent fact, and I think we are doing right in bringing it to light and finally confronting the situation. We must dispel the confusion of opinions which prevails even among ourselves. It is commonly held that the Society departed from its original programme, in so far as it is now more political than scientific. Actually we ourselves have refuted this qualification only occasionally, in the course of debate, but not systematically and in well-defined terms, which only encouraged adverse public opinion. Nothing is more dangerous than ill-defined concepts.

I do not claim that the disinterested search for scientific truth demands that the scientist isolate himself from real life, or repress in his soul all those feelings which tie human beings in full possession of their spiritual and physical forces to the life that sparkles around them. I do not claim that he should isolate himself from the community of men of action. The human essence, as well as the interest of science itself, would protest against that. How true are Goethe's words: 'Auch in den Wissenschaften kann man nichts wissen, es will immer getan sein.' (One cannot acquire knowledge even in science: one has to act!)

The sociologist has to accomplish in real life what the physicist, the chemist, the psychologist can achieve in the laboratory: subject his logical deductions to the control of cognition perceived.

For the laboratory of the sociologist is social existence and experience itself; 'Selbsterleben' is the sensation that becomes the
ultimate proof of our present notions, and the fertile source of
new knowledge. Hence the programme which the first president of
the Soçiety, the honoured and distinguished scientist and politician, Ágost Pulszky, proposed at the moment of its foundation
was indeed intelligent and correct:

> We are called upon in the first place to express concern for
> science and spread scientific principles at our meetings, con-
> ferences, as well as in the journal sponsored by the Society.
> It does not follow from this, however, that our concerns
> should have no effect on the public.... We have no direct
> political objectives; what is more, we definitely reject any
> direct political involvement which might coincide with the
> activities of any political party or regime, or even with the
> interests of a particular social class. On the other hand, we
> will constantly endeavour to arouse public feeling, to create
> an atmosphere in which social factors can bear salutary fruit;·
> indirectly, therefore, our activities are bound to affect actual
> social organizations. Under the present circumstances in
> Hungary there is at least as much need for the creation of
> such an atmosphere as elsewhere in the world.

Considering these words, nobody can claim that the subsequent
activities of the Society have departed qualitatively from the original progreamme. For its first president, a distinguished scientist
who was by no means a political radical, had set practical effect
as the goal of our activities. The Society was only acting in the
spirit of this programme when it contributed 'to create an atmosphere in which social factors can bear salutary fruit' for the
solution of Hungary's most urgent practical problems.
  I dare declare that the Society as such, as a scientific organization, has faithfully remained aloof from the positions of a party
or a social class. Witness the twenty-six volumes of 'Huszadik
Század' as well as our conferences and polls, we made room for all
honest opposition; what is more, we did everything possible to
make room in our journal and our debates for the most contradictory opinions, the most contrasting convictions: suffice to mention
the debates on social development, the reform of secondary education, on eugenics and, more recently, on art and society. I do
not believe anyone could cite even a single Hungarian association
in the area of intellectual life where such divergent views are
given free vent, only to find clarification in the heat of the debate.
  It is not our fault that the Hungarian intellectual climate is far
from being ripe for such impartial intellectual athletics. It is not
our fault that the freedom of speech so often cited in our country
does not cover the publication of contrary opinions, that the state
shamelessly expects that only those tenets which preserve the
interests of the ruling classes should come to light - whether they
be true or not. In the area of social sciences, moreover, where

scientific truth or the discovery of social laws results in direct practical application affecting our very lives, both the scientific and practical work of the Society has met with these restrictions. In its scientific as well as in its propagandistic activities our Society tried its best to be objective; and to what extent it has succeeded in achieving this is clearly indicated by the fact that to this day we encounter resistance, not merely from one side but, I dare say, from all sides, including the side of those with whose party or class interests our enemies have often identified the Society. (If perchance – to the regret of all – there may have been some from our own ranks who have repaid the impatience of our opponents with impatience towards well-meaning adversaries, this is a symptom not of the general tendency within our Society, but rather of the spirit which prevails in Hungarian public life.) Can we wonder then, under such circumstances, that in this atmosphere which has become red-hot from constant friction from all sides, unusual light effects have projected some of the actions and words of its politically committed members into the Society?

Who could blame the Society, moreover, for having defended the freedom of scientific research both against persecution by authorities and against the explicit boycott of official social and scientific circles? The task was to create an atmosphere which was absolutely essential for the proper functioning of the Society and without which it would be simply impossible to pursue science.

Or who could blame us if, in the process of creating such a civilized public opinion, the Society has turned a considerable part of its efforts to the popularization of science? To elicit, in ever widening circles, feelings of love and respect towards scientific endeavour which contribute the most important element of a public opinion actively sympathetic to objective scientific research. Nevertheless, the Society has not forgotten the other aspect of its dual task: pure sociology. Countless articles that have appeared in 'Huszadik Század' and the monographs published by the Society attest to that fact: they include works by Spencer, Loria, Giddings, Ward, Westermarck, Le Dantec, Guyau, etc. What better proof do we need that the spirit which strives for pure knowledge of social laws without consideration of any other motive has always prevailed in this Society?

In this sense, the Society indeed has not departed from the set of tasks which its learned president outlined for it at its founding meeting. But if we ask whether we have also remained true to our programme, in the sense that our primary and most important task is to pursue pure social science and to consecrate the best of our efforts and energy to the scholarly inquiry: to this question we must reply in the negative.

On a war footing on all sides, under circumstances which do not favour scientific investigation either materially or spiritually, our activities have indeed lost the balance between research, on the one hand, and the preparation or popularization of research, on the other. One might almost concede: we have hardly had the time for thoughts amidst all the action. It is hardly necessary to list

the extenuating circumstances: the lack of differentiation in our
society, the lack of development in the social division of labour,
the lack of an atmosphere conducive to scientific investigation,
etc. We are familiar with these factors, and we have admitted
them as the causes of our present predicament. Nor is it necessary for me to repeat that, while in comparison with foreign sociological societies we are less engaged in theoretical work, among
Hungarian learned societies there is probably none which has
introduced such a mass of new theoretical knowledge as our own.
If sociology is recognized today as an independent branch of
knowledge, most of the credit for that is due to the Sociological
Society.

Yet because our expectation is that our work should be measured
not by local, but by absolute standards, we must decide at this
solemn moment of introspection whether it might not be possible to
re-establish the proper balance in the division of our energies. I
am well aware, of course, that this is not merely a matter of
decision or determination. I am well aware that, as a result of a
strange concatenation of circumstances, an important part of the
work which has been going on for a century toward a bourgeois
transformation of Hungary rests on the shoulders of precisely
those persons who are also called upon to carry out the scientific
function of our Society. And I know very well that most of them
have spent all their energy in the performance of this twofold task.
We cannot create new forces out of nothing. But we can use our
existing resources better, more purposefully, with proper organization.

If I examine the roster of our members, and if I also consider
those societies in the capital and in the provinces which sympathize with our endeavours or support us - and now, please do not
misunderstand me - I become frightened. There are so many of us
tending towards the same goals that the danger seems to be almost
that, while certainly not in the country, but in the extensive
sections of society where our sympathizers can be found, we may
obtain the majority before long. Which means that the functions of
the Society may become identical with that of a large crowd.

If we consider the scientific functions of the Society as its primary task, we should fear such an outcome. Nobody will think, I
hope, that I am resorting to some kind of ethical evaluation when
warning of such a possibility. Or that we should forget not only
the obligations of gratitude, but also of respect, for these are the
ties which have bound the members, leaders and all the friends of
our Society in the course of our common struggle. Indeed, the
first decade of the existence of this Society and of its journal are
an almost unique, hence extremely significant and valuable, manifestation of the sort of progress which makes scientific research
independent of the state and of the rich sponsors. It is thanks to
you, dear friends, that it was possible to reach this stage here
in Hungary, that a Hungarian learned society and a periodical are
not forced to sell out their right to independent free research. It
is thanks to those thousands who have persevered, in good times

and bad, in spreading around the country a public spirit that relies only on itself, that is independent of power and of conventions, and which alone is able to bear, understand and dedicate itself to the spirit of free and independent scholarship. That we became what we are – we owe to the public spirit you represent; and if we mean to improve in the future, if we want to develop in the direction I have indicated – we know full well we cannot do it without your assistance.

What I have in mind is a separation of functions. There are tremendous forces among the masses which are simply indispensable today for social progress. Let us try to imagine contemporary society without that powerful tension elicited by the wants of the masses, without that instinctive force with which the masses strive to achieve their desires, without that will that admits of no hesitation; every conscious, intelligent and purposeful will can receive strength only from this collectively and individually existing instinctive will. But the foresighted and purposeful will is the product not of instinct, but of the intellect: of science that researches, dissects and reorganizes relationships, analyses determinations and designates the necessary order of our actions. All this in the perfect form of scientific truth: purely, simply, transparently, apart from anything incidental, it can appear only where one instinct predominates over all others; namely, the yearning for truth.

Since in its present degree of differentiation society orients the instincts of the great majority of mankind towards the realization of other needs, the instinct and will of scientific work exist only among a very few, a negligible minority. Hence it is not possible as yet – and perhaps never will be – that scientific truth should dwell among the masses. One of our excellent colleagues, who is mentioned proudly and lovingly among those whose entire activity is based upon the masses, described in an article several years ago the process of the inevitable distortion of ideas when it comes to their realization.

Thus we must not cease to fear the day when we, as a Society, should reach the realization of our truths. Even if sociological tenets have no other verification than practice, action, life, and even if the true thing is not that which survives only in the world of ideas, but which also survives in reality: still, let us not forget that the road to the realization of truth is slow, and by the time it is achieved science has already discovered new truths based on the development of old results. And new truth means a different truth.

Even if this danger is, for the moment, purely academic, we would not believe in the truth of our principles if we did not expect that some day they may become applied, and that our principles will get their chance to withstand the final test of validity. Let us then beware that this practical test does not consume our truth. Let us beware and hurry! The process of verification has already begun, it is taking place right before our eyes: as our ideas spread, they become realized. Let us make certain that the deficit that comes about whenever a truth is actualized should always be balanced out by new positive truths. Our theories must not fall behind. Our knowledge has to be continually revised. We must assimilate the consequences of practical tests, and gain new knowledge. Our investigation must penetrate more deeply into the laws of society. That is true science; that is what we must accomplish if we wish to remain true to our name and our programme.

The Sociological Society should dedicate itself more to its scientific function: this is what we have to decide upon today, in good faith. This is the purpose for which we have attempted to reorganize our resources. If you, who have come here in such numbers and with such enthusiasm to celebrate along with us, will consent, then something can indeed be done to that effect.

The Sociological Society can proudly claim that it was able to overcome its isolation in public life. Those who were formerly indifferent and whose interest, friendship and help we have managed to win, nay, even former opponents often greet our initiatives and accomplishments with pleasure and respect. Our membership, relatively large by Hungarian standards, the proliferation of our branches in the provinces, the long list of organizations which sympathize with our Society or derive directly from it, succeeded to place a social stratum of significant size and quality at the service of Hungarian society.

Would it not be possible, ladies and gentlemen, to apply the principle of the social division of labour to our community as well? Would it not be possible to base such a division of labour on the differentiation of functions? What I have in mind is to consciously enhance a process that is already in course. Much of that important task that, according to Wilhelm Ostwald, in terms of saving energy, is equivalent to that of the inventor which consists in the organization of ideas, is already being performed by other organizations. Their work of organization and propaganda is preparing the terrain that responds to the endeavours of our Society. Let these come to our aid even more, so that the Sociological Society can concentrate its energies on scholarship. In addition to these spiritual prerequisites of scientific work, let them help us obtain the material means for the functioning of our Society, so that those who want to work in and through the Society should not find their energies dissipated in doing scientific propaganda that is less akin to them.

I believe that the time has arrived for our scientific re-evaluation. We have to carry it out for the benefit of the Society as well as for all related endeavours. Nothing can be more important than the needs, the demands of the day. If we do not meet these we will not be able to accomplish tomorrow's work either. Help us get a start, and I can vouch that we will carry it out with utmost dedication.

WHAT IS READ AND WHAT
SHOULD BE

Szabó spent virtually his entire adult life working in libraries
as a librarian. In 1900 he became librarian of the Budapest
Chamber of Commerce, in 1904 he was entrusted to organize
the Municipal Library of which he became the first director
in 1911. It has been noted that 'the air of the library characterized all his writings' in the sense that he was a passion-
ate bibliographer and an extremely well-read man; but also
his socialist educator conviction characterized his librarianship. Oriented on the American pattern of the 'public library',
he designed an entirely new institution for central Europe
and began to put it into reality in Budapest; a central research library with a social-science orientation augmented by
branch libraries for the wider reading public. In his writings
on librarianship, a collection of which has been edited by A.
Tiszay (Budapest, 1959, with a bibliography of foreign language publications on libraries, pp. 611-13) he also utilized,
though critically, the concepts of the German, Walter Hofmann, who advocated 'propagandistic' workers' libraries.
Szabó's achievements in the library can be gauged from his
annual reports in 'Zentralblatt für Bibliothekswesen' for 1912,
1913, 1917 and 1918: in those years the Municipal Library was
almost the only 'practical' activity he pursued, having been
disappointed by the Social Democratic - and the short-lived
syndicalist - movements in Hungary. In order to represent
this important field of Szabó's literary activity, we include
an article, originally published in 'Népmivelés' (Popular
Education), vol. 6, no. 2 (1911), pp. 60-4.

The main difference between the old and the new libraries is that
the former were built to have a place where books could be kept;
should a researcher occasionally find his way into the library,
that would be all right - but if he did not, that was even better.
Today, on the other hand, libraries are founded in order to have
a place whence books can be disseminated so that they may reach
more and more readers. The libraries exist to educate and enter-
tain people. Hence the modern library has but one main task: the
dissemination of books. Everything else, be it the building, per-
sonnel, or installations, exists only for this purpose, and can only
be of secondary importance.

With what books are we able to obtain the desired effect? What
can we do that this effect becomes deeper and wider? We can

answer either question only once we know the public upon which
we want to have an effect. We must know the human material we
are dealing with. Theoretically the public library is meant for everyone. It does
not declare that only graduates may enter, nor does it exclude
the person of learning. But the 'everyone' is different everywhere.
The public is not the same in a village, in a small town, or in a
city. In vain would I proclaim, in the village, that the library
belongs to everyone. The landlord will have no use for it, if it is
frequented by the peasants. And if the peasants have no use for
it, then it belongs to no one at all! And in the small town it is
mainly the petty-bourgeois clerk who comes to the library, or
rather his wife and daughter. Only in the city, especially in the
industrial city, does the library really belong to everyone. There
are cities in which the class distribution of the users of the library matches almost exactly the class or professional breakdown
of the population at large. And even if this parallel is not always
perfect we can accept as a rule that all classes of people visit and
use the library.

What kind of reading should therefore be offered by the urban
library? Most likely it must begin with what the public is inclined
to read. We must relate our efforts to an existing, perhaps puri-
fied need, in order to obtain an effect. This is where the dis-
agreement begins. There are librarians and library-politicians who,
while residing in the city, regard the people from the point of
view of the land-owner. They consider that those who are poor in
material possessions must also be poor in emotional and intellectual
goods, that their reading material is in accordance with their
poverty; that they like the wishy-washy, sentimental, effeminate,
or 'popular' novelists, stories and travelogues filled with adven-
tures, and particularly bad detective stories and other kinds of
pornography. On the other hand, they are assumed not to read
what the learned persons read: the classics and the sophisticated
moderns, or serious non-fiction. And we must not try to induce
them to read these kinds of books.

These library-politicians base their opinion on the statistics provided by certain public libraries. They could base their opinion
on other evidence as well: on how certain sociologists evaluate the
modern proletariat. In his work 'Das Proletariat' Werner Sombart
provides a description of the urban industrial worker which would
lead us to believe that their readings are of the most primitive
kind.

But is this really so? Is it true that the proletarians do not read
good books because they cannot appreciate them? Or is it rather
that they are given bad books and have access to the good ones
only with difficulty, if at all? There are librarians who argue the
latter. We should consider the statistics of those libraries whose
holdings include good literature and bad. In these libraries the
statistics provide a different image of the proletariat.

In the town of Plauen, near Dresden, Walter Hofmann compiled
accurate data about every reader and their reading during a

period of two years. He strictly differentiated the proletarian
from the petty-bourgeois readers, and the latter from the intellectuals. The latter, however, did not play a significant role in
his library, hence only the first two categories are statistically
significant. It appears from the data that the percentage of
didactic literature borrowed was 40.7 per cent for the first category, 35.46 per cent for the second. Nor is the division between
the branches of science to the disadvantage of the proletariat.
While the lighter geographical and ethnological descriptions were
more widely perused by the proletariat (25.01 per cent versus
20.73 per cent) in the natural sciences the proletariat read 15.73
per cent as opposed to 13.69 per cent for the petty bourgeois,
whereas in economics and sociology the former read 4.11 per cent
and the latter only 2.42 per cent. And so on.(1)

The results from the Krupp library in Essen confirm the serious
interest of proletarian readers when it comes to belletristic works.
(2) Among the thirty most frequently read writers we find only
one of the lighter kind, and that is Marlitt, who stands in the
twenty-first place. Schiller comes first, and 76 per cent of his
readers belong to the proletarian class. He is followed by Lessing,
Kleist, Dickens, Scott, Goethe, Anzengruber, Rosegger, C. F.
Meyer, etc. All this tends to indicate that the most typical industrial worker can also appreciate and love the greatest and finest
poets and writers.

Therefore it is in no way necessary to use different standards
to measure the requirements, equipment, or holdings of a library
meant for proletarian readers. The reading needs of the proletarian are in no way inferior to the reading need of the so-called
man of learning. (At the same time, this is the best argument
against the description provided by Sombart.) Hence, in building
the collection of a modern public library, we must disregard the
differences between the so-called higher and lower classes. Bad
books are read equally in all social circles, and each of these
circles has the potential to appreciate good literature as well.
Hence we must have but one criterion in electing holdings: the
need of the most sophisticated and most appreciative reader.

The difference we must deal with in the public library is not the
difference in taste, but a difference in knowledge, in intellectual
background. And in two ways at that. The proletarian readers do
not read reviews, and literature is not the prevailing subject of
conversation in their social life. Hence they cannot know, off-
hand, which are the good books, which books should they request
from the librarian. They are uninformed in bibliography. The
other difference in knowledge appears in the area of science. The
interest of an industrial worker in mathematics, philosophy, or
chemistry may be a hundred times greater than that of many men
of learning; but since he attended no university, and may not
even have finished secondary school, he necessarily lacks the
preparation to understand the higher science, a preparation the
children of middle-class families obtained in school.

The librarian may concentrate his activities on these two gaps

in order to increase the use of his library and improve its quality.
To cope with the lack of information in bibliography the librarian
may prepare lists of books selected strictly according to literary
standards, and educating the readers to its use. On the other
hand, in the acquisition of scientific literature he should be concerned with the varying degrees of difficulty and take care that
every reader receives appropriate materials.
The librarian should not exceed this framework. If he wants to
provide the reader with more than the literature appropriate to
his or her individual taste and understanding, if he tries to
impose his political or moral views, if he wants to be paternalistic,
even with the best of intentions, a reaction sets in immediately,
and it usually amounts to a decrease in library usage. For, just
as the man of learning does not tolerate paternalism, neither does
the industrial worker. The result of any such attempt would be a
conflict with the basic purpose of the public library which is the
greatest possible accessibility. Let us learn that the library is
not an elementary school, but a school for adults; in other words,
a free school!

NOTES

1 Cf. Walter Hofmann: Die Organisation des Ausleihendienstes
   in der modernen Bildungsbibliothek. 'Volksbindugsarchiv',
   vol. I, p. 291, and passim.
2 Ibid., p. 307.

'PROLETARIAN POETRY'
(To the book of Zseni Várnai's poems)

.

The first of these two articles appeared in 'Nyugat' (The West), the representative magazine of modern Hungarian literature, (1914, pt 1, pp. 643-5) à propos a volume of fairly mediocre poems (one of which, however, 'To my soldier son', with the cadence 'Don't shoot my son - I shall be there myself!', played an important role in the revolutionary propaganda in 1918. The review led to a heated exchange between the literary critic of the party and Szabó in the 17 May 1914 Sunday issue of 'Népszava', about the possibility of a proletarian literature and the relationship of base and superstructure, in general. Bresztovszky came out in favour of the movement's immediate political interests in literature, while Szabó, who in his youth had been an advocate of proletarian culture, argued for the autonomy of art. Emphasizing that some features of intellectual and creative life may not fit into the categories of superstructure and class-character, he arrived at propositions which were accepted by Marxist philosophy and aesthetics only decades after his death. Thus, far 'ahead of his time', it is no wonder that Szabó, in the heat of the debate, oversimplified, for example, the argument about the possibility and role of an advanced ideology preceding its 'adequate' socio-economic base. We have selected the opening article and Szabó's most elaborate reply from the series of exchanges.

There seem to be socialists, especially some so-called Marxists, who measure the aesthetic value of all contemporary Hungarian poetry on the basis of what it includes or omits from the programme of the party; this has been the criterion according to which they decide that so and so is a great poet, or so and so is not a poet at all. On the other hand, there have been, and will continue to be, professional critics and literary historians who are inclined to banish a literary work from the realm of literature simply on the grounds that its subject, its characters, or its ideology and convictions do not appeal to them.

It is hardly necessary to point out that the judgment of party aestheticians, as well as that of the official critics have equally little to do with true art. Neither feel nor understand the essence of artistic creation. Art does not depend on the raw material from which it was made, but rather on what it became and how it was made. Are we not dealing with knowledge, creativity? Are we not richer with new forms, colours and modes of expression?

Nobody would deny that beyond the material prerequisites of artistic creativity, the subject is not at all indifferent. The other prerequisite of any work of art is honesty: the sincerity of the feelings and thoughts expressed. There can be no doubt that a work of art can only be successful if the writer or artist has experienced its contents. And it is likewise undeniable that we appreciate completely different emotional, intellectual and moral qualities in a writer whose universe is the whole world, rather than the four walls of his room.

A stupid person, an unlearned person, a lazy person will never be a great artist. Assuming that both have artistic ability, Goethe will be necessarily a greater artist than, let us say, Mihály Szabolcska, 'if only' because he was more intelligent, more erudite, more serious, because even the slightest resonance of the universe affected the chords of his soul. Because he could see more, because he knew more, because he wanted to see more, the mass and intensity of his inner experience were so much greater.

Another way of saying this would be: I measure the artist on the strength of his work, I measure the man on the subjects he chooses. Since I claim that there is progress in the concept of man, and whereas the artist cannot be imagined apart from the human community, I must conclude from his materials, from his subjects, that the artist has those attributes of a human being without which he cannot be a great artist: the comprehensive understanding, love, respect of what makes the world move.

Genius is determined by the capacity to create, and an appreciation of the potentials of mankind. The artist can hardly be an artist without a spark of genius.

Because of this, and also because the appreciation of possibilities and the nature of genius include the concepts of impossibility and infinity, the true artist cannot be judged within the limitations of any kind of party programme, not even the most radical one. Every party programme is a compromise between certain interests of the masses and the practical possibilities. Such pragmatism, such more or less rational insight, such cautious compromise obviously implies the restriction of feeling and will; how could it then determine the boundaries of artistic imagination and creation?

A person may be basically socialist or anarchist, Catholic or feudal, and still remain a great artist; but if we can dress him into the points of the programme of the Social Democratic Party, the Popular Party, or the Constitutional Party, and note that they fit perfectly - he cannot be an artist. If his imagination never transcends the frontiers of the useful and practical, if he never has iconoclastic thoughts or does not express them - he may be good at occasional verse, may be a good agitator, or journalist, but has little to do with art.

Hence it is not possible to speak of proletarian science, proletarian philosophy, proletarian sociology, or proletarian technology; no more than we can speak of bourgeois poetry, feudal science, or Catholic mathematics. No one will deny a certain social determinism in art and science. Neither artistic nor scientific

production is possible without a certain surplus of social energy
and wealth, and certain social realities tie the feet of the soaring
genius to the ground: ideologies, tendencies, the limits of knowledge, success, the need to make a living. But proletarian poetry:
what on earth would that be?

Most often this designation is applied to the poetry which deals
with episodes from the life of the poorest classes. But we have
seen that the poetic nature of a work does not depend on the
material itself. And we know that the greatest portraitists of the
life of the poor, Dickens and Zola, Verhaeren or Dehmel, were
never card-carrying party members, and the sword-bearers of
the notion of proletarian aesthetics would never recognize them
as 'proletarian poets'.

Could the proletarian origin of the poet be what counts? Such a
background, of course, does not imply genius, nor ideology, nor
curiosity, nor conviction. The naive verses of a worker do not
make poetry, and the editors of the 'Népszava' reject by the
dozen the limping verse submitted by its faithful readers. The
proletarian or socialist ideology was actually conceived by non-
proletarians. Socialist ideology is not simply the consequence of
proletarian living conditions. These living conditions are perfectly
compatible with the darkest ignorance, the most obscurantist
superstition, the most naive religiosity, the greatest humility and
submissiveness; we would have much more right to refer to this
as the proletarian spirit, for the time being, than the socialist
ideology. That, however, was shaped by non-proletarians from the
materials of 'bourgeois' philosophy and 'bourgeois' science and, of
course, proletarian living conditions; because they too, like all
true scientists and thinkers, built on the work of their
predecessors.

Could it be that the poet's principles provide the proletarian
character of his poetry? But what are these principles, in their
most general terms? Freedom, happiness for all mankind, love,
peace among men. These principles have also been the principles
of the rising bourgeoisie. Béranger and Schiller, Petőfi and Ady
invoke them as enthusiastically as the socialist troubadours. The
'Realpolitik' requirements found in party programmes can surely
be dismissed as nothing more than the specific ways and means
towards the accomplishment of these common principles.

There is no artistic element, therefore, which would allow us to
differentiate between art and art, and consider it as the product
peculiar to a particular class. There is but one art. Within it there
are degrees. There is greater or lesser, richer or poorer, more
universal and more limited art. The bases for these evaluations
have to be the creative force, the wealth and beauty of colours,
of forms, of tones.

Only the critics are qualified to evaluate the poems of Zseni
Várnai. My feeling is that some of her poems deserve better than
to be classified as 'proletarian poetry'.

VULGAR MARXISM
A reply to Ernö Bresztovszky

In his charming utopia the 'Isle of the Penguins' Anatole France
speaks of poetry in a socialist society as follows: 'Nowadays all
poets do is say delicate things which make no sense and have no
syntax - the language is as much their own as is the rhythm, the
assonances, or the alliterations.' In other words, according to
the great socialist poet, poetry in a socialist society will be nothing but games with words.
   I will never be a poet, hence I have no right to play around
with words, either today or tomorrow. If my essay on 'proletarian
poetry' was nevertheless such that it was possible to understand,
in all good faith, the exact opposite of what I intended, then I am
not even a writer; then, as a matter of fact, even this reply makes
no sense.
   What had I written, according to Bresztovszky? If I have understood him correctly, something like this. Differences in the realm
of art, as well as among social phenomena, are not determined by
class characteristics. There is no proletarian mortality. If the
topic of poetic creation is taken from social life, it is to be excluded from the domain of art. There is no such thing as religious
poetry, or patriotic poetry, there is only poetry. Genius, therefore, is unquestionably devoid of party or conviction. Hence we
must proscribe from 'true' literature all card-carrying party members: for example, Maxim Gorki, George Bernard Shaw, and
Anatole France.
   Many crazy ideas have been expressed in as many sentences.
How can I demonstrate that not only have I said nothing of the
sort, but that these ideas are not even implied anywhere in my
writings? Shall I refer to the fact that in the very second sentence
of my article I reject the point of view of professional aesthetes,
which regards the object or tendency of the artistic creation as
the criterion of artistic value? If I argue that it is inappropriate
to exclude someone from art because his themes or tendencies are
not to my liking, I cannot possibly be arguing that those with
whom I sympathize should be excluded.
   Should I repeat that in my article I wrote of those 'whose basic
tendency is socialist or anarchist, Catholic or feudal - and are
great poets?' Therefore I certainly do not advocate that persons
be excluded from the rank of poets simply because they have convictions. Shall I repeat that Dickens and Zola, Verhaeren and
Dehmel, Petöfi and Ady are great poets? They are geniuses. Yet
even I know that they had political tendencies, definite social
convictions and principles.

I should think all this would be superfluous, inasmuch as my article under attack has been written entirely to prove that the volume of poetry by Zseni Várnai, entitled 'To my soldier son' is indeed art. I do not know, but I assume that Várnai, the author of the poems that appear on the pages of the Social Democratic newspaper 'Népszava', and whose volume appears under the imprint of the paper's publishing house, is a member of the party; and I know from its contents that she is a proletarian and a convinced socialist. Yet I claim she is a poet. Why would I require that Shaw, France, or Gorki be without principles, or else I should kick them out of literature?

Clearly every statement my critic claims to have derived from my words is nonsense, and finds denial in my own article. This is my answer to his criticism. Nevertheless, it might be worth exploring how a person of goodwill can come to such conclusions about my article. There can be but one explanation for it: the mistakes can only be ascribed to that frightening fanaticism with which a good many of those who claim to be Marxists apply Marx's theory of class struggle to all the affairs of the world. This fanaticism is incompatible with science.

In what does the Marxist theory consist? Reduced to its simplest form: the mode of production determines the distribution of wealth; the social, political and intellectual processes are dependent on the economic structure of society, that is the organization of production and the competition for profits – commonly referred to as the class struggle.

This theory does not imply by any means that every social phenomenon is directly determined by class struggle, or that everything in society is connected to the interests of one particular class, and that there are no social phenomena in which several classes might have an interest.

Should anyone reach such a conclusion logically from the Marxist thesis, he must keep silent if the facts prove otherwise. This is required by the true spirit of science which, I am firmly convinced, was also that of Marx. Was it not he who declared that ideologies were mostly historical illusions, states of false consciousness? Did he not direct science to seek the relationships between facts and the laws governing the phenomena? The fanaticism of class struggle, like any other fanaticism, is incompatible not only with science, but with Marxism as well.

Marxian theory does not entitle anyone to declare any social manifestation as a class manifestation, unless he can support this assertion with factual relationships. To generalize all manifestations as class manifestations would represent a watering down and 'popularization' of Marxian theory much like that simplistic sequel to the classical school of economics, which Marx derogatorily baptized 'vulgar economics'. Vulgar Marxism!

These vulgar Marxists labelled all classes beside the working class a 'single reactionary mass' – until Marx slapped them and warned them about the essence of class. The 'single reactionary mass' does not derive its income from a single source, hence cannot be lumped all in one. Engels himself, the other initiator of the theory of historical materialism, had to rehabilitate ideologies in contrast to this vulgar Marxism.

It is this same vulgar Marxism which loudly proclaims the general theory of class struggle, while it allies itself at times with the bourgeoisie, at times with the land-owners, in pursuit of common goals, for common class interests, in other words, in social solidarity with them.

It is this same vulgar Marxism which cannot admire the wonders of science and art without seeking out the economic phenomena from which they are derived, or the class interest which gave them birth. Only it does not realize that, for the time being, we are not even sufficiently familiar with the laws regarding the interrelationship of the legal, political and moral superstructure, which lies much closer to the economic base, let alone the more removed ideologies which, we assume, are more independent of the economic base.

This same vulgar Marxism, hot-headed as it is, ends up by kicking its own base from under itself. It disregards the Marxian thesis that the transformation of the economic structure is followed, not preceded by the transformation of the superstructure. It speaks of proletarian science, of proletarian philosophy, of proletarian poetry when we are still up to our necks in the capitalist mode of production, and even the socialist legal and political superstructure remain problems for the future. It speaks of proletarian music and proletarian aesthetics, when we do not even have 'proletarian production' and 'proletarian distribution of wealth'. Or rather, what we do have is a class living in misery, bitterly struggling for its everyday existence, for a little light, a little freedom, a little happiness. It has practically no bread, it has no knowledge, it has no pleasures - but a science of its own, and an art, and a literature, yes, that it has! An admirable sort of Marxism, indeed!

CULTURE AND CULTIVATION

This last writing of Szabó may be read as his spiritual last
will and testament, the more so as he wrote it for 'Szabad-
gondolat' (Free Thought), the journal of the progressive
youth organization, Galilei Circle, where the anti-militarist
young followers of his last years of life came from. (The
words in the title and the text are difficult to translate; they
refer to 'Bildung' versus 'Kultur', but also play on the
homophony in Hungarian of 'intelligence' and 'intelligentsia'.)
It was published in the July issue of 1918 (pp. 33-7). Having
advocated a non-aligned social science a few years earlier,
then advocating a non-political sphere for the arts, Szabó
now, plagued but also enlightened from the crisis of the war,
felt that the leadership of society should belong to the ethically, and not intellectually, superior 'knights of culture'.
Parallel to his sympathies for the ethical idealists in the last
philosophical debates, Szabó embraced a position very far
from his militant class-loyalty of only a few years before. We
felt that this piece, succinctly anticipating Julien Benda's
'Trahison des clercs' and Lukács's 'Responsibility of the
Literates' by many decades, could serve well as the closing
paper.

Among all the realizations which sociology owes to the war there
is one which subsequent experience will probably never amend:
the bankruptcy of the intelligentsia. By intelligentsia I do not
mean the philosophical or psychological concept of intelligence. To
be sure, it would be justified to discuss the concept of intelligence
in a journal the name of which, as a fighting motto, could easily
be considered the exclusive voice of rationalism and intellectualism
in this country. Here, however, I want to discuss the social class
whose working tools are reason and knowledge, differentiated from
other classes by its function, which is not material production,
but the conservation, communication and development of the intellectual workers, the educated, the intelligentsia.

No matter how materialistic our age may be, ethically speaking,
it nevertheless adopted the respect for science and intellectual
work from other periods in which - we are told - social prestige
was not as exclusively based on wealth and fortune as in the bourgeois society. It is the frenetic rate of the creative economic
forces of contemporary capitalism which accounts for the fact that
the most terrible barbarism and most appalling philistinism have

spread to the highest levels of social and public life. But were there not similar barbarians and philistines among the first generation in earlier historical periods, among the great seigneurs who reached the upper echelons thanks to their physical prowess, their bravery, or their cunning? It implies greater respect for the intellectuals that, in our age, the importance of wealth, material strength and financial status for achieving social positions is often criticized, and seems to need excuses. The same is suggested by the seigneurs of new wealth rivalries in obtaining the passport to the upper echelons of society: by acquiring intellectual qualifications and 'patronizing' the arts and sciences. How could they know that diplomas and money do not signify culture!

While our society may not appreciate its intellectuals sufficiently, there never has been an epoch when so many scientists, writers and artists have attained relatively high social or material positions. Not for a moment did these intellectuals miss the opportunity to claim suitable maintenance and a leading role in the direction of state and society for intelligence and knowledge. Indeed, it is precisely in our society that such a great demand for 'intellectual workers' has been created, because of the complexity of the system of economic production and distribution, and also because of the hitherto unheard of omnipotence of state power: there was probably never a period in which the intellectual class played a more decisive role than in ours.

On what did the entire intelligentsia - professors and other scientists, writers and, in particular, the most numerous group, the higher-ranking bureaucrats of various sorts - base their right and their claim to lead society and state? On what we commonly refer to as culture. Something by which most people mean a certain degree of education, a certain amount of knowledge. The thinking elite means something more by it: a moral and intellectual, but mostly intellectual preparation which enables the person to order his life with thought, knowledge and perception. On this basis the intellectual class has claimed as its function to guide and lead the fate of those whose life takes place predominantly under the pressure of instincts, of feelings and of the environment, and who have a lower capacity for judging and understanding, because of their 'lack of culture'.

Indeed, can there be a nobler, more beautiful, more rewarding task! To discover the secrets of life, the laws that govern society! To teach new generations of outstanding intellectuals, to show them the way! To lead those who are stumbling in the darkness of their ignorance, caught in the net of their passions! To open their minds and raise them to the level of a rational independent life! This was the social function the intellectuals claimed for themselves. Had they carried out this function, who would deny them the highest recognition? Who would question their calling for the leadership of state and society?

The European intelligentsia attempted to prove its calling not only by practical political and social activity, but also by the fact that the scientists and writers challenged that function of religion

which no amount of force can extinguish from the soul of humanity: to seek, determine and illuminate the laws governing our
relationship to infinity and to the universe. The intelligentsia has
indicated the principles and the road to follow, especially as far
as the relationship of the individual to the whole is concerned,
with a gesture of authority. Their writings were full of praise
and encouragement of humanism, philanthropy, brotherhood, uni-
versality, internationalism, science, insight, work and creativity.
The criterion for European culture was whether one subscribed to
these principles as the postulates of scientific cognition or not.

'It is not enough to know, one must be able to apply knowledge;
it is not enough to want, one must also act', says Goethe. The
higher the claim of a theory to be able to explain ever deeper
layers, wider circles, or longer-term trends of social occurrences,
the more we should demand from its proponents that even amidst
world-shaking events they show by fitting acts the validity of
the theories and their ability to apply them.

The outbreak of the war was that historical event which put the
theories about the leadership of the intelligentsia to a real test;
and there has never been a more shameful defeat for the mind,
for intelligence! All over Europe the war-hawks, the witch-hunters
and the bewitched, the instigators, the spy-detectors, the traitor-
seekers and other ecstatics took over; and who danced the most
frenetic dance among them? Precisely the intellectuals! Those who
all their life have been preaching the superiority of mind and
knowledge! Who thought of themselves as the only ones destined
to lead the masses, dominated by their instincts, on to the path
of understanding! Those who constructed the most perfect systems
of ideas about the potential, the necessity, the ineluctability of a
harmonic order of mankind! How many of them have been seen
wallowing together with the mobs in the morass of the most primitive passions, and how many of them did it out of cold calculation,
and how many more who bent their necks under the yoke of the
mass frenzy out of servile cowardice or of self-forgotten uncons-
ciousness! What became of the superiority of reason, when the
monist Haeckel, the internationalist Ostwald, the rationalist Anatole France and the philosopher Bergson alike distinguished themselves from the crazy European mob only by yelling louder, by
gesticulating more frantically than the run of the mill? If the
leading minds behaved thus, what could we expect from the others,
the second-rate ones, the truly numerous intelligentsia?

We are still in the midst of the war, and we can see the wielders
of the mind-tool at work. Can anyone deny that, not only during
the first moments of inebriation, but also month after month, year
after year, unimpressed by the bitter suffering, it is the so-
called cultured who fulfil the basest functions from the point of
view of war economy and politics, and the most senseless ones
from that of social rationality.

Is it necessary to mention these well-known facts when discussing the new generation of cultured who, it is to be hoped, will
take up the fight for the rule of reason and humanism. We must

redefine the concept of culture, and by the same token, the social function of culture as well. Let them call culture a certain quantity of knowledge, a certain polish of understanding, a certain extension of existential requirements.

After our recent experiences, however, nobody can pretend that these qualities be considered sufficient, that they should serve as the basis for the leadership role of the intellectuals.

We have seen that neither the greatest mind nor the greatest amount of knowledge is sufficient in itself to enable its possessor to become a reliable leader of others. Often they have not even proved sufficient to be entrusted with the care of the sciences, of knowledge, or of the naked truth.

The kind of cultivation which alone would suffice for this purpose is not simply a matter of intellectual qualities. Its requirements are not even primarily in the mental but rather in the moral and social spheres. The basic quality is the harmony of all human abilities, the highest development and harmony of the forces of the intellect, of feelings and of action. Those whose self is not permeated by feeling – no matter how knowledgeable they might be – those who, while knowing what is good and bad 'pro foro interno' have nevertheless not taken a stand deep in their hearts, irrevocably, stalwartly on the side of good, cannot be truly cultured. Nor should we entrust ourselves to those who, while they proclaim convictions, remain in the realm of words and of beautiful principles. Every conviction is worth only as much as is realized of it through action by its protagonist. Let us not take the word of those who, out of slyness or out of naive self-delusion, attempt to convince us of the excellence and sublimeness of their theories and ideals by recognizing only the distant future as their legitimate judge.

The relationship of people to one another and to society can be reduced to a few simple and lasting moral principles that can be continually validated in practice. The most high-falutin utopia is but the theoretical application of a few or several of these principles. He who does not find the means in his everyday life to practise his principles in everyday action may be the most perfect thinker, but is nevertheless a person of weak convictions and weak will. If he surrenders in small matters, right from the beginning, how can we expect him to take his stand in matters of import? Hence those who know and proclaim the good, but want to realize it with means that are contrary to their moral convictions, are not truly cultured, and are not worth of leadership. It is better to allow the bad to remain than to change it by immoral means.

The complete harmony of the soul: that is true culture. The welding together of knowledge, feeling and will. To study everything, to select the best, to believe in it with the power of love, and to realize every day all that is possible with heroic determination – that is the ideal; that is the cultivation of the soul, in contrast to the culture of the mind. And the only true, reliable leaders are not the 'cultured', but the paragons of cultivation.

INDEX